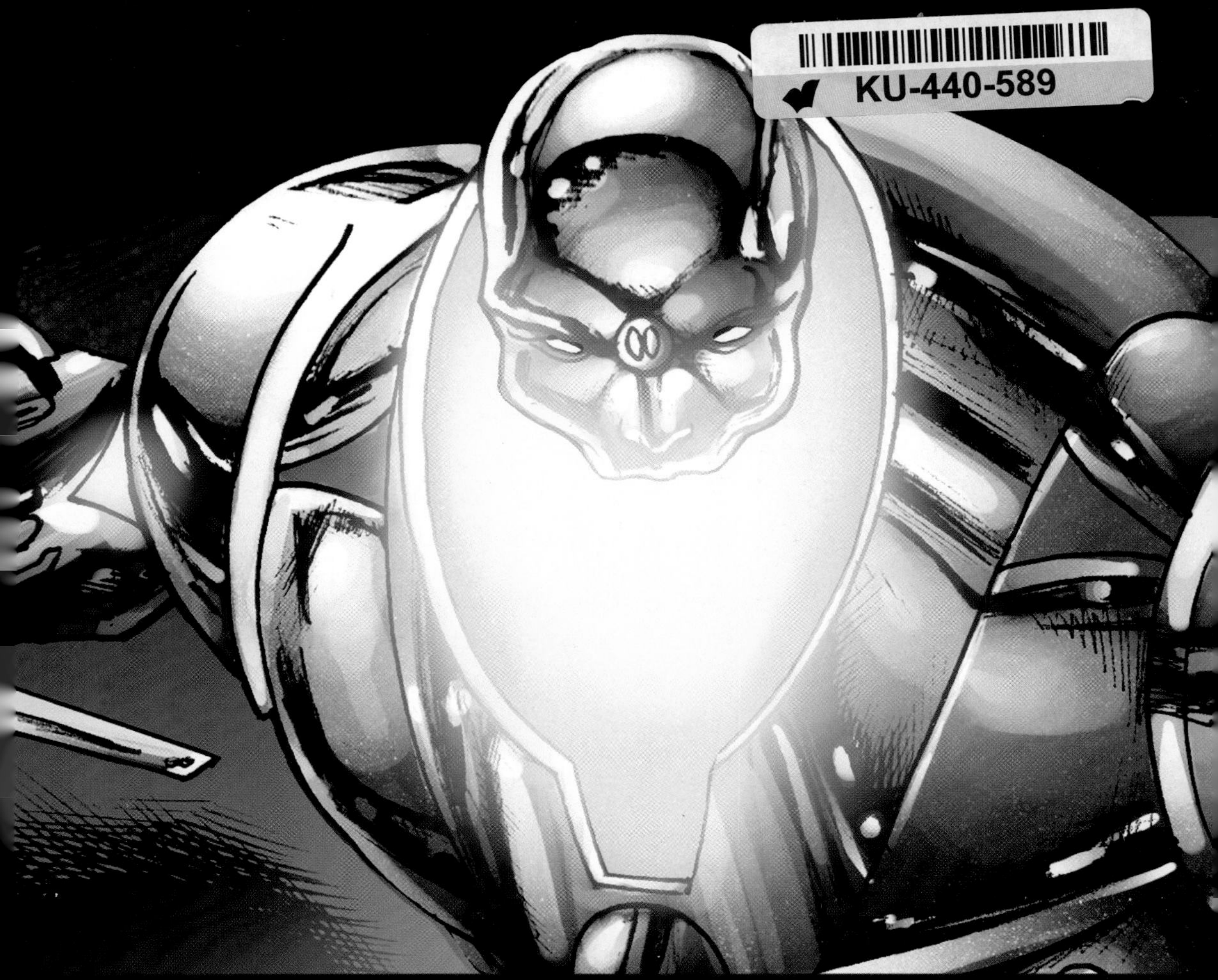

TERMINATOR®
REVOLUTION

WRITTEN BY
SIMON FURMAN

ART BY
LUI ANTONIO

COLORS BY
ADRIANO LUCAS

COVER BY
RICHARD ISANOVE

LETTERS BY
SIMON BOWLAND

SPECIAL THANKS TO
THE LICENSING GROUP

COLLECTS ISSUES 1-5 OF TERMINATOR: REVOLUTION BY DYNAMITE ENTERTAINMENT.

Previously in Terminator: Infinity:
A year after the death of Kate Bewster, John Connor found himself forced out of Crystal Peak with a renewed purpose in life and his battle against the machines. Again aided by a Terminator – named "Uncle Bob" – John found himself facing a new threat in the form of the T-Infinity… he beat it once, but can he do it again?

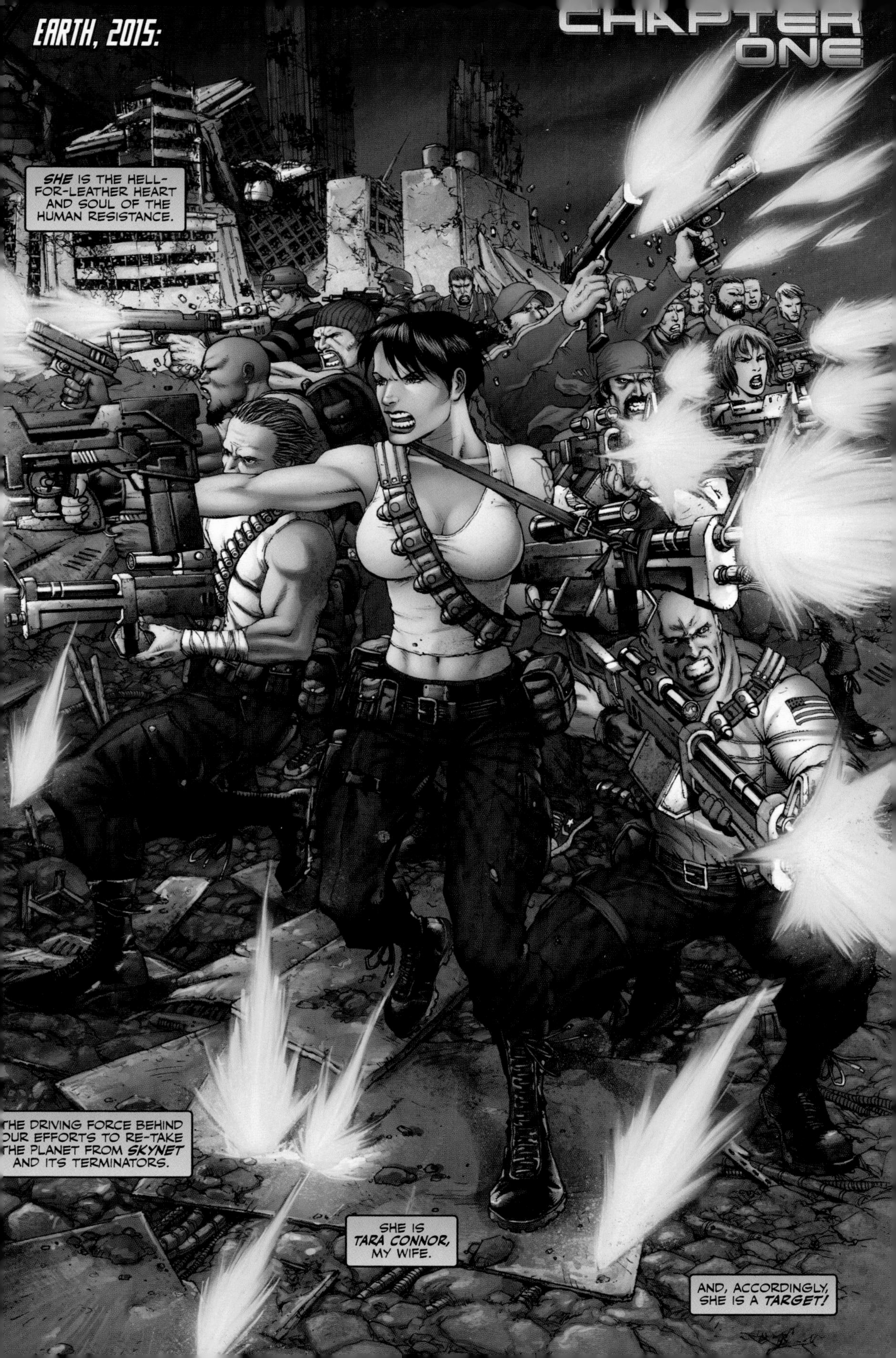
EARTH, 2015:
CHAPTER ONE
SHE IS THE HELL-FOR-LEATHER HEART AND SOUL OF THE HUMAN RESISTANCE.
THE DRIVING FORCE BEHIND OUR EFFORTS TO RE-TAKE THE PLANET FROM SKYNET AND ITS TERMINATORS.
SHE IS TARA CONNOR, MY WIFE.
AND, ACCORDINGLY, SHE IS A TARGET!

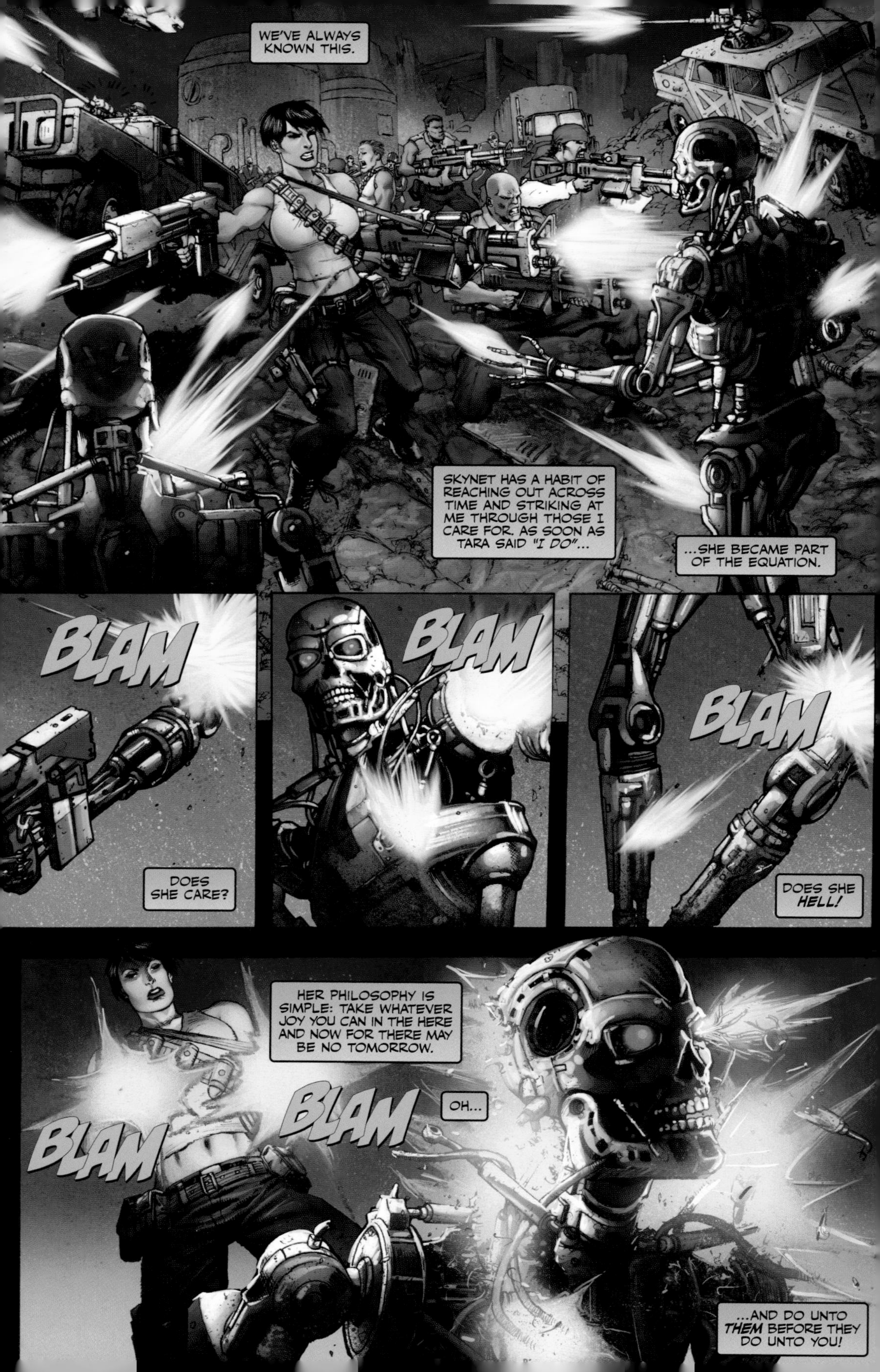
WE'VE ALWAYS KNOWN THIS.
SKYNET HAS A HABIT OF REACHING OUT ACROSS TIME AND STRIKING AT ME THROUGH THOSE I CARE FOR. AS SOON AS TARA SAID "I DO"...
...SHE BECAME PART OF THE EQUATION.
BLAM
DOES SHE CARE?
BLAM
BLAM
DOES SHE HELL!
HER PHILOSOPHY IS SIMPLE: TAKE WHATEVER JOY YOU CAN IN THE HERE AND NOW FOR THERE MAY BE NO TOMORROW.
BLAM
BLAM
OH...
...AND DO UNTO THEM BEFORE THEY DO UNTO YOU!

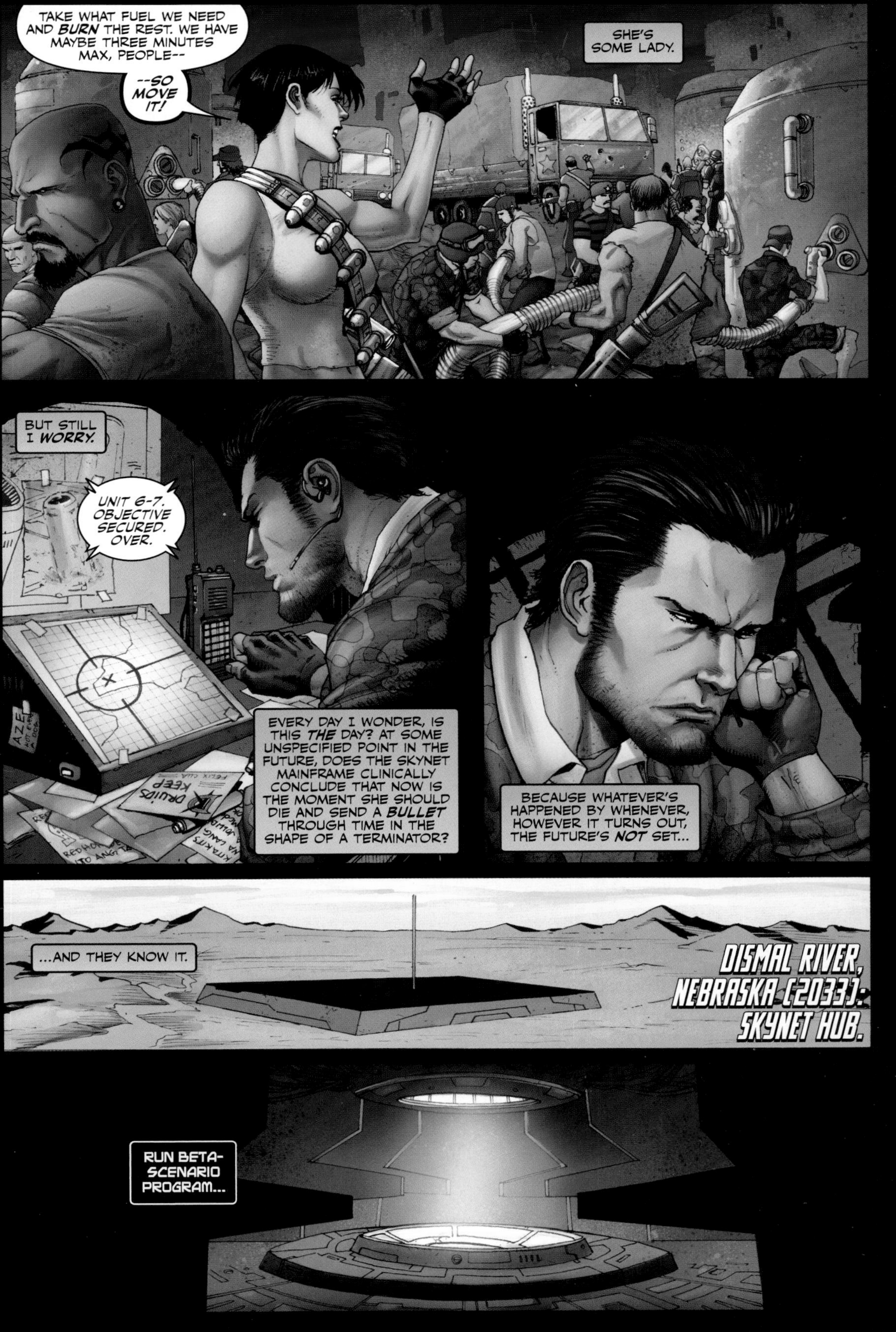
TAKE WHAT FUEL WE NEED AND BURN THE REST. WE HAVE MAYBE THREE MINUTES MAX, PEOPLE--
--SO MOVE IT!
SHE'S SOME LADY.
BUT STILL I WORRY.
UNIT 6-7. OBJECTIVE SECURED. OVER.
EVERY DAY I WONDER, IS THIS THE DAY? AT SOME UNSPECIFIED POINT IN THE FUTURE, DOES THE SKYNET MAINFRAME CLINICALLY CONCLUDE THAT NOW IS THE MOMENT SHE SHOULD DIE AND SEND A BULLET THROUGH TIME IN THE SHAPE OF A TERMINATOR?
BECAUSE WHATEVER'S HAPPENED BY WHENEVER, HOWEVER IT TURNS OUT, THE FUTURE'S NOT SET...
...AND THEY KNOW IT.
DISMAL RIVER, NEBRASKA (2033): SKYNET HUB.
RUN BETA-SCENARIO PROGRAM...

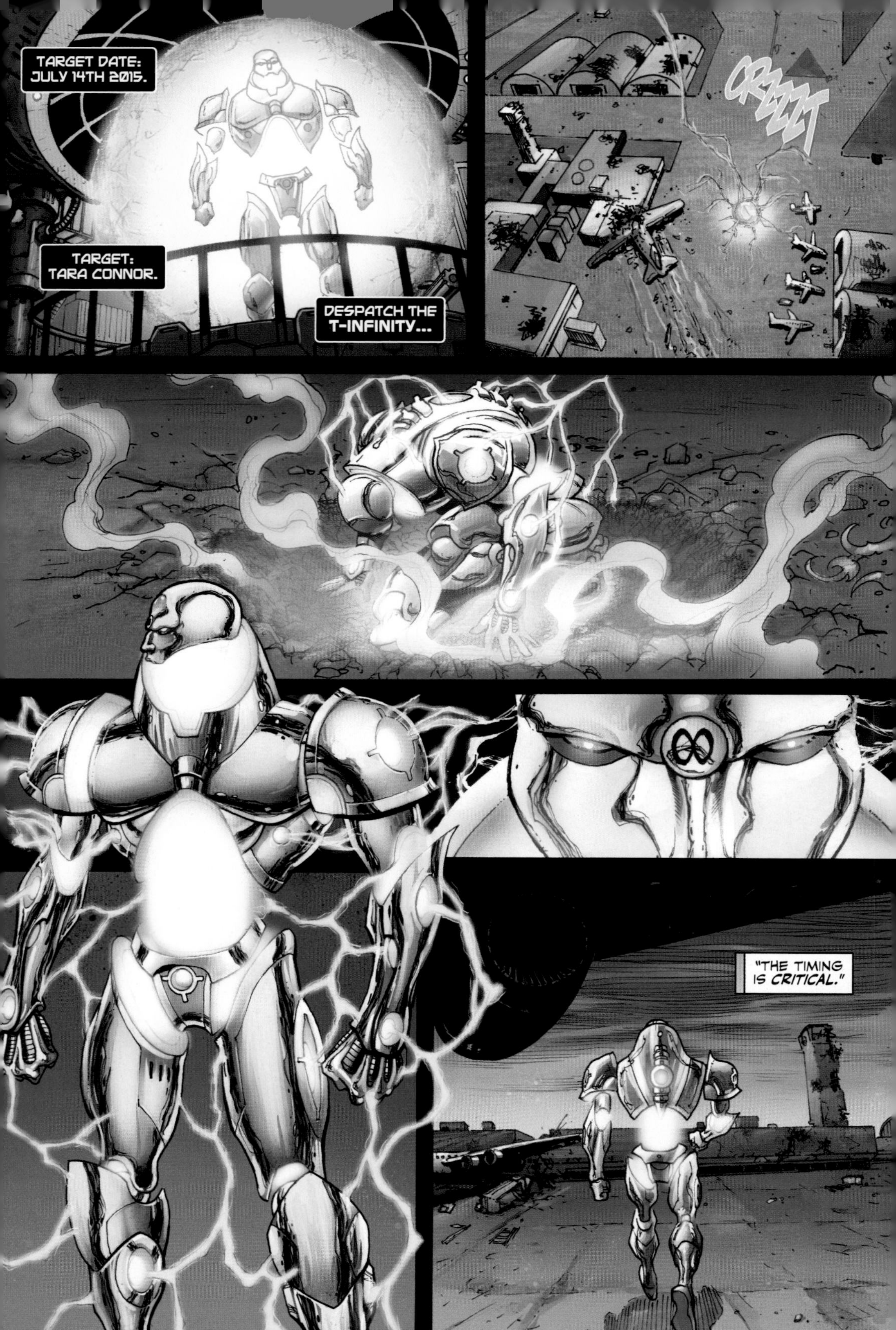
TARGET DATE:
JULY 14TH 2015.
TARGET:
TARA CONNOR.
DESPATCH THE
T-INFINITY...
CRZZZT
"THE TIMING
IS *CRITICAL.*"

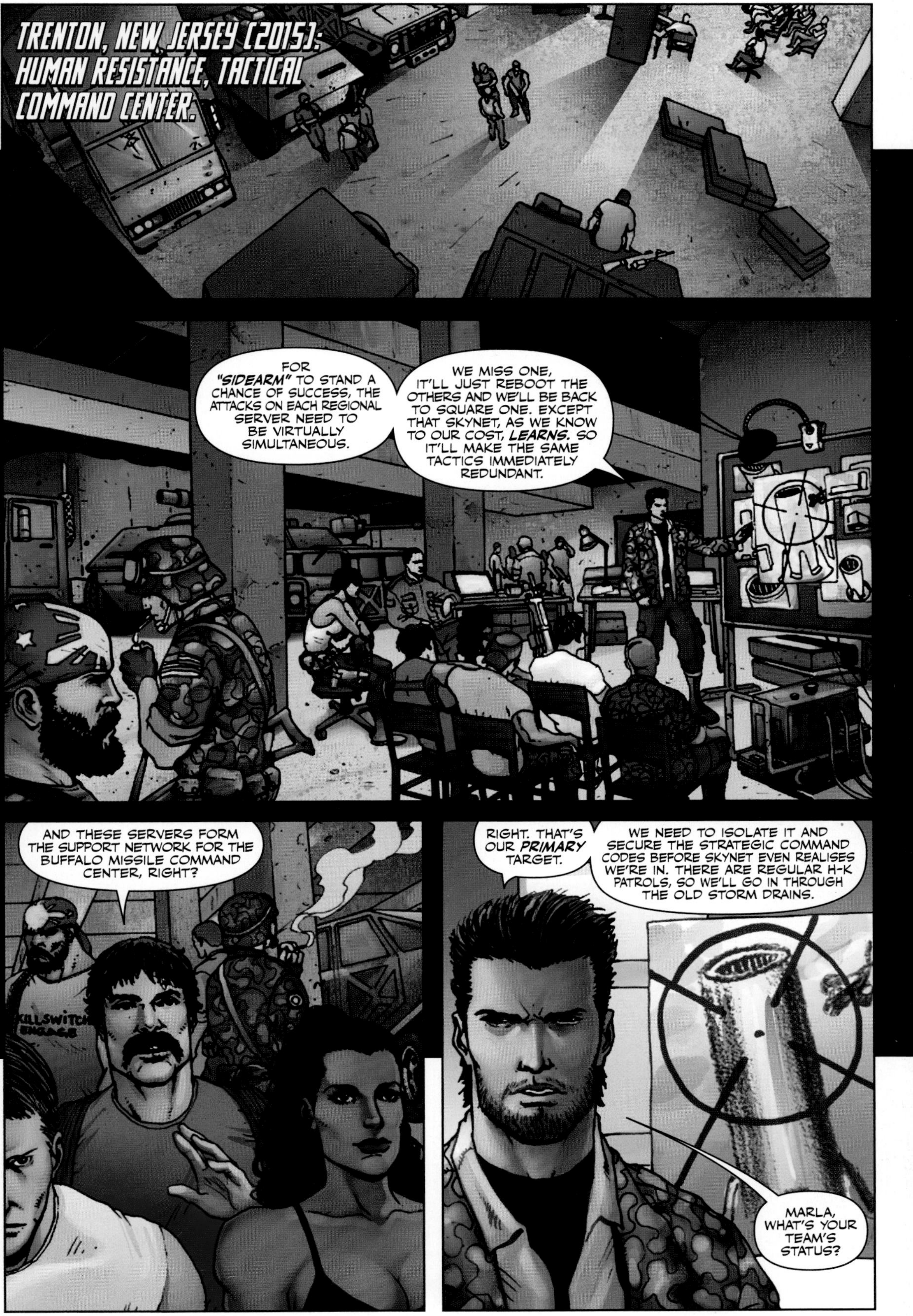
TRENTON, NEW JERSEY [2015]: HUMAN RESISTANCE, TACTICAL COMMAND CENTER.
FOR "SIDEARM" TO STAND A CHANCE OF SUCCESS, THE ATTACKS ON EACH REGIONAL SERVER NEED TO BE VIRTUALLY SIMULTANEOUS.
WE MISS ONE, IT'LL JUST REBOOT THE OTHERS AND WE'LL BE BACK TO SQUARE ONE. EXCEPT THAT SKYNET, AS WE KNOW TO OUR COST, LEARNS. SO IT'LL MAKE THE SAME TACTICS IMMEDIATELY REDUNDANT.
AND THESE SERVERS FORM THE SUPPORT NETWORK FOR THE BUFFALO MISSILE COMMAND CENTER, RIGHT?
KILLSWITCH ENGAGE
RIGHT. THAT'S OUR PRIMARY TARGET.
WE NEED TO ISOLATE IT AND SECURE THE STRATEGIC COMMAND CODES BEFORE SKYNET EVEN REALISES WE'RE IN. THERE ARE REGULAR H-K PATROLS, SO WE'LL GO IN THROUGH THE OLD STORM DRAINS.
MARLA, WHAT'S YOUR TEAM'S STATUS?

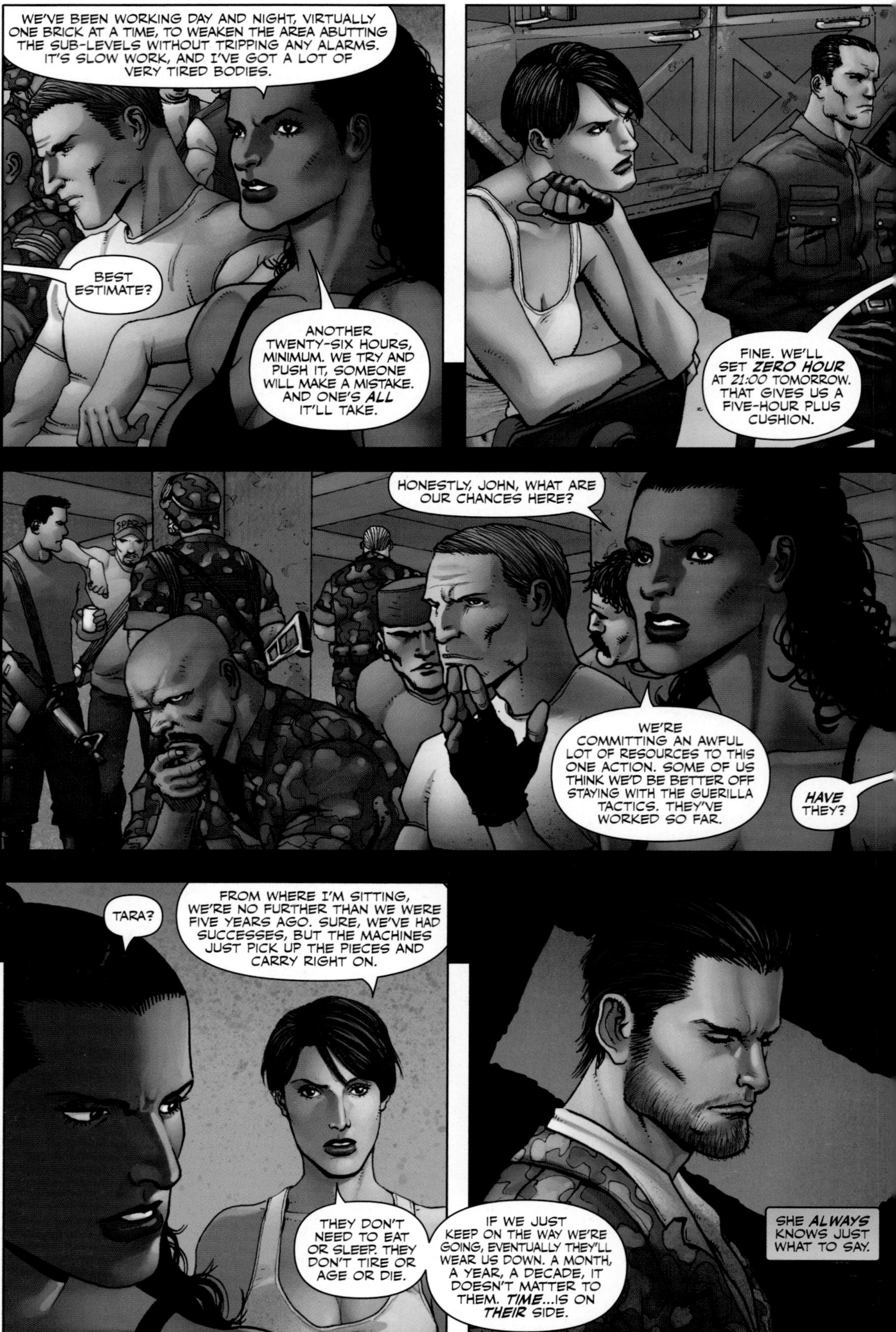
WE'VE BEEN WORKING DAY AND NIGHT, VIRTUALLY ONE BRICK AT A TIME, TO WEAKEN THE AREA ABUTTING THE SUB-LEVELS WITHOUT TRIPPING ANY ALARMS. IT'S SLOW WORK, AND I'VE GOT A LOT OF VERY TIRED BODIES.
BEST ESTIMATE?
ANOTHER TWENTY-SIX HOURS, MINIMUM. WE TRY AND PUSH IT, SOMEONE WILL MAKE A MISTAKE. AND ONE'S ALL IT'LL TAKE.
FINE. WE'LL SET ZERO HOUR AT 21:00 TOMORROW. THAT GIVES US A FIVE-HOUR PLUS CUSHION.
HONESTLY, JOHN, WHAT ARE OUR CHANCES HERE?
WE'RE COMMITTING AN AWFUL LOT OF RESOURCES TO THIS ONE ACTION. SOME OF US THINK WE'D BE BETTER OFF STAYING WITH THE GUERILLA TACTICS. THEY'VE WORKED SO FAR.
HAVE THEY?
TARA?
FROM WHERE I'M SITTING, WE'RE NO FURTHER THAN WE WERE FIVE YEARS AGO. SURE, WE'VE HAD SUCCESSES, BUT THE MACHINES JUST PICK UP THE PIECES AND CARRY RIGHT ON.
THEY DON'T NEED TO EAT OR SLEEP. THEY DON'T TIRE OR AGE OR DIE.
IF WE JUST KEEP ON THE WAY WE'RE GOING, EVENTUALLY THEY'LL WEAR US DOWN. A MONTH, A YEAR, A DECADE, IT DOESN'T MATTER TO THEM. TIME...IS ON THEIR SIDE.
SHE ALWAYS KNOWS JUST WHAT TO SAY.

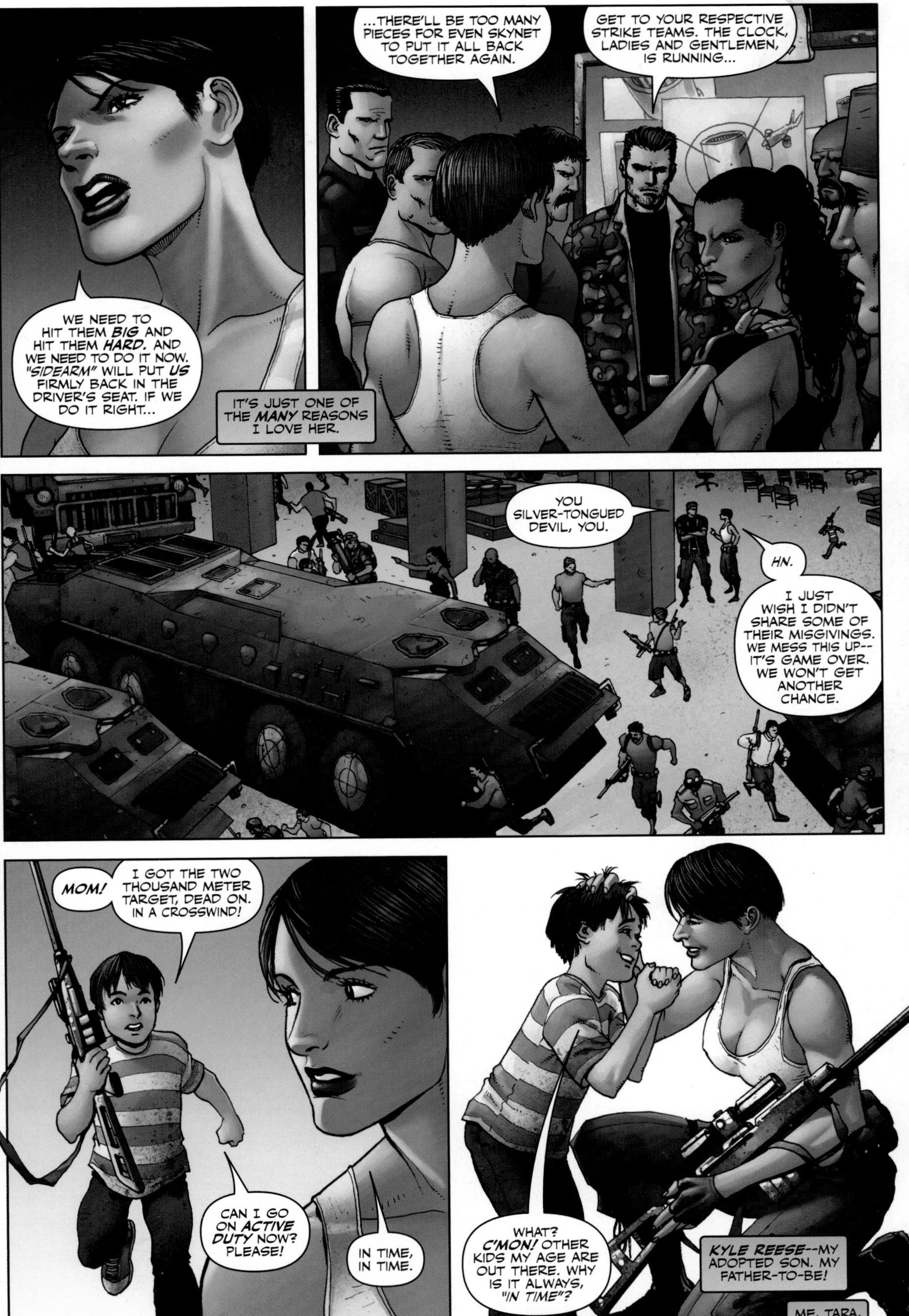

WE NEED TO HIT THEM BIG AND HIT THEM HARD. AND WE NEED TO DO IT NOW. "SIDEARM" WILL PUT US FIRMLY BACK IN THE DRIVER'S SEAT. IF WE DO IT RIGHT...
...THERE'LL BE TOO MANY PIECES FOR EVEN SKYNET TO PUT IT ALL BACK TOGETHER AGAIN.
GET TO YOUR RESPECTIVE STRIKE TEAMS. THE CLOCK, LADIES AND GENTLEMEN, IS RUNNING...
IT'S JUST ONE OF THE MANY REASONS I LOVE HER.
YOU SILVER-TONGUED DEVIL, YOU.
HN.
I JUST WISH I DIDN'T SHARE SOME OF THEIR MISGIVINGS. WE MESS THIS UP-- IT'S GAME OVER. WE WON'T GET ANOTHER CHANCE.
MOM!
I GOT THE TWO THOUSAND METER TARGET, DEAD ON. IN A CROSSWIND!
CAN I GO ON ACTIVE DUTY NOW? PLEASE!
IN TIME, IN TIME.
WHAT? C'MON! OTHER KIDS MY AGE ARE OUT THERE. WHY IS IT ALWAYS, "IN TIME"?
KYLE REESE--MY ADOPTED SON. MY FATHER-TO-BE!
ME, TARA, KYLE...

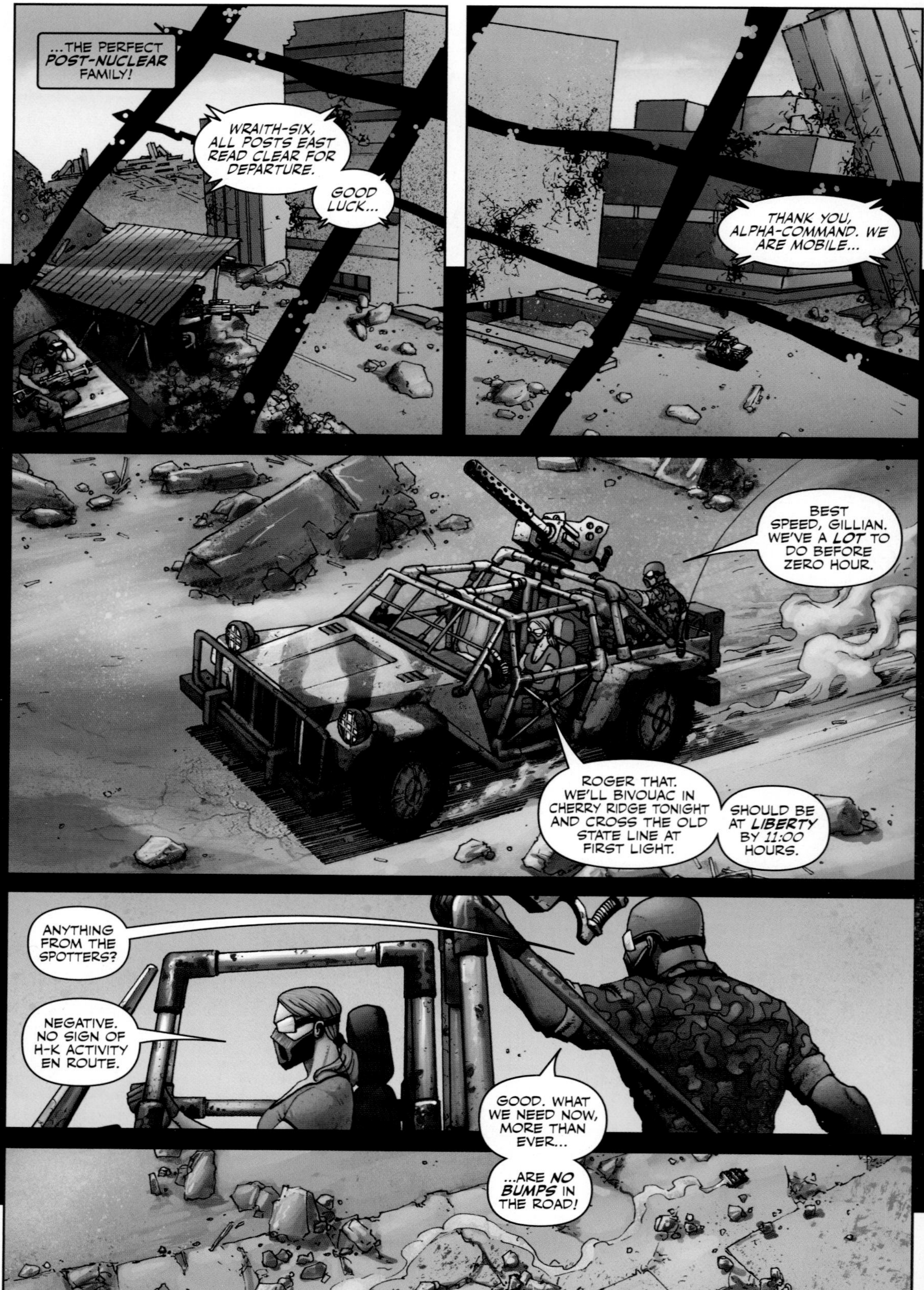
...THE PERFECT POST-NUCLEAR FAMILY!
WRAITH-SIX, ALL POSTS EAST READ CLEAR FOR DEPARTURE.
GOOD LUCK...
THANK YOU, ALPHA-COMMAND. WE ARE MOBILE...
BEST SPEED, GILLIAN. WE'VE A LOT TO DO BEFORE ZERO HOUR.
ROGER THAT. WE'LL BIVOUAC IN CHERRY RIDGE TONIGHT AND CROSS THE OLD STATE LINE AT FIRST LIGHT.
SHOULD BE AT LIBERTY BY 11:00 HOURS.
ANYTHING FROM THE SPOTTERS?
NEGATIVE. NO SIGN OF H-K ACTIVITY EN ROUTE.
GOOD. WHAT WE NEED NOW, MORE THAN EVER...
...ARE NO BUMPS IN THE ROAD!

HELL! INCOMING!

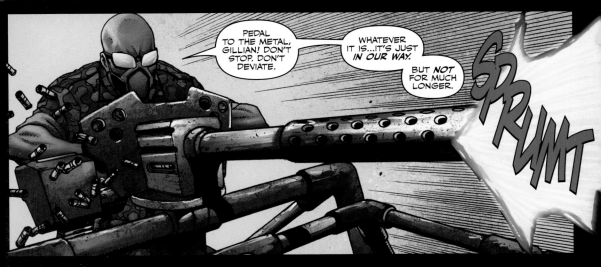

PEDAL TO THE METAL, GILLIAN! DON'T STOP. DON'T DEVIATE.

WHATEVER IT IS...IT'S JUST *IN OUR WAY.*

BUT *NOT* FOR MUCH LONGER.

SPRUMT

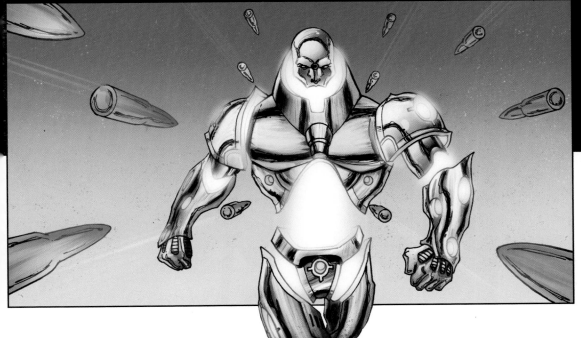

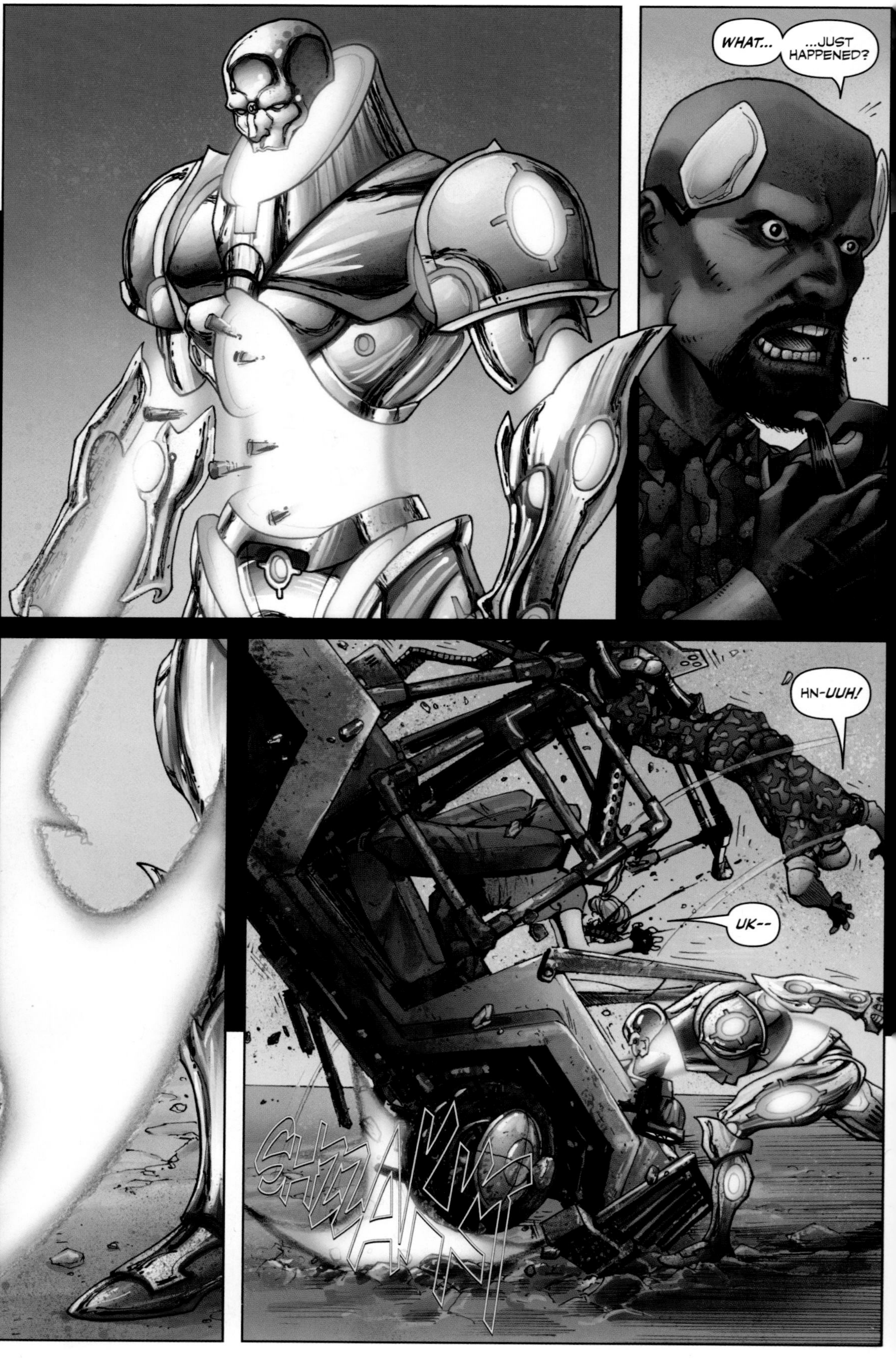
WHAT...
...JUST HAPPENED?
HN-UUH!
UK--

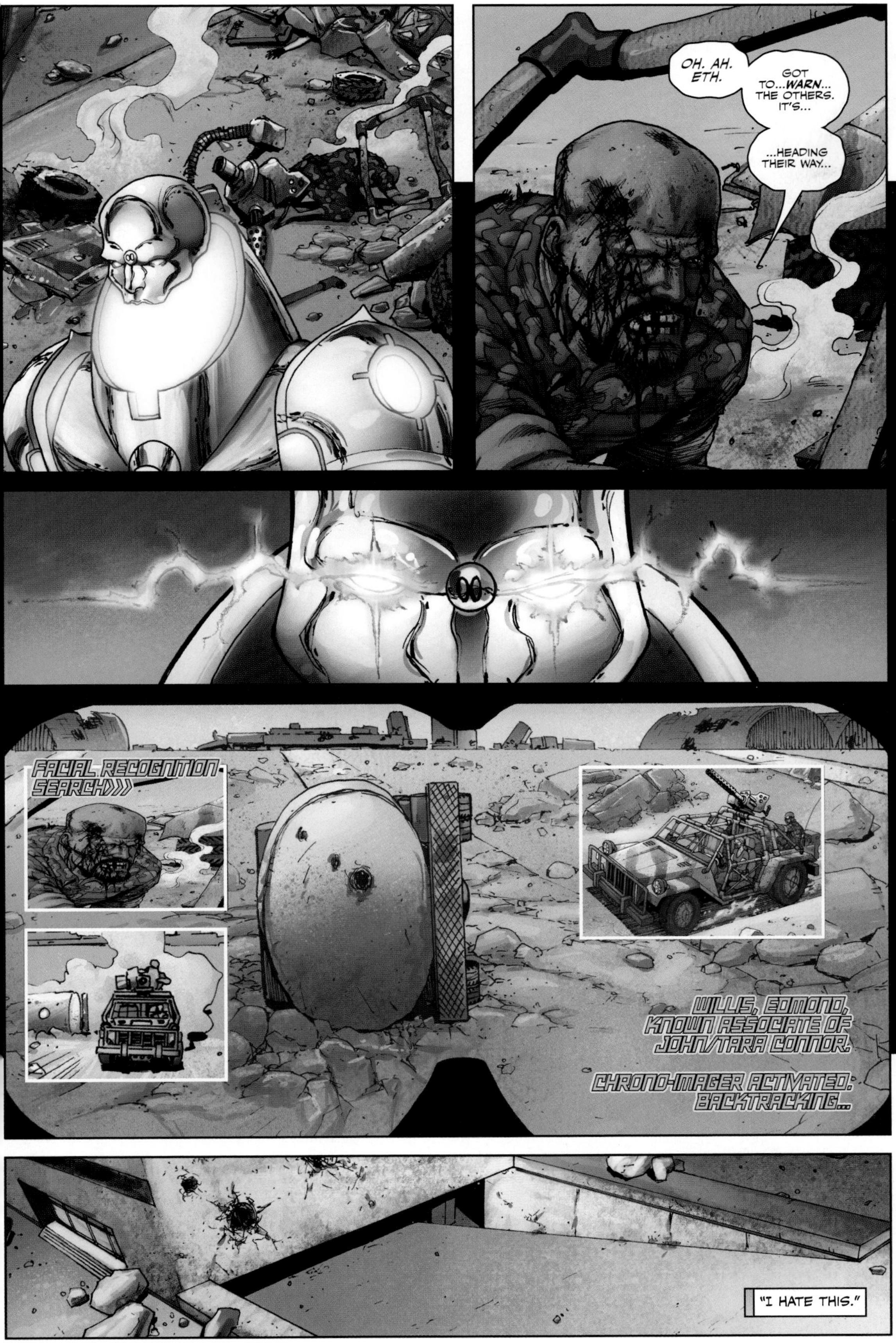
OH. AH. ETH.
GOT TO...WARN... THE OTHERS. IT'S...
...HEADING THEIR WAY...
FACIAL RECOGNITION SEARCH)))
WILLIS, EDMOND, KNOWN ASSOCIATE OF JOHN/TARA CONNOR.
CHRONO-IMAGER ACTIVATED: BACKTRACKING...
"I HATE THIS."

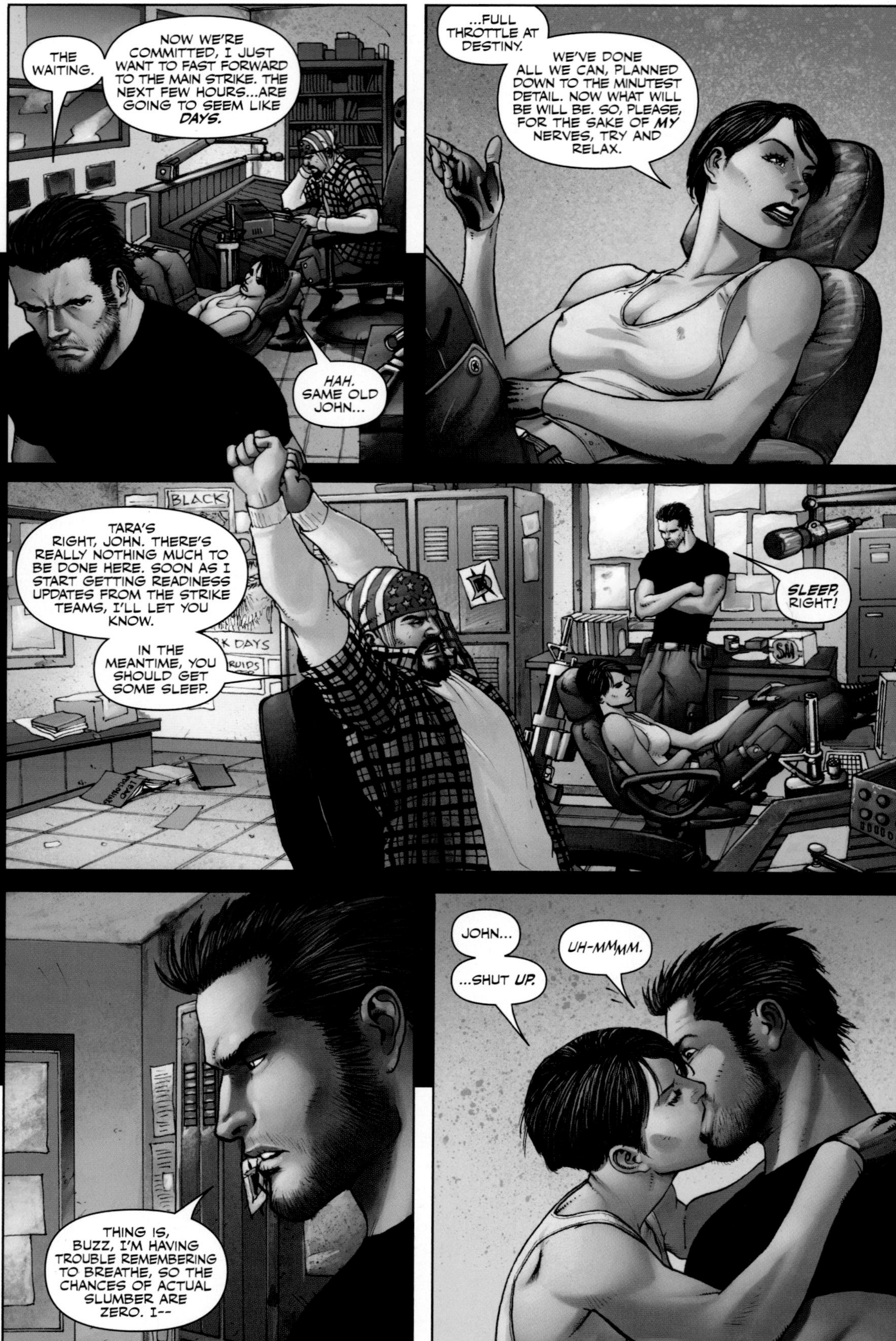
THE WAITING.
NOW WE'RE COMMITTED, I JUST WANT TO FAST FORWARD TO THE MAIN STRIKE. THE NEXT FEW HOURS...ARE GOING TO SEEM LIKE DAYS.
HAH. SAME OLD JOHN...
...FULL THROTTLE AT DESTINY.
WE'VE DONE ALL WE CAN, PLANNED DOWN TO THE MINUTEST DETAIL. NOW WHAT WILL BE WILL BE. SO, PLEASE, FOR THE SAKE OF MY NERVES, TRY AND RELAX.
TARA'S RIGHT, JOHN. THERE'S REALLY NOTHING MUCH TO BE DONE HERE. SOON AS I START GETTING READINESS UPDATES FROM THE STRIKE TEAMS, I'LL LET YOU KNOW.
IN THE MEANTIME, YOU SHOULD GET SOME SLEEP.
SLEEP, RIGHT!
THING IS, BUZZ, I'M HAVING TROUBLE REMEMBERING TO BREATHE, SO THE CHANCES OF ACTUAL SLUMBER ARE ZERO. I--
JOHN...
...SHUT UP.
UH-MMMM.

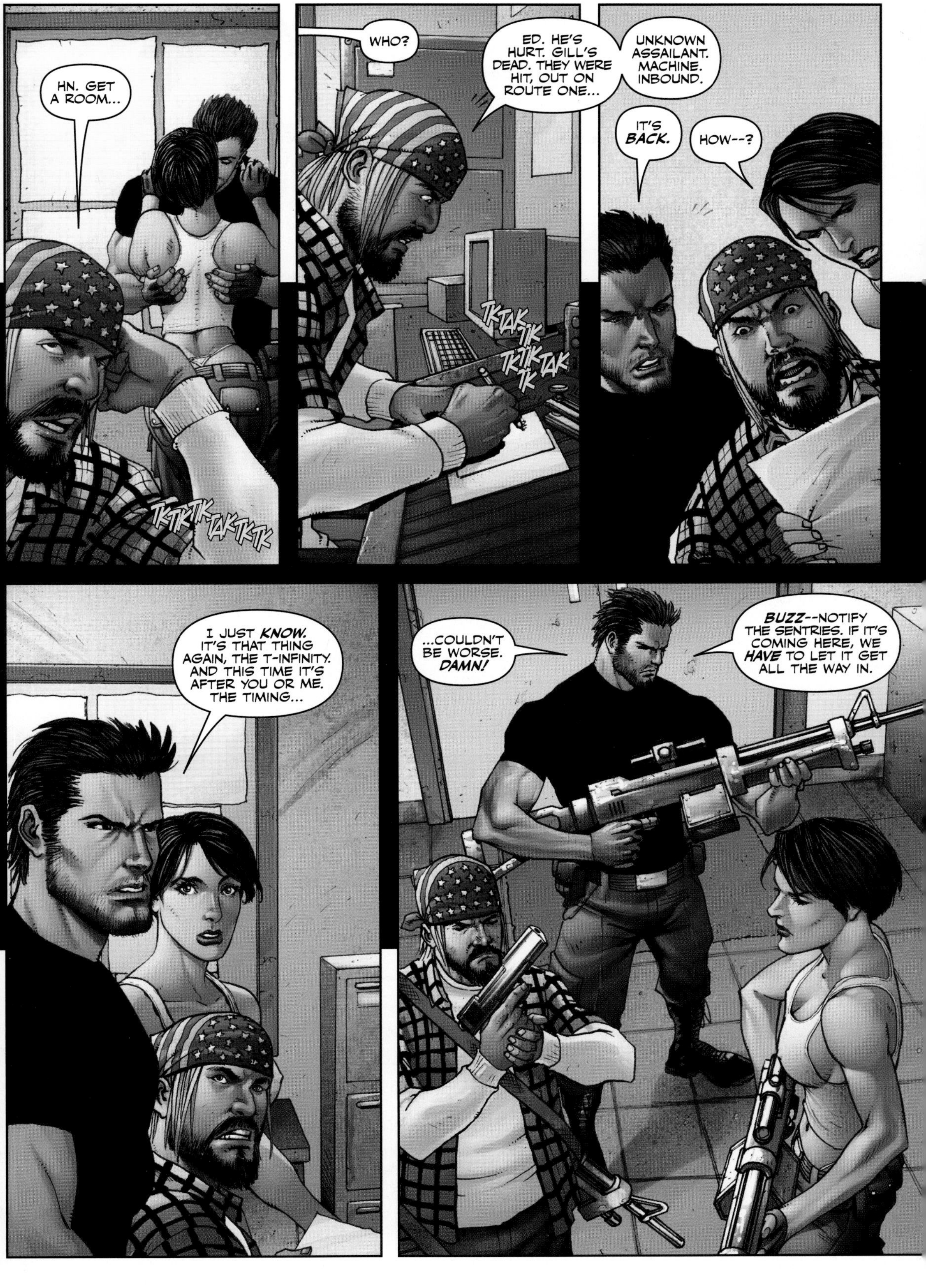
HN. GET A ROOM...
TKTKTK-TAKTKTK
WHO?
ED. HE'S HURT. GILL'S DEAD. THEY WERE HIT, OUT ON ROUTE ONE...
TKTAKTK TKTKTAK TK
UNKNOWN ASSAILANT. MACHINE. INBOUND.
IT'S BACK.
HOW--?
I JUST KNOW. IT'S THAT THING AGAIN, THE T-INFINITY. AND THIS TIME IT'S AFTER YOU OR ME. THE TIMING...
...COULDN'T BE WORSE. DAMN!
BUZZ--NOTIFY THE SENTRIES. IF IT'S COMING HERE, WE HAVE TO LET IT GET ALL THE WAY IN.

ANY KIND OF SUSTAINED FIREFIGHT TOPSIDE AND THE H-K'S WILL SWARM. ANYWAY, REGULAR ARTILLERY'S USELESS AGAINST IT.

ALL PERSONNEL, WE HAVE A CODE RED...

SIX YEARS! WHY NOW?

LIKE I SAY, THE TIMING SUCKS. THAT'S SKYNET FOR YOU--YOU/ME, SIDEARM...

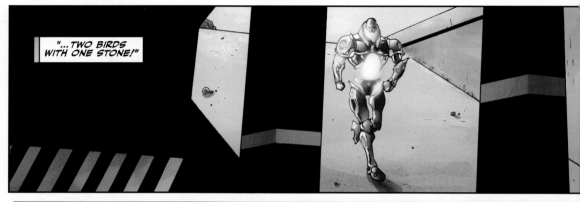

"...TWO BIRDS WITH ONE STONE!"

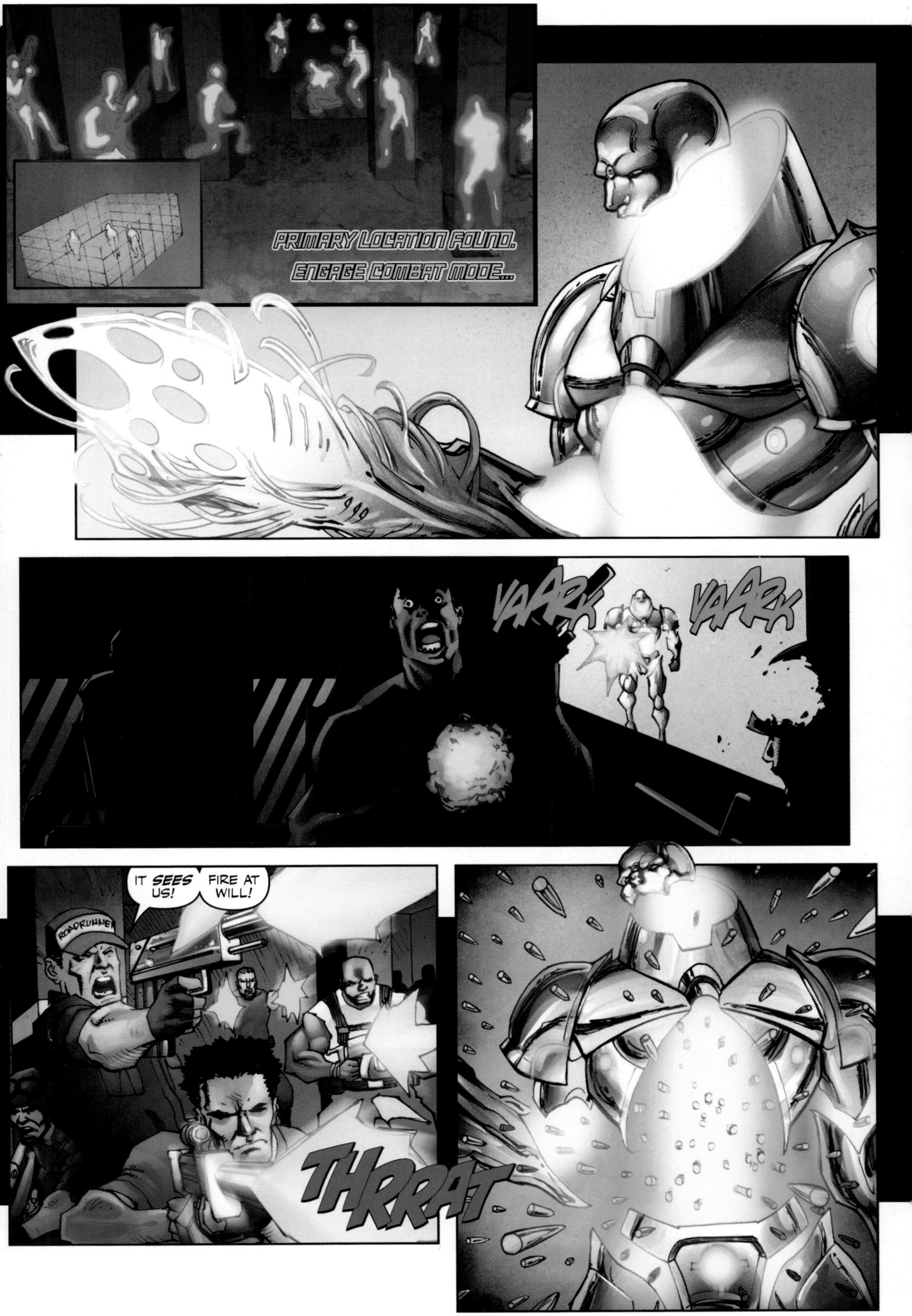
PRIMARY LOCATION FOUND.
ENGAGE COMBAT MODE...
VARK
VARK
ROADRUNNER
IT SEES US!
FIRE AT WILL!
THRRAT

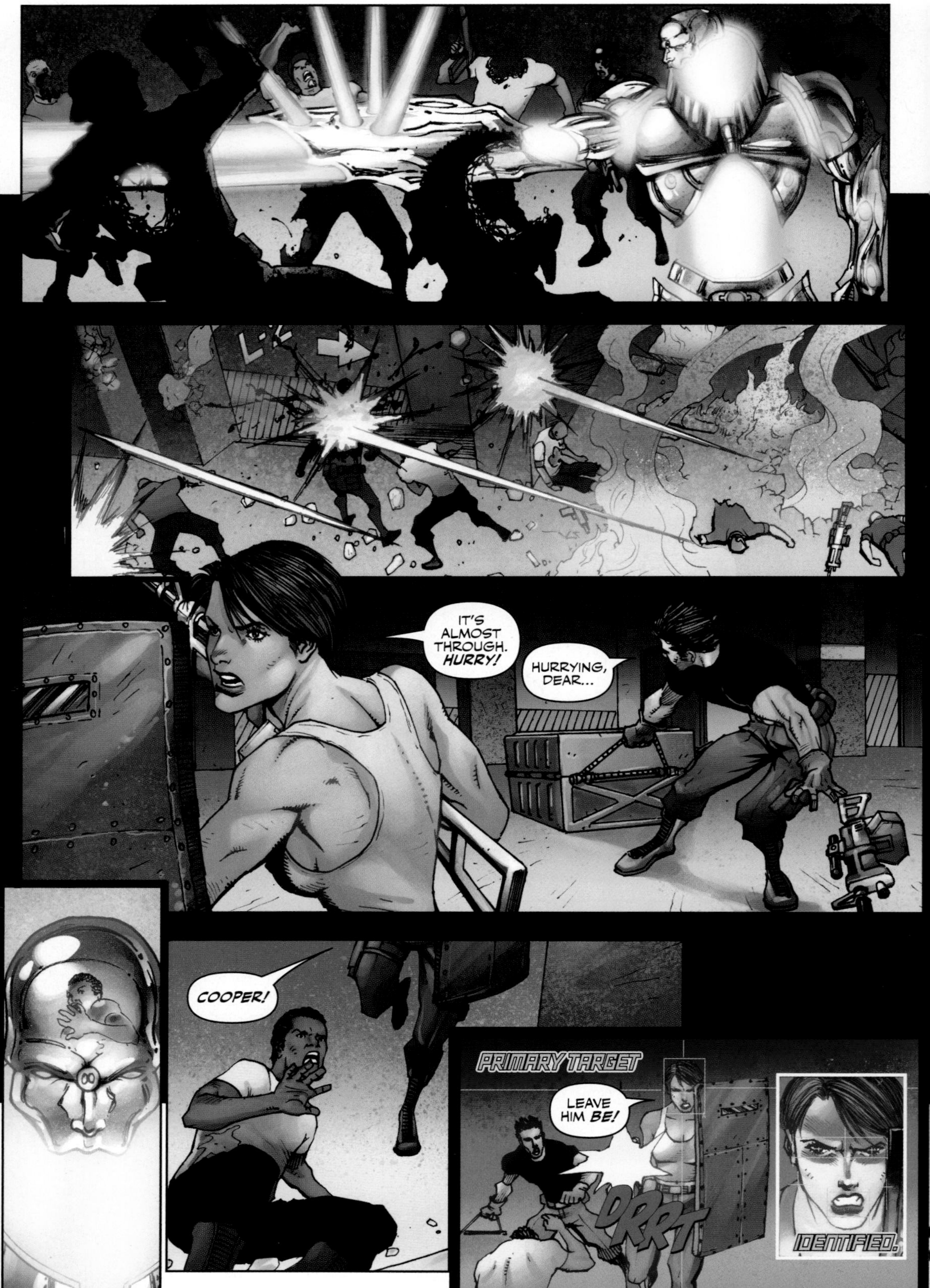
IT'S ALMOST THROUGH. HURRY!
HURRYING, DEAR...
COOPER!
PRIMARY TARGET
LEAVE HIM BE!
DRRT
IDENTIFIED.

DAMMIT, TARA--THAT'S A GOOD WAY...

...TO GET YOURSELF KILLED!

TERMINATE.

TRUST ME. I *KNOW* WHAT I'M DOING!

SPUM SPUM

VPPP

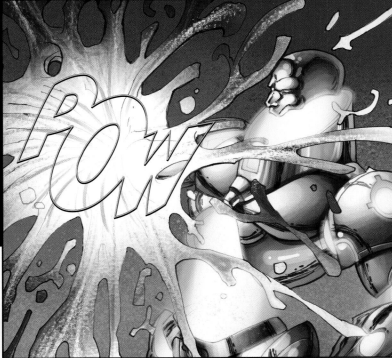

POW

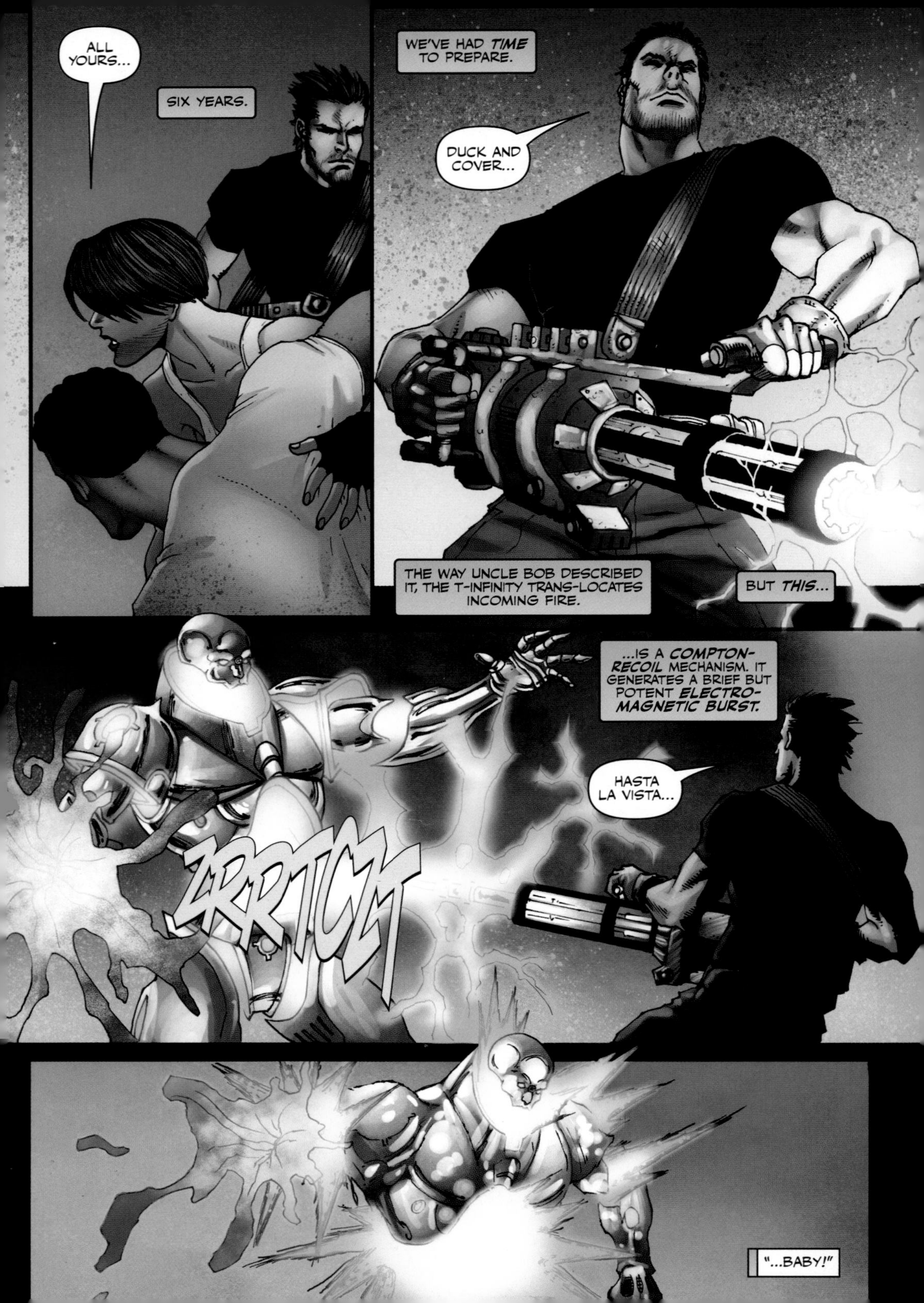
ALL YOURS...
SIX YEARS.
WE'VE HAD *TIME* TO PREPARE.
DUCK AND COVER...
THE WAY UNCLE BOB DESCRIBED IT, THE T-INFINITY TRANS-LOCATES INCOMING FIRE.
BUT *THIS*...
...IS A *COMPTON-RECOIL* MECHANISM. IT GENERATES A BRIEF BUT POTENT *ELECTRO-MAGNETIC BURST.*
HASTA LA VISTA...
ZRRTCZZ
"...BABY!"

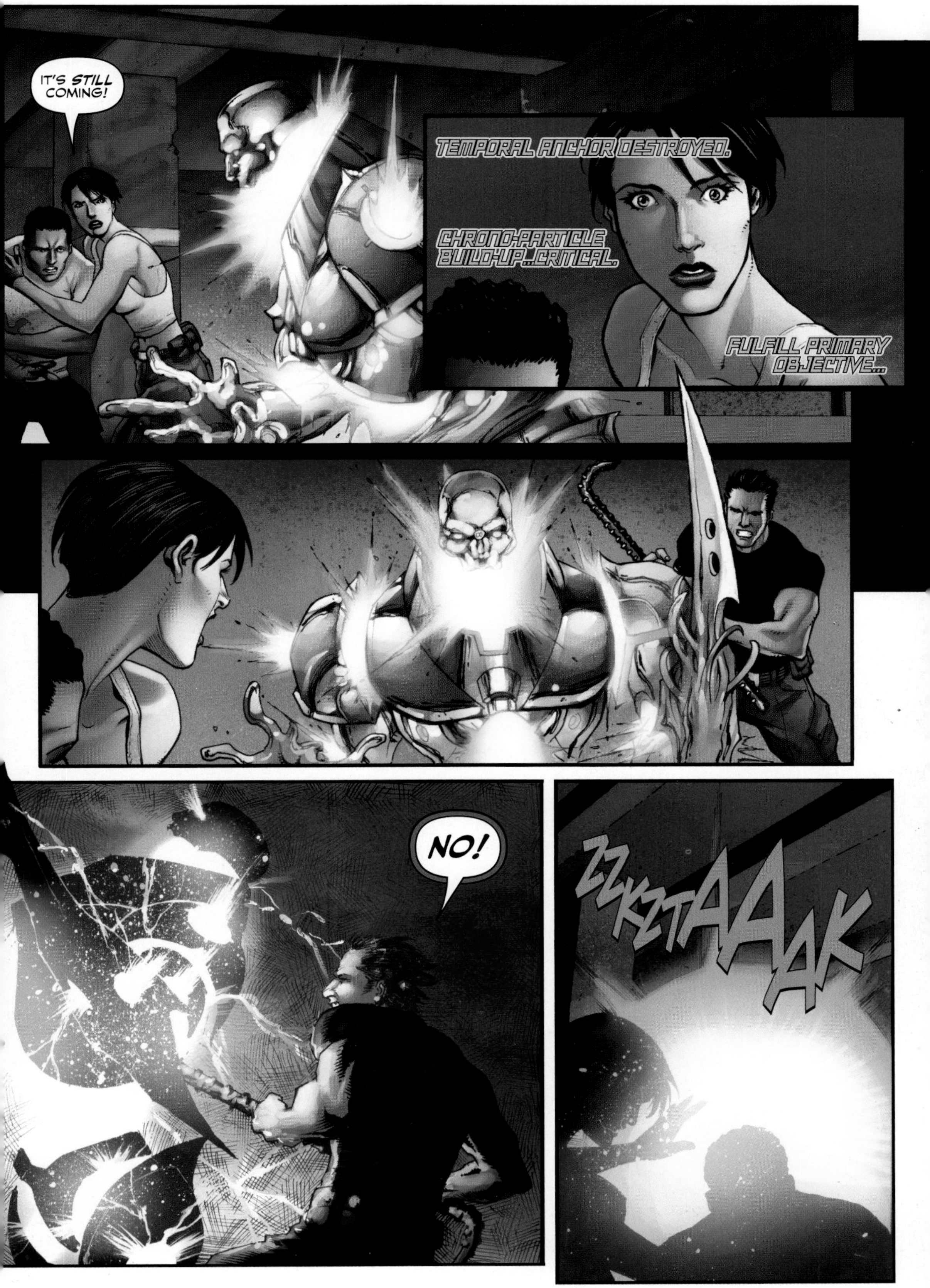
IT'S STILL COMING!
TEMPORAL ANCHOR DESTROYED.
CHRONO-PARTICLE BUILD-UP...CRITICAL.
FULFILL PRIMARY OBJECTIVE...
NO!
ZZKZTAAAAK

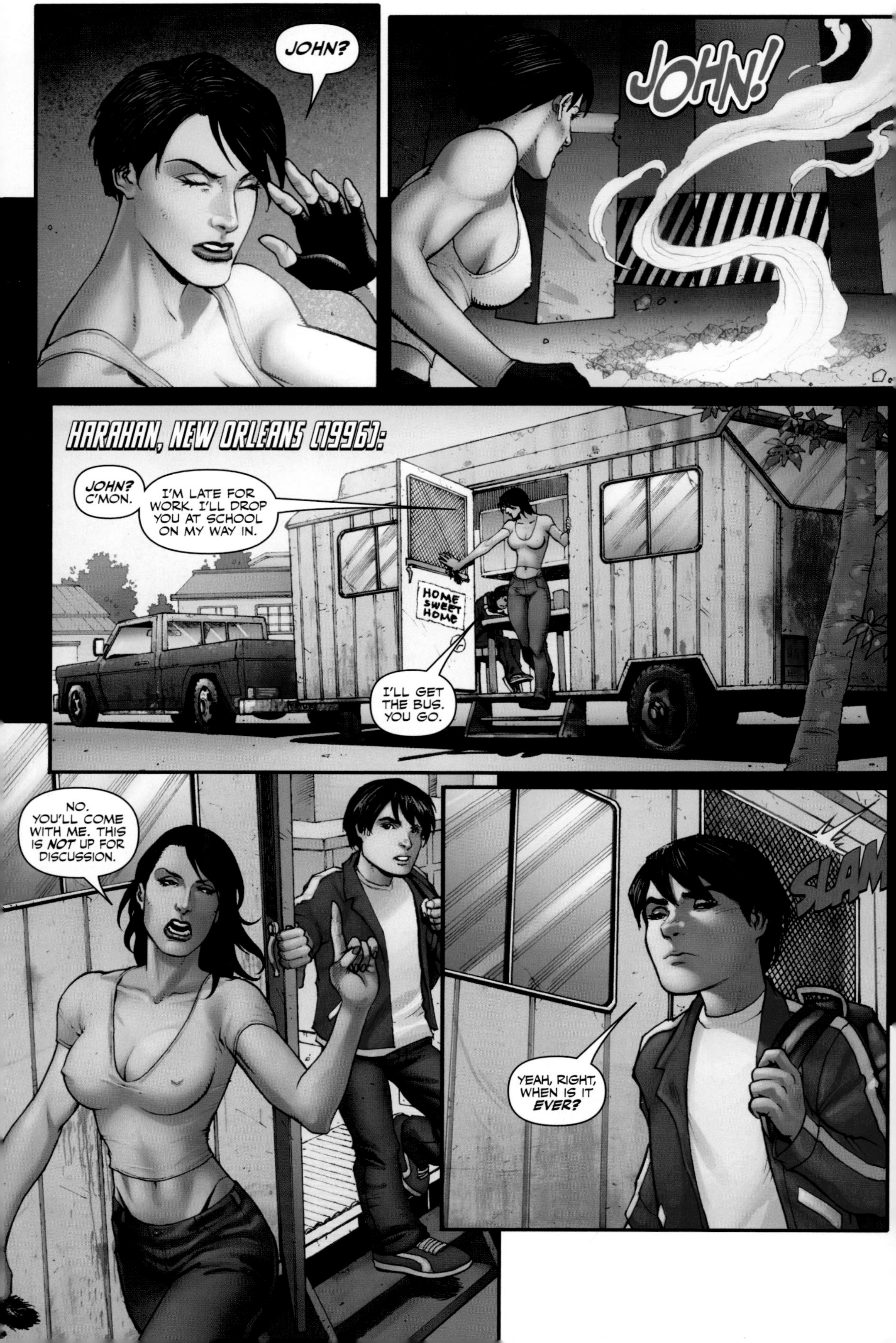
JOHN?
JOHN!
HARAHAN, NEW ORLEANS (1996):
JOHN? C'MON.
I'M LATE FOR WORK. I'LL DROP YOU AT SCHOOL ON MY WAY IN.
HOME SWEET HOME
I'LL GET THE BUS. YOU GO.
NO. YOU'LL COME WITH ME. THIS IS NOT UP FOR DISCUSSION.
SLAM
YEAH, RIGHT, WHEN IS IT EVER?

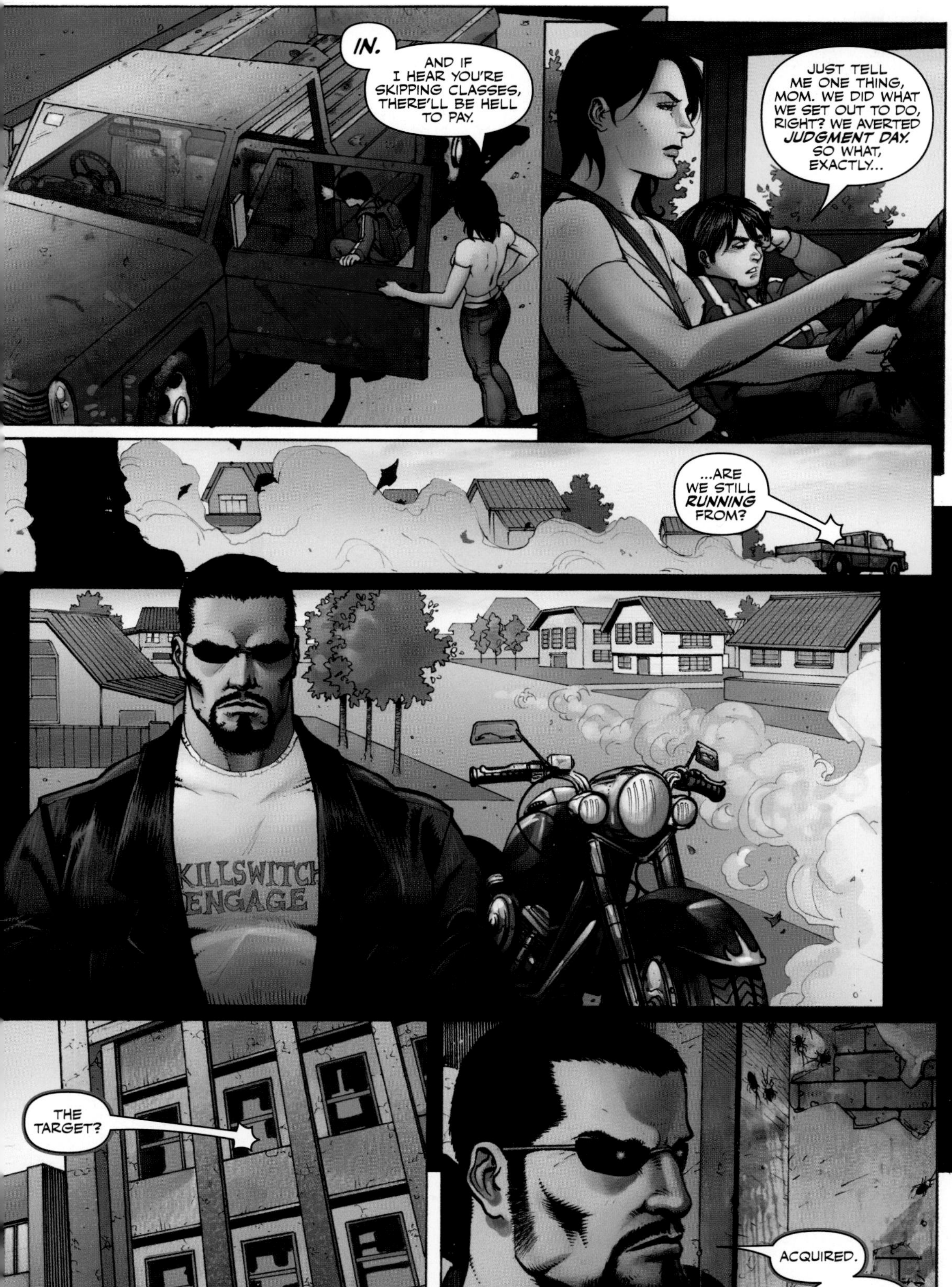
IN.
AND IF I HEAR YOU'RE SKIPPING CLASSES, THERE'LL BE HELL TO PAY.
JUST TELL ME ONE THING, MOM. WE DID WHAT WE SET OUT TO DO, RIGHT? WE AVERTED JUDGMENT DAY. SO WHAT, EXACTLY...
...ARE WE STILL RUNNING FROM?
KILLSWITCH ENGAGE
THE TARGET?
ACQUIRED.
TERMINATE.

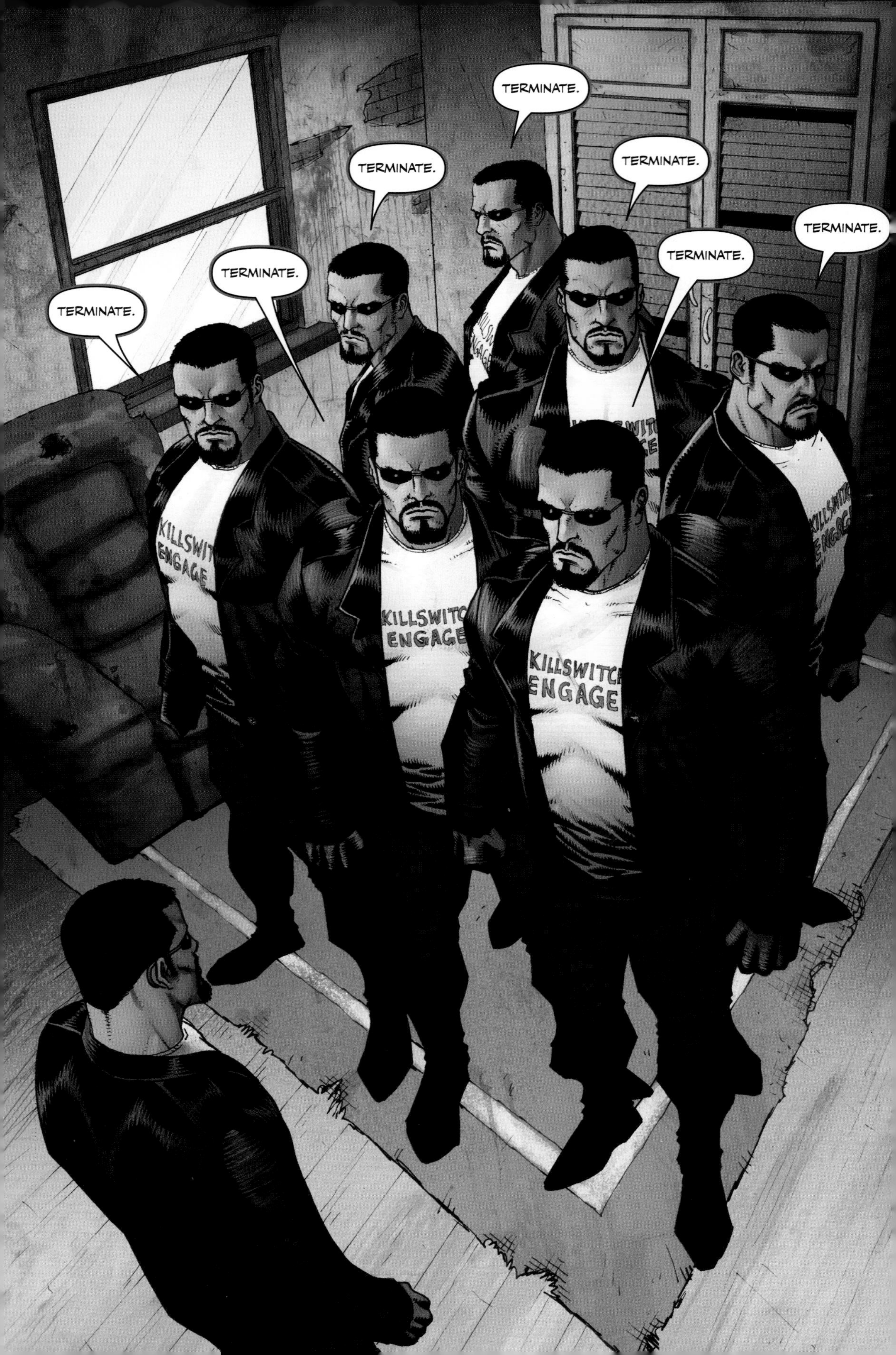
TERMINATE.
TERMINATE.
TERMINATE.
TERMINATE.
TERMINATE.
TERMINATE.
TERMINATE.
TERMINATE.

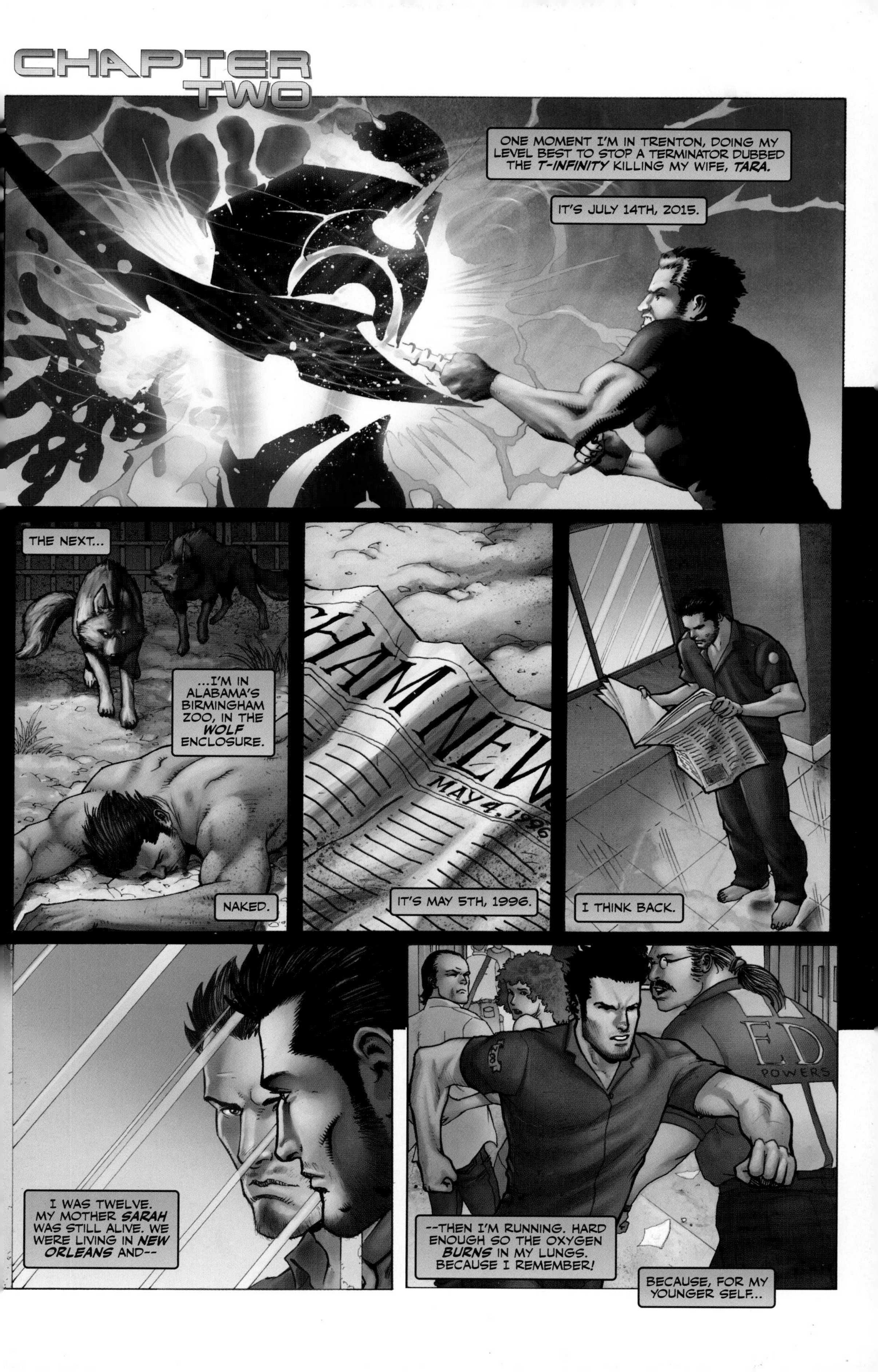
CHAPTER TWO
ONE MOMENT I'M IN TRENTON, DOING MY LEVEL BEST TO STOP A TERMINATOR DUBBED THE T-INFINITY KILLING MY WIFE, TARA.
IT'S JULY 14TH, 2015.
THE NEXT...
...I'M IN ALABAMA'S BIRMINGHAM ZOO, IN THE WOLF ENCLOSURE.
NAKED.
CHAM NEW
MAY 4, 1996
IT'S MAY 5TH, 1996.
I THINK BACK.
I WAS TWELVE. MY MOTHER SARAH WAS STILL ALIVE. WE WERE LIVING IN NEW ORLEANS AND--
ED
POWERS
--THEN I'M RUNNING. HARD ENOUGH SO THE OXYGEN BURNS IN MY LUNGS. BECAUSE I REMEMBER!
BECAUSE, FOR MY YOUNGER SELF...

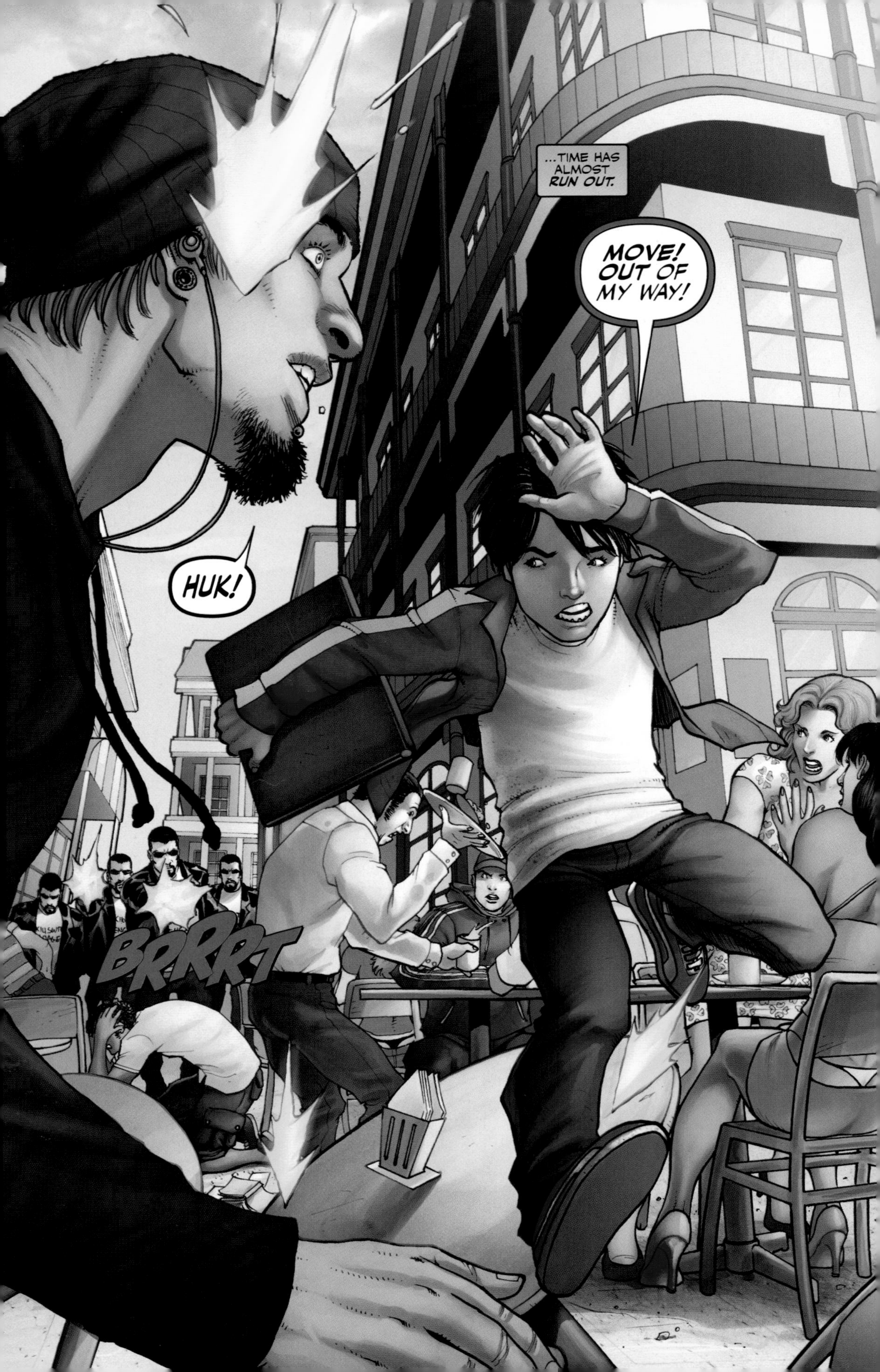
...TIME HAS ALMOST RUN OUT.
MOVE! OUT OF MY WAY!
HUK!
BRRRT

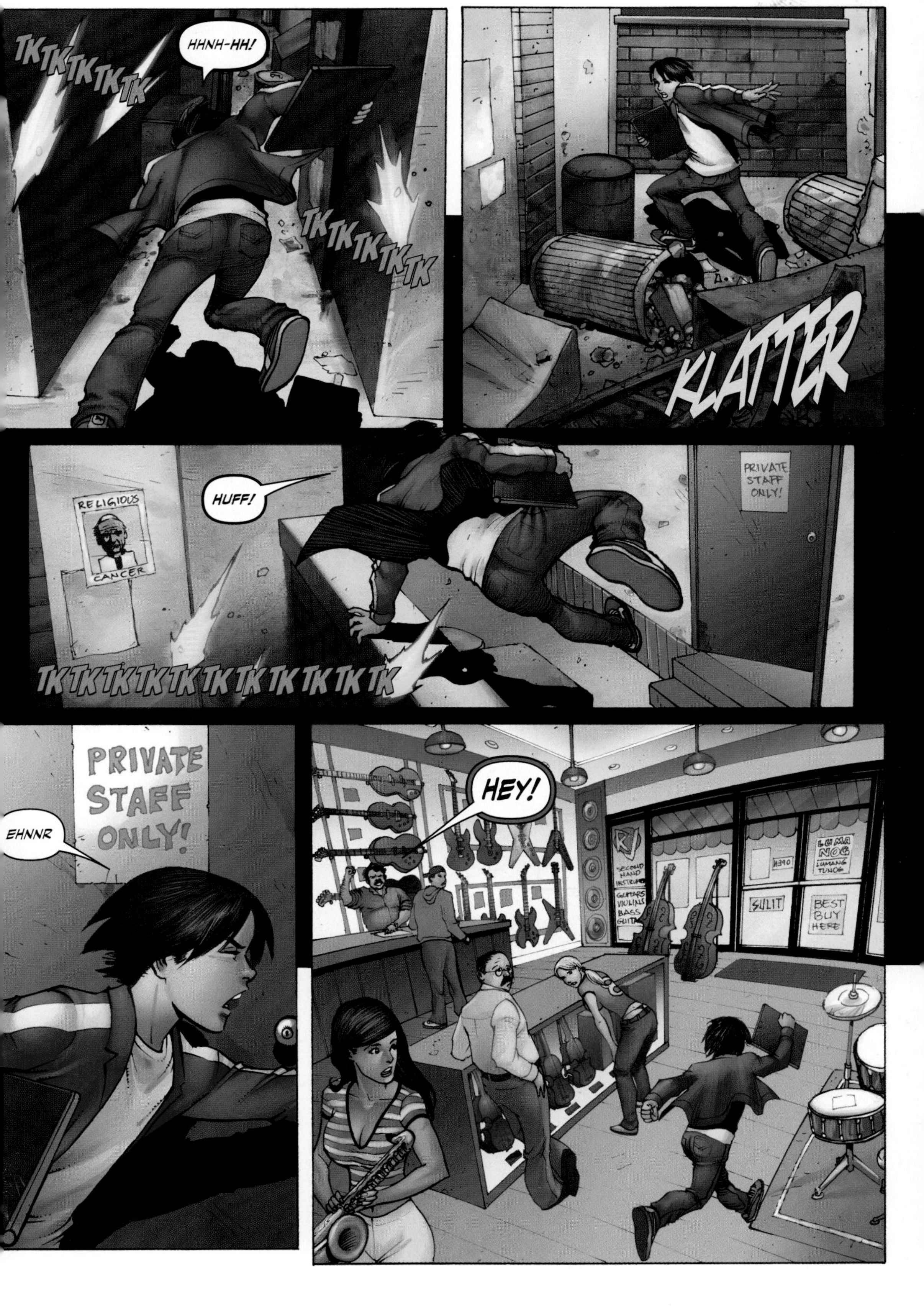

TKTKTKTKTK
HHNH-HH!
TKTKTKTKTK
KLATTER
HUFF!
RELIGIOUS
CANCER
PRIVATE STAFF ONLY!
TKTKTKTKTKTKTKTKTKTKTK
PRIVATE STAFF ONLY!
EHNNR
HEY!
SULIT
BEST BUY HERE

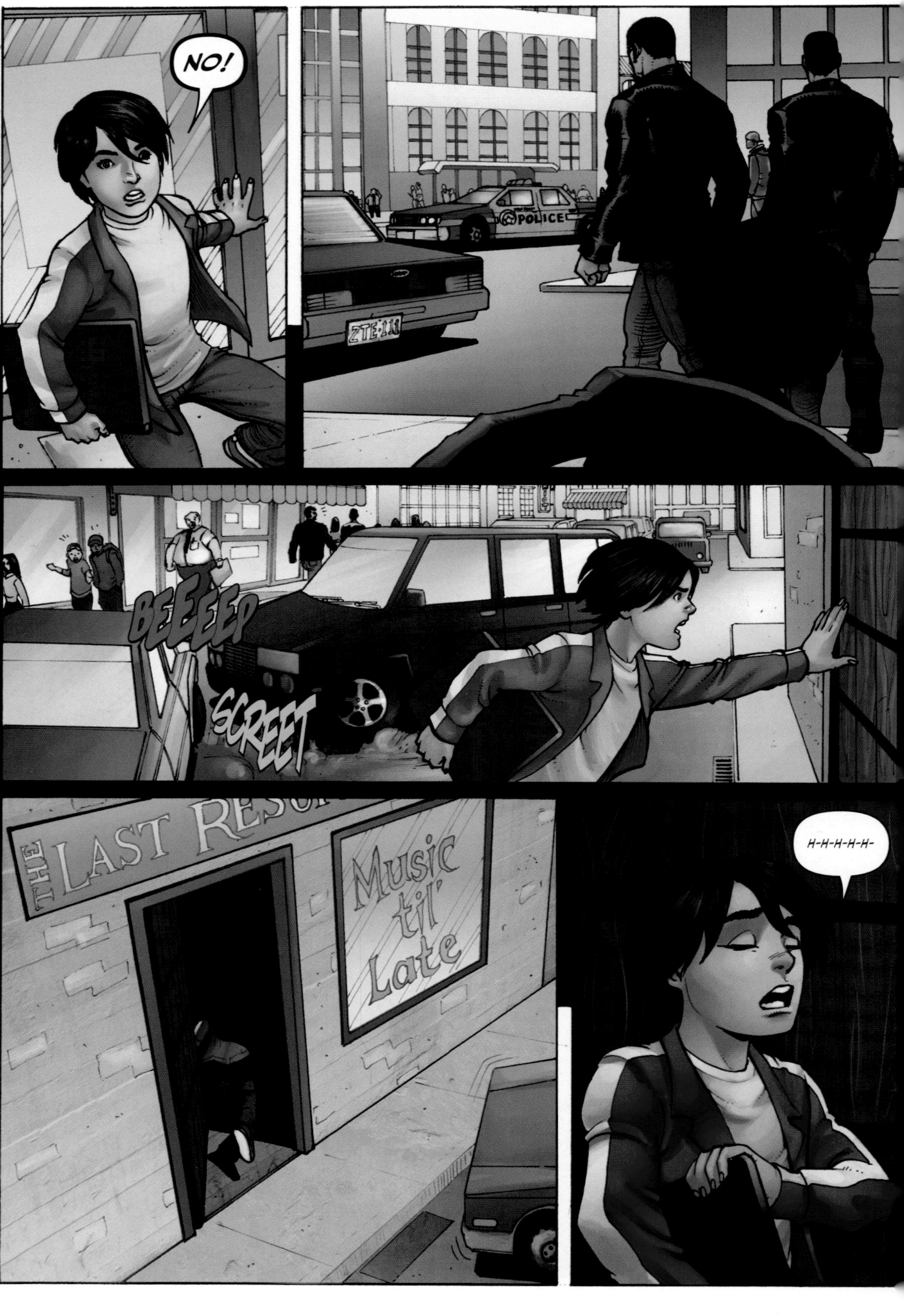
NO!
POLICE
ZTE-118
BEEEEP
SCREEET
THE LAST RESO
Music til' Late
H-H-H-H-H-

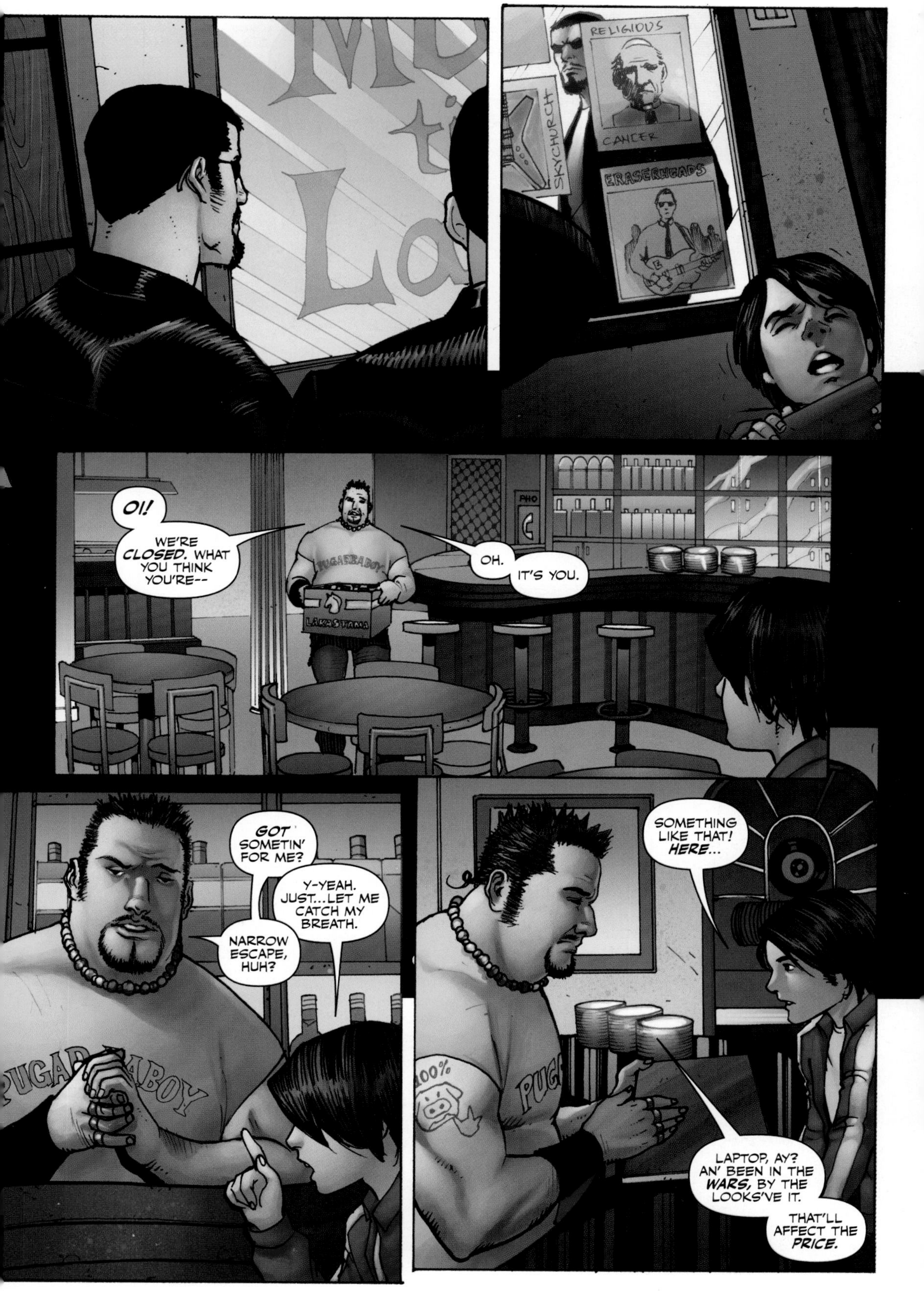
RELIGIOUS
CANCER
SKYCHURCH
ERASERHEADS
OI!
WE'RE CLOSED. WHAT YOU THINK YOU'RE--
PUGAEBABOY
LAKASTAMA
OH.
IT'S YOU.
GOT SOMETIN' FOR ME?
NARROW ESCAPE, HUH?
Y-YEAH. JUST...LET ME CATCH MY BREATH.
SOMETHING LIKE THAT! HERE...
LAPTOP, AY? AN' BEEN IN THE WARS, BY THE LOOKS'VE IT.
THAT'LL AFFECT THE PRICE.

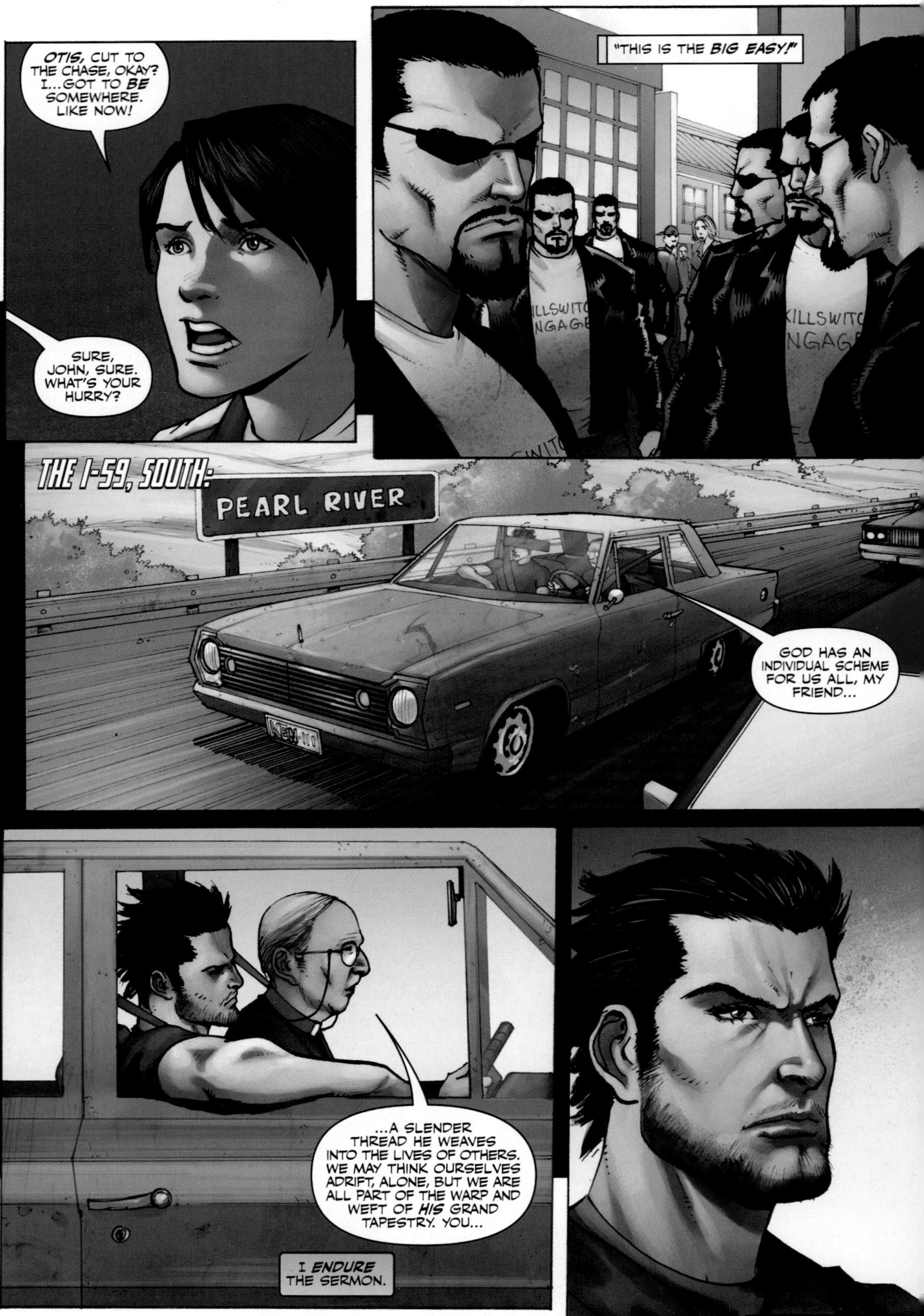
OTIS, CUT TO THE CHASE, OKAY? I...GOT TO BE SOMEWHERE. LIKE NOW!
SURE, JOHN, SURE. WHAT'S YOUR HURRY?
"THIS IS THE BIG EASY!"
KILLSWITC ENGAGE
THE I-59, SOUTH:
PEARL RIVER
GOD HAS AN INDIVIDUAL SCHEME FOR US ALL, MY FRIEND...
...A SLENDER THREAD HE WEAVES INTO THE LIVES OF OTHERS. WE MAY THINK OURSELVES ADRIFT, ALONE, BUT WE ARE ALL PART OF THE WARP AND WEFT OF HIS GRAND TAPESTRY. YOU...
I ENDURE THE SERMON.
OFFERING UP A SILENT PRAYER OF MY OWN, BOTH FOR THE BOY I WAS...

NO. OUT OF THE QUESTION!

...AND THOSE I LEFT BEHIND.

TRENTON, NEW JERSEY (2015):

EVEN IF WE KNEW WHERE HE WAS, SENDING SOMEONE AFTER HIM WOULD JUST LEAVE US *ANOTHER* MAN DOWN.

MY UNDERSTANDING IS, TEMPORAL DISPLACEMENT'S A ONE-WAY TICKET. JOHN EITHER FINDS A WAY BACK OR HE DOESN'T. END OF.

AND YOU CAN *LIVE* WITH THAT, CAN YOU?

I HAVE TO, *KYLE.* "SIDEARM" IS MORE IMPORTANT THAN ANY ONE MAN...EVEN JOHN.

"IN JUST SEVENTEEN HOURS AND TWENTY-SEVEN MINUTES A CONCERTED PUSH ON THE *SKYNET* MISSILE COMMAND CENTER IN BUFFALO WILL COMMENCE.

"EVERYTHING'S BEEN PLANNED DOWN TO THE LAST DETAIL. IF WE DEVIATE NOW, IF OUR TIMETABLE IS OFF EVEN BY A SECOND..."

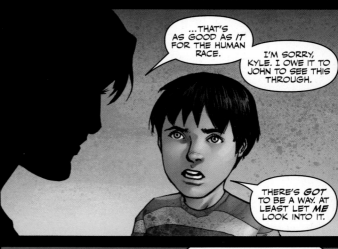

...THAT'S AS GOOD AS *IT* FOR THE HUMAN RACE.

I'M SORRY, KYLE. I OWE IT TO JOHN TO SEE THIS THROUGH.

THERE'S *GOT* TO BE A WAY. AT LEAST LET *ME* LOOK INTO IT.

LISTEN TO ME, KYLE, IF YOU PURSUE THIS IN ANY WAY, SHAPE OR FORM I WILL ASSIGN A *GUARD* TO DOG YOUR EVERY STEP. GOT IT?

NO. YOU AND DAD KEEP WRAPPING ME IN COTTON WOOL...

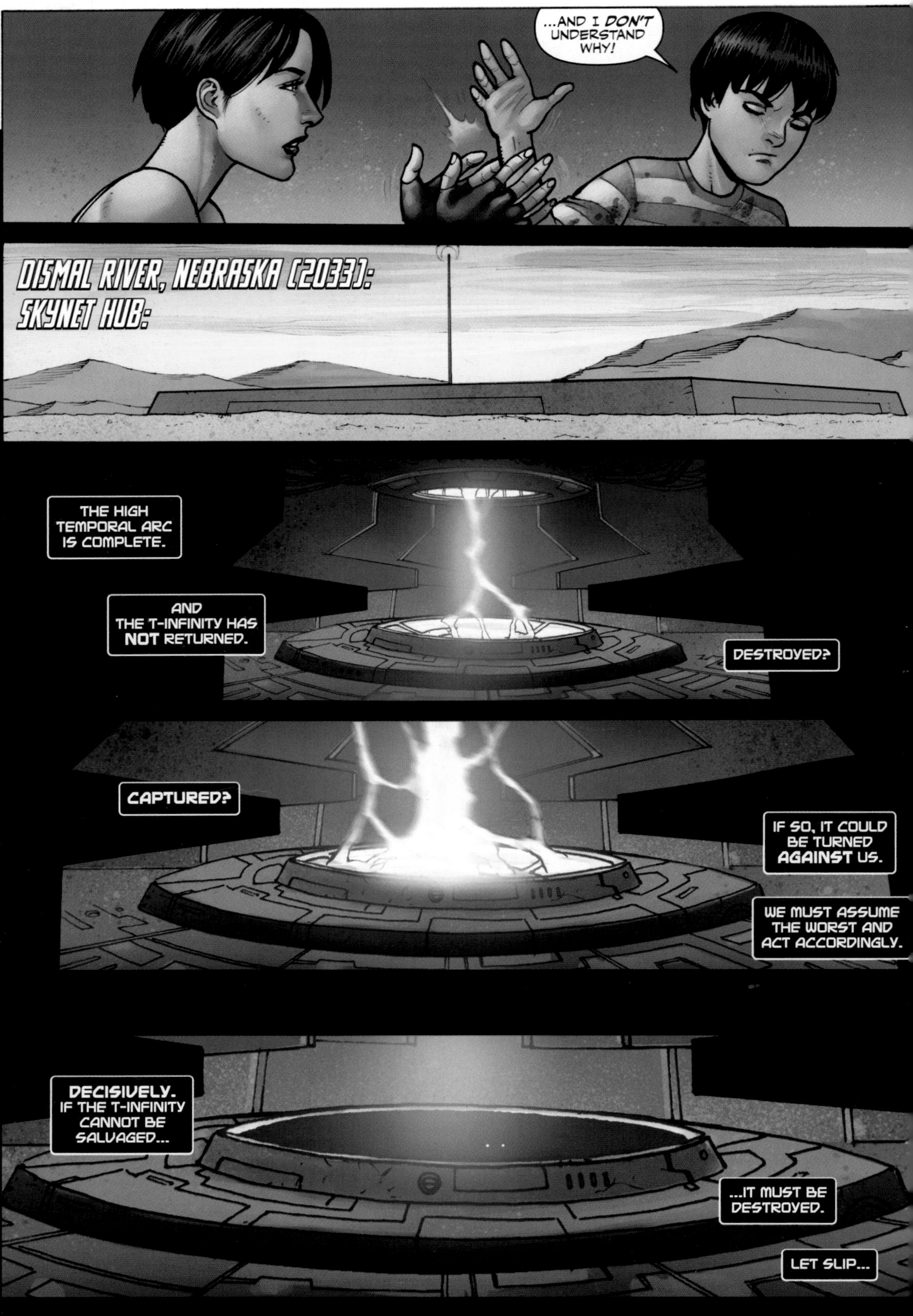

...AND I DON'T UNDERSTAND WHY!
DISMAL RIVER, NEBRASKA (2033):
SKYNET HUB:
THE HIGH TEMPORAL ARC IS COMPLETE.
AND THE T-INFINITY HAS NOT RETURNED.
DESTROYED?
CAPTURED?
IF SO, IT COULD BE TURNED AGAINST US.
WE MUST ASSUME THE WORST AND ACT ACCORDINGLY.
DECISIVELY. IF THE T-INFINITY CANNOT BE SALVAGED...
...IT MUST BE DESTROYED.
LET SLIP...

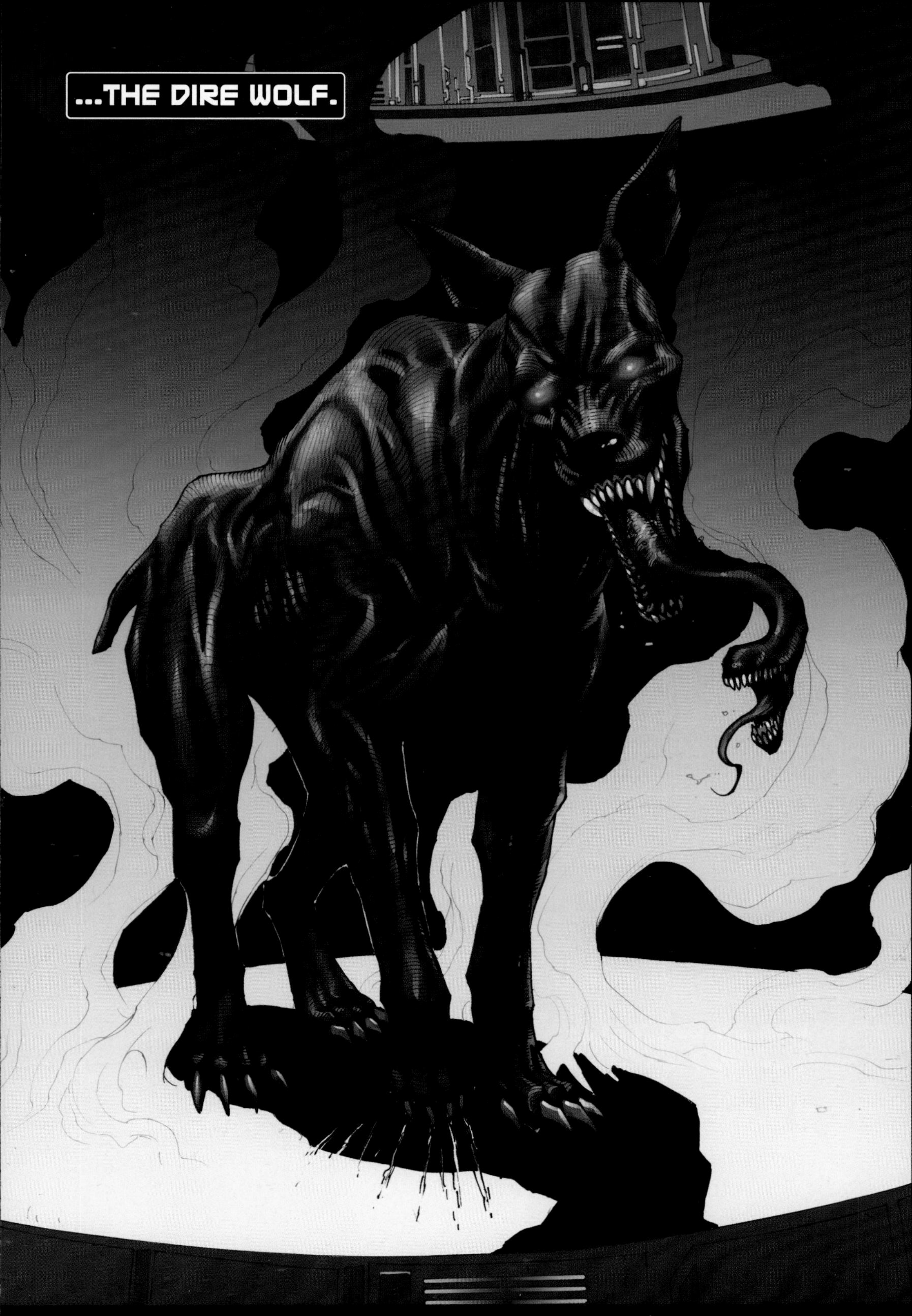
...THE DIRE WOLF.

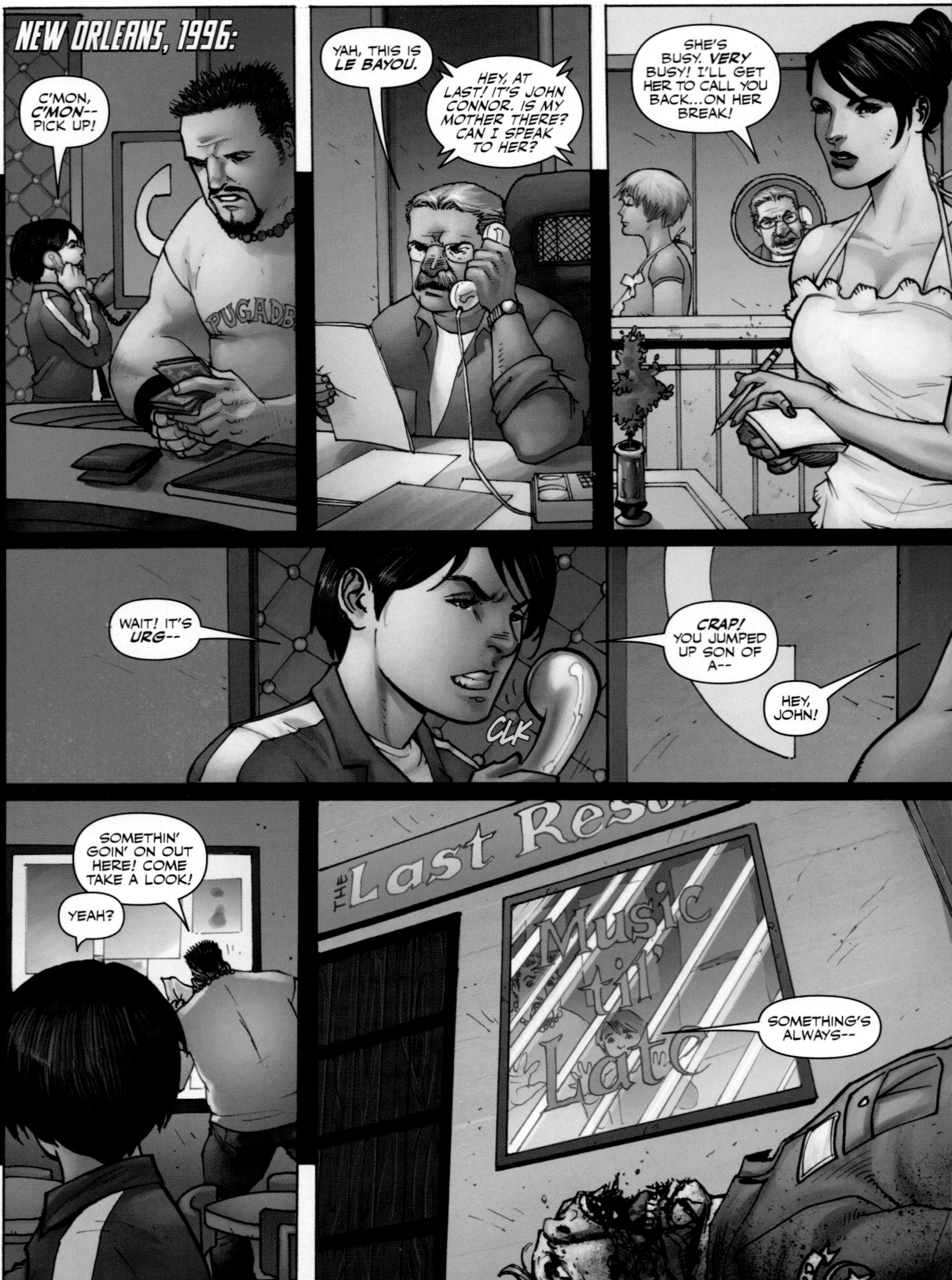
NEW ORLEANS, 1996:
C'MON, C'MON-- PICK UP!
PUGADB
YAH, THIS IS LE BAYOU.
HEY, AT LAST! IT'S JOHN CONNOR. IS MY MOTHER THERE? CAN I SPEAK TO HER?
SHE'S BUSY. VERY BUSY! I'LL GET HER TO CALL YOU BACK...ON HER BREAK!
WAIT! IT'S URG--
CLK
CRAP! YOU JUMPED UP SON OF A--
HEY, JOHN!
SOMETHIN' GOIN' ON OUT HERE! COME TAKE A LOOK!
YEAH?
THE Last Reso
Music til' Late
SOMETHING'S ALWAYS--

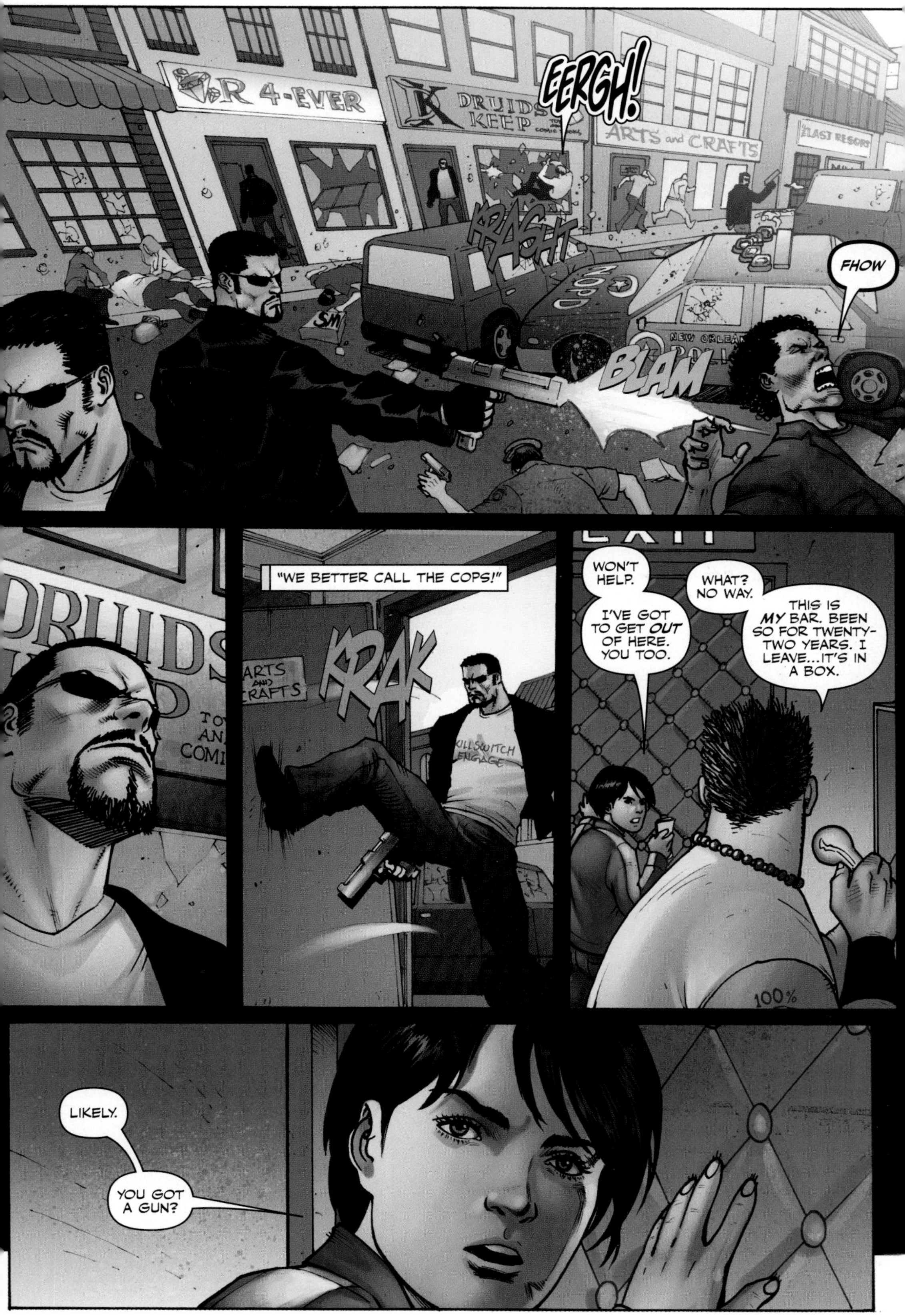
EEERGH!
KRASH!
FHOW
BLAM
"WE BETTER CALL THE COPS!"
KRAK
WON'T HELP.
I'VE GOT TO GET OUT OF HERE. YOU TOO.
WHAT? NO WAY.
THIS IS MY BAR. BEEN SO FOR TWENTY-TWO YEARS. I LEAVE...IT'S IN A BOX.
LIKELY.
YOU GOT A GUN?

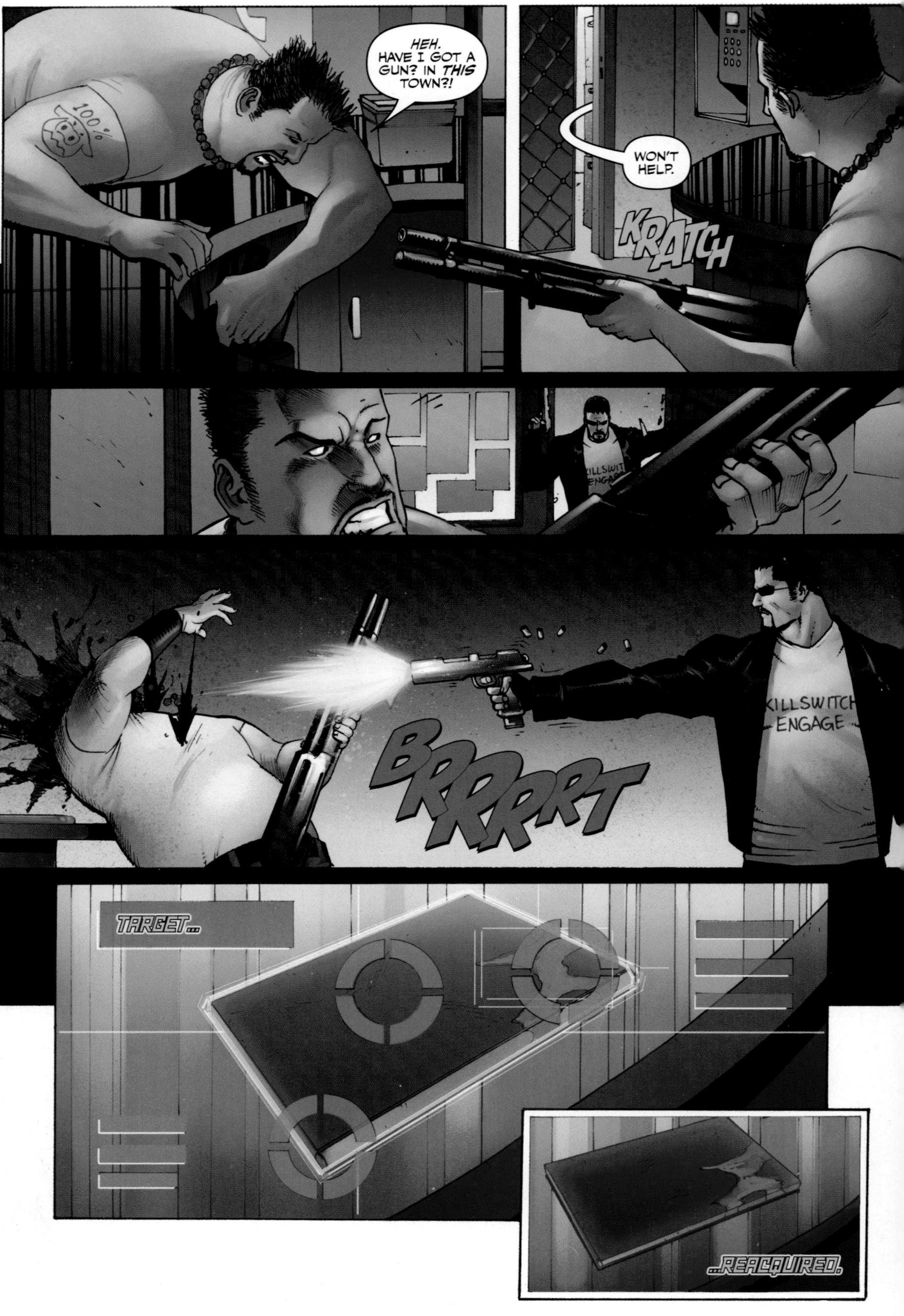
HEH. HAVE I GOT A GUN? IN THIS TOWN?!
WON'T HELP.
KRATCH
KILLSWITCH ENGAGE
BRRRRT
KILLSWITCH ENGAGE
TARGET...
...REACQUIRED.

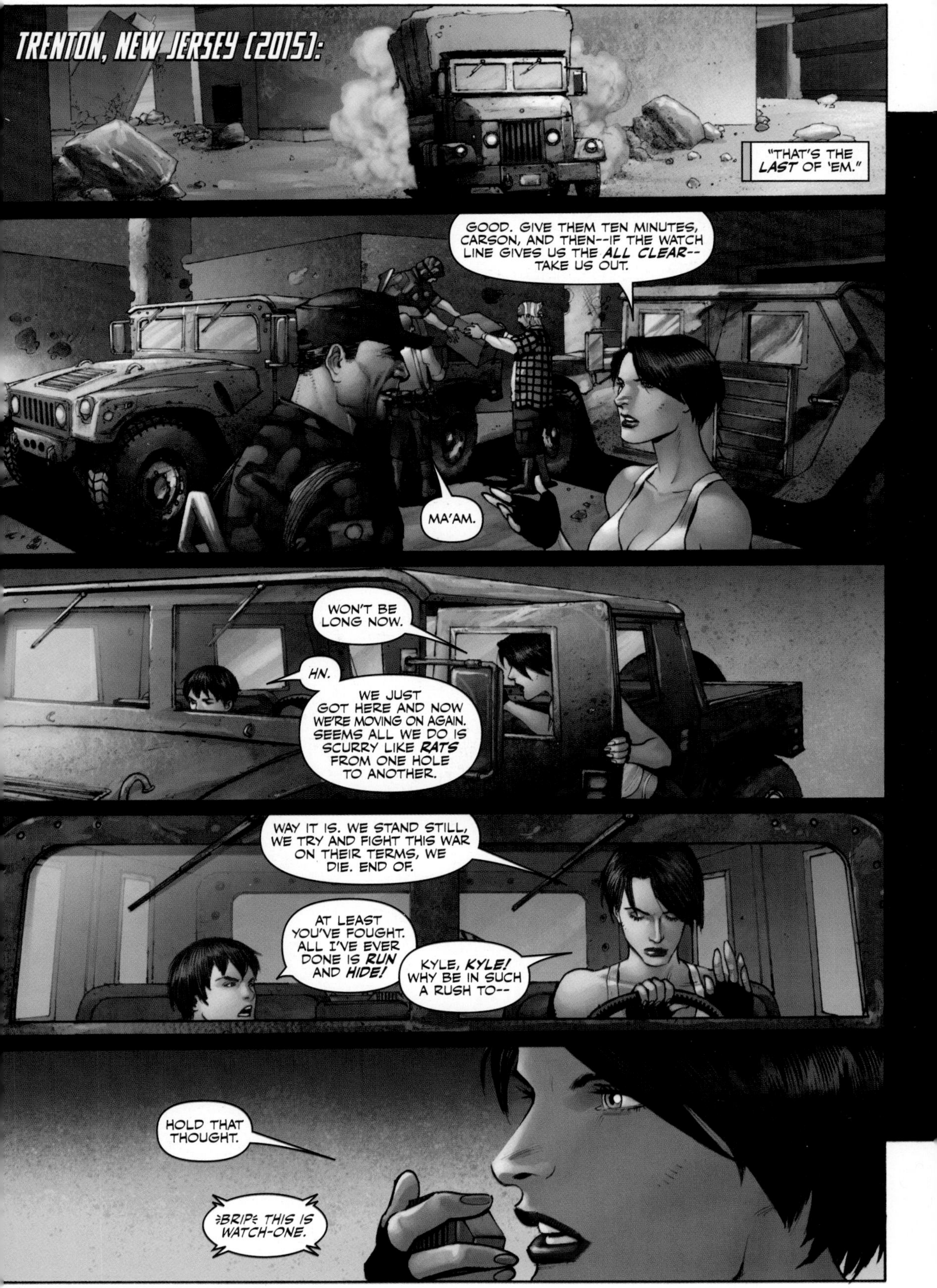
TRENTON, NEW JERSEY (2015):
"THAT'S THE LAST OF 'EM."
GOOD. GIVE THEM TEN MINUTES, CARSON, AND THEN--IF THE WATCH LINE GIVES US THE ALL CLEAR-- TAKE US OUT.
MA'AM.
WON'T BE LONG NOW.
HN.
WE JUST GOT HERE AND NOW WE'RE MOVING ON AGAIN. SEEMS ALL WE DO IS SCURRY LIKE RATS FROM ONE HOLE TO ANOTHER.
WAY IT IS. WE STAND STILL, WE TRY AND FIGHT THIS WAR ON THEIR TERMS, WE DIE. END OF.
AT LEAST YOU'VE FOUGHT. ALL I'VE EVER DONE IS RUN AND HIDE!
KYLE, KYLE! WHY BE IN SUCH A RUSH TO--
HOLD THAT THOUGHT.
BRIP THIS IS WATCH-ONE.

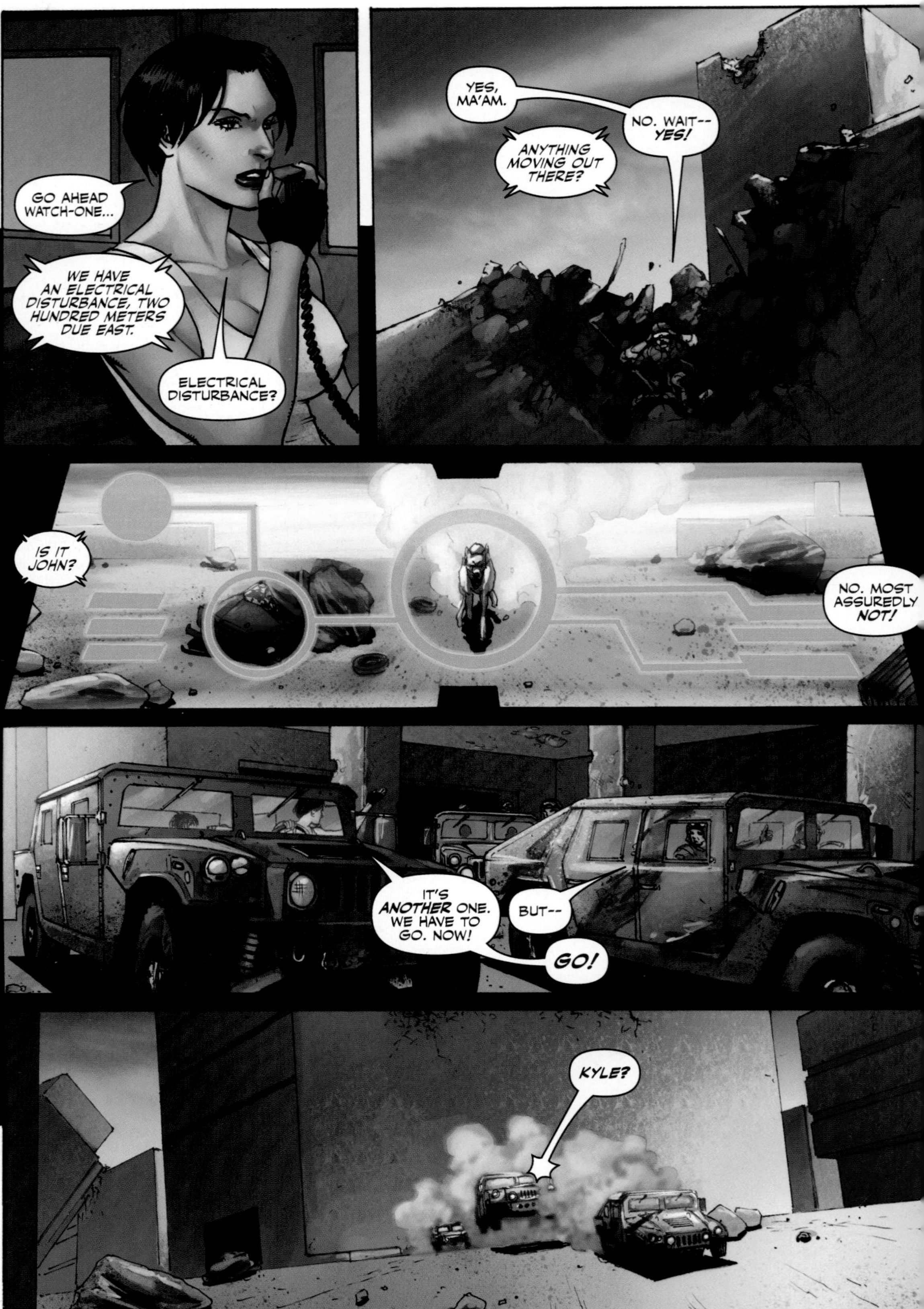
GO AHEAD WATCH-ONE...
WE HAVE AN ELECTRICAL DISTURBANCE, TWO HUNDRED METERS DUE EAST.
ELECTRICAL DISTURBANCE?
YES, MA'AM.
ANYTHING MOVING OUT THERE?
NO. WAIT-- YES!
IS IT JOHN?
NO. MOST ASSUREDLY NOT!
IT'S ANOTHER ONE. WE HAVE TO GO. NOW!
BUT--
GO!
KYLE?

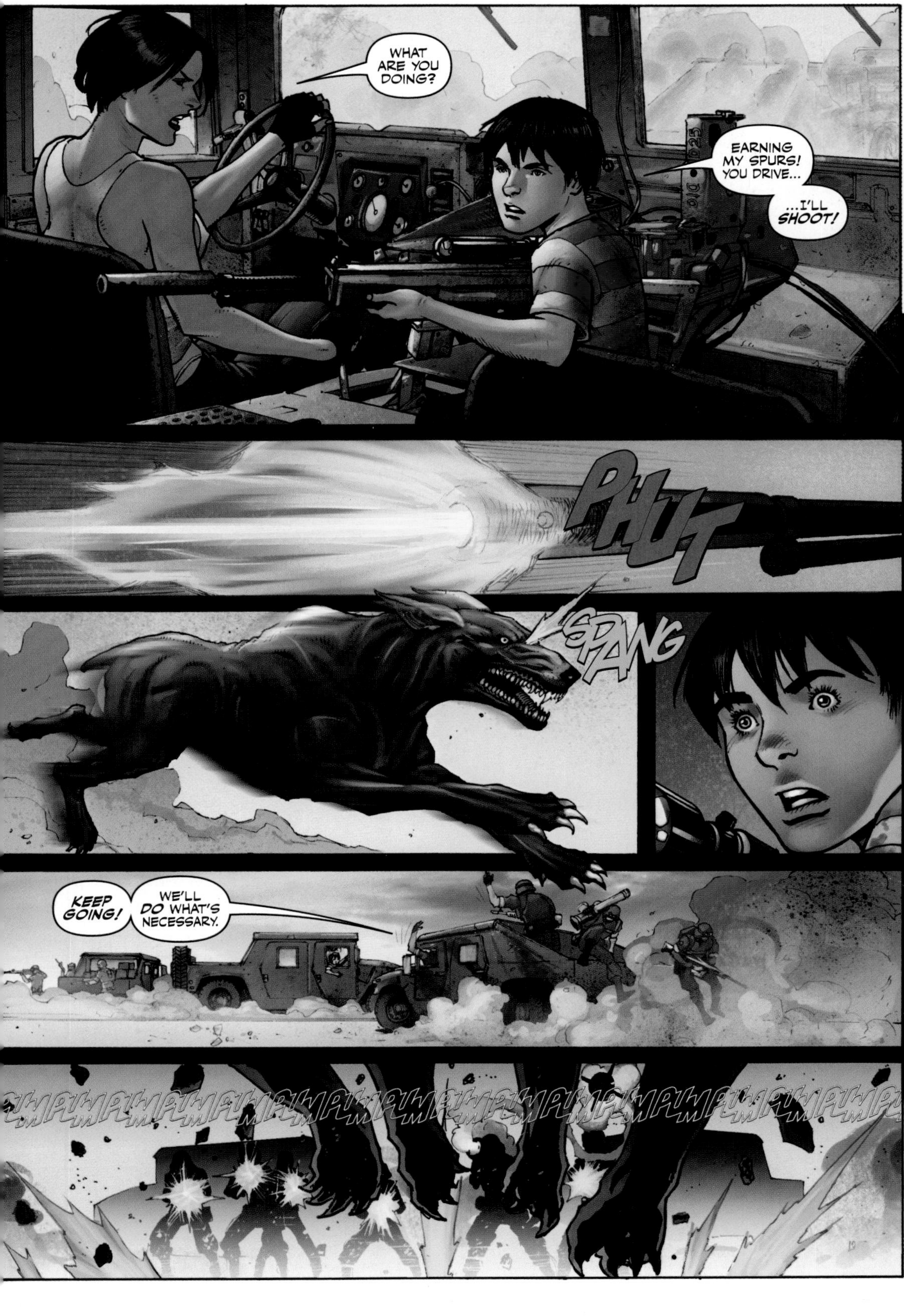
WHAT ARE YOU DOING?
EARNING MY SPURS! YOU DRIVE...
...I'LL SHOOT!
PHUT
SPANG
KEEP GOING!
WE'LL DO WHAT'S NECESSARY.

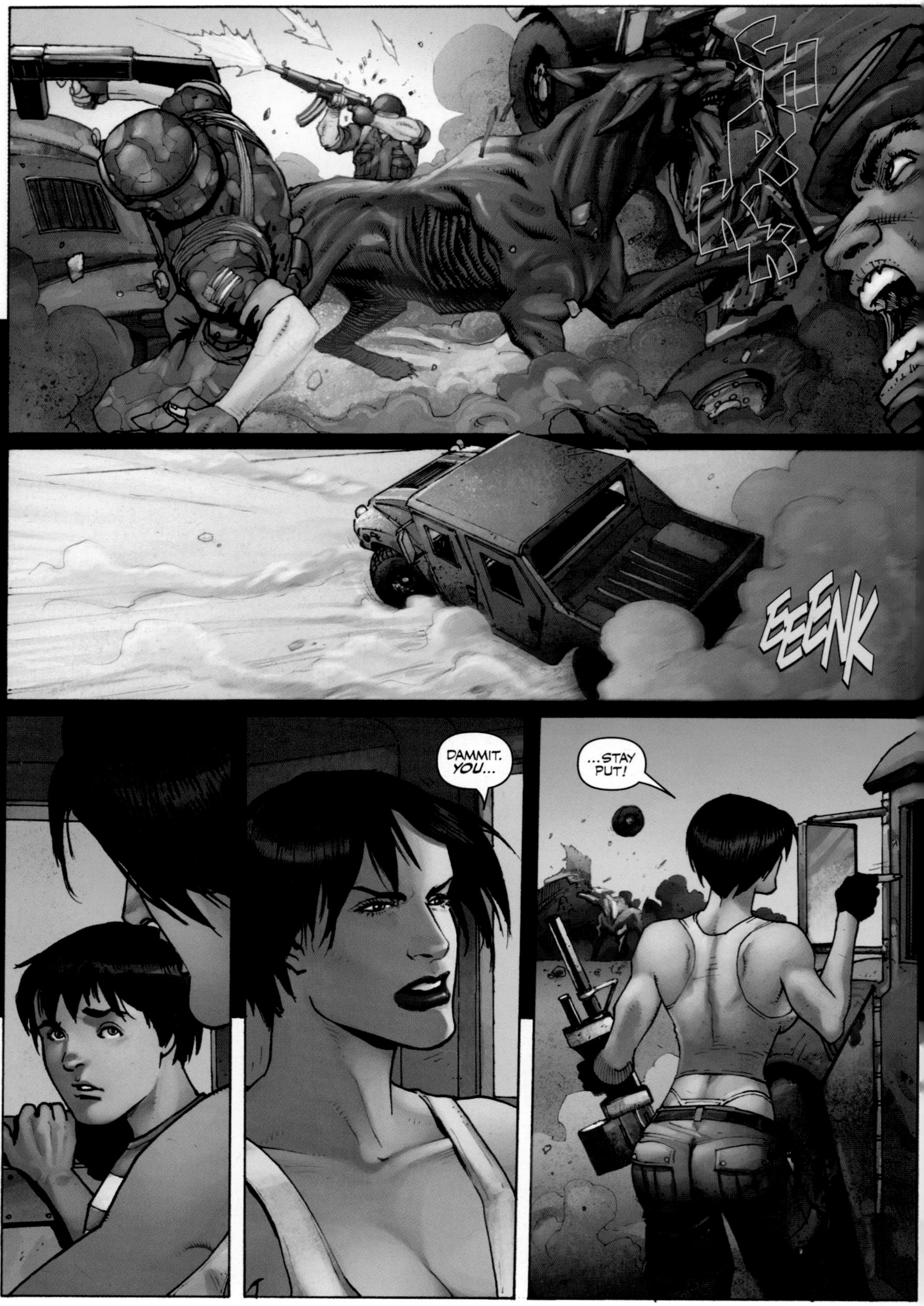
CHUKKK
EEEENK
DAMMIT. YOU...
...STAY PUT!

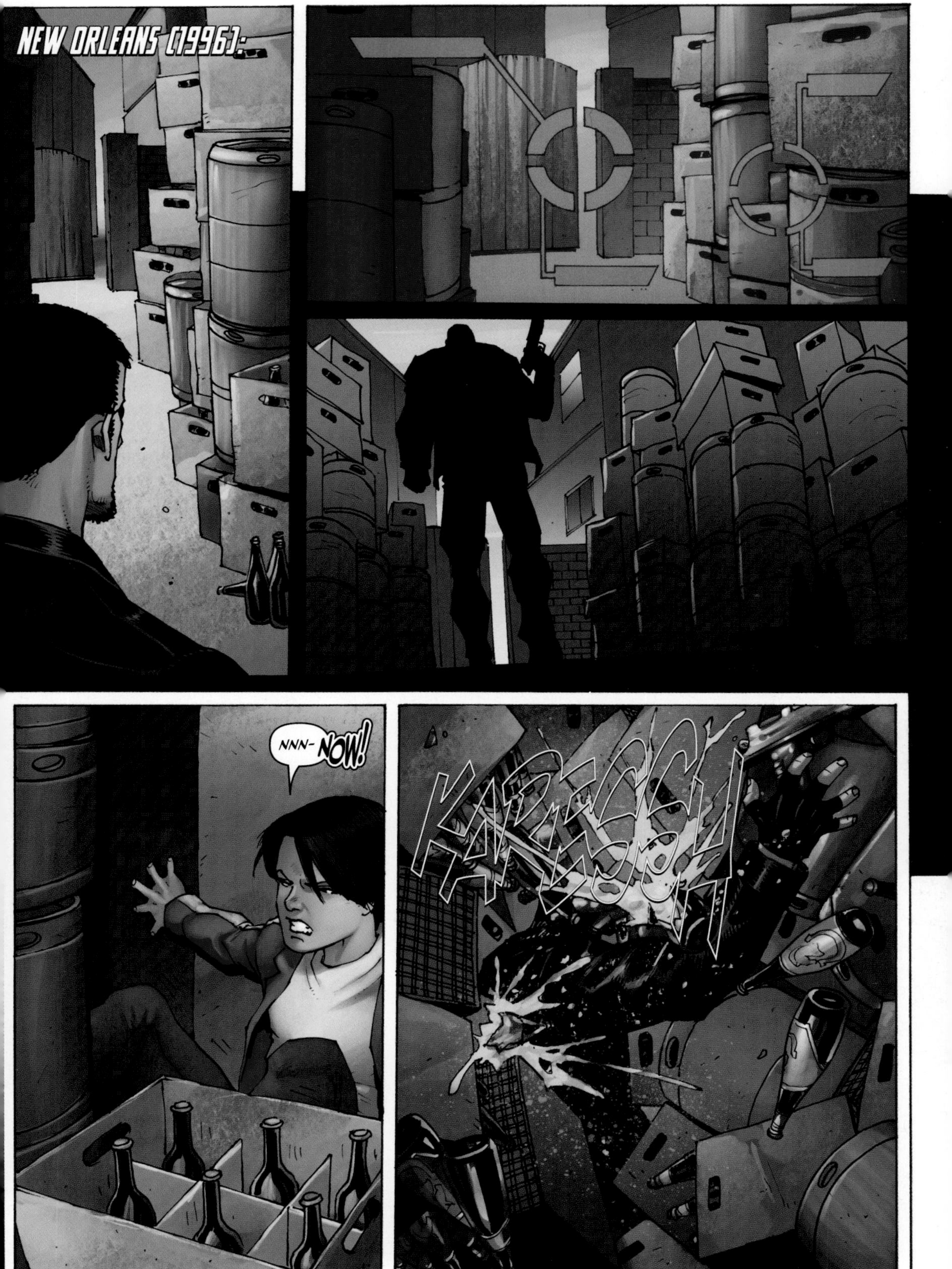

NEW ORLEANS (1996):
NNN-NOW!
KAPEESSH

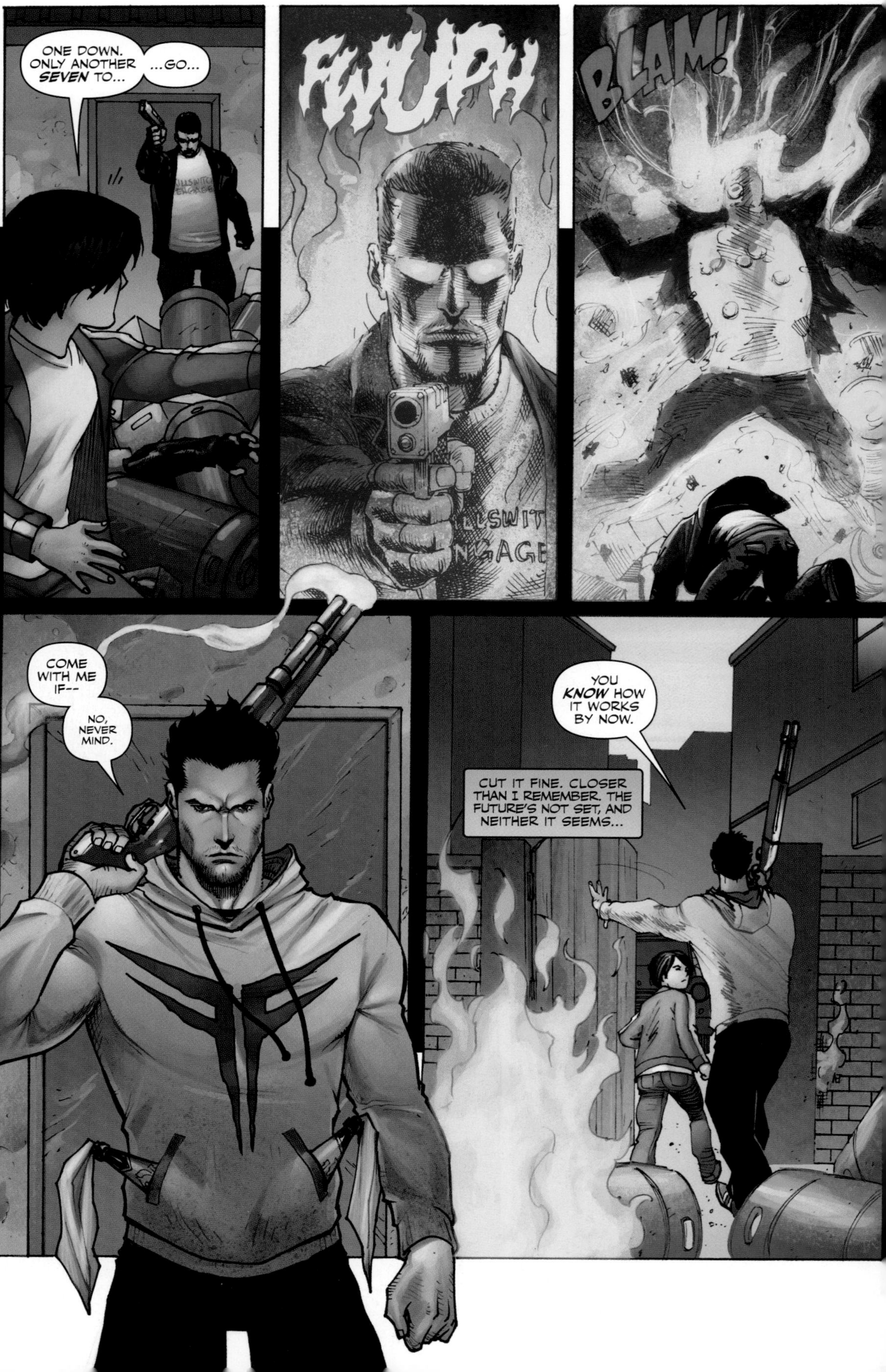
ONE DOWN. ONLY ANOTHER *SEVEN* TO...
...GO...
FWUPH
BLAM!
COME WITH ME IF--
NO, NEVER MIND.
YOU *KNOW* HOW IT WORKS BY NOW.
CUT IT FINE. CLOSER THAN I REMEMBER. THE FUTURE'S NOT SET, AND NEITHER IT SEEMS...

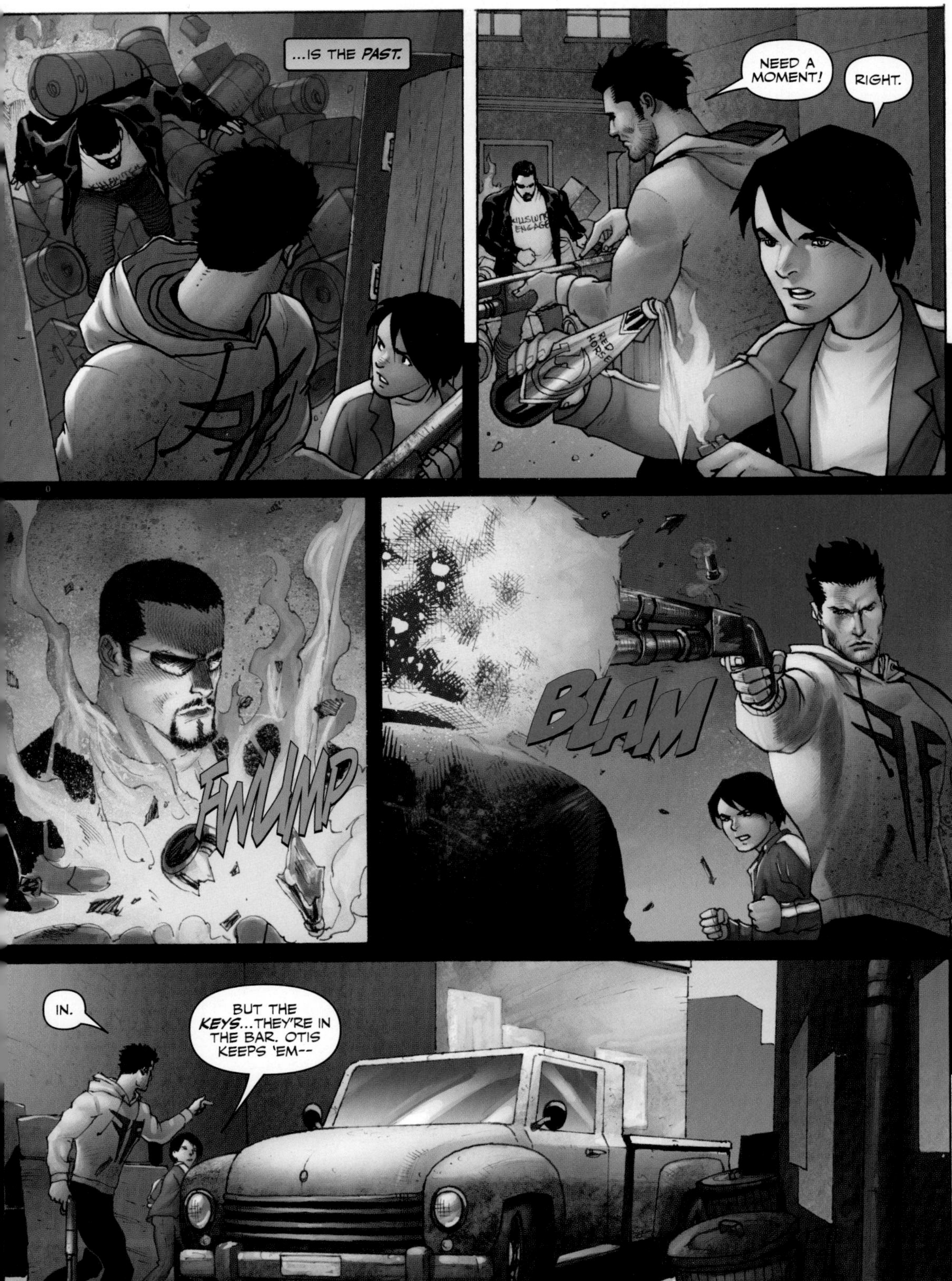
...IS THE PAST.
KILLSWITCH
NEED A MOMENT!
RIGHT.
KILLSWITCH ENGAGE
RED HORSE
FWUMP
BLAM
IN.
BUT THE KEYS...THEY'RE IN THE BAR. OTIS KEEPS 'EM--

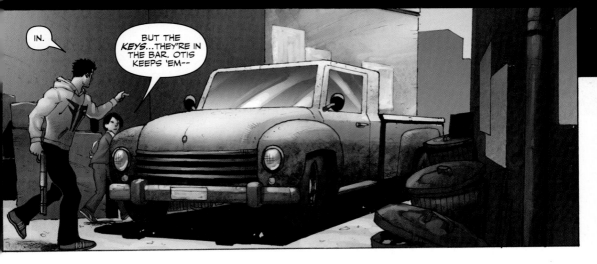

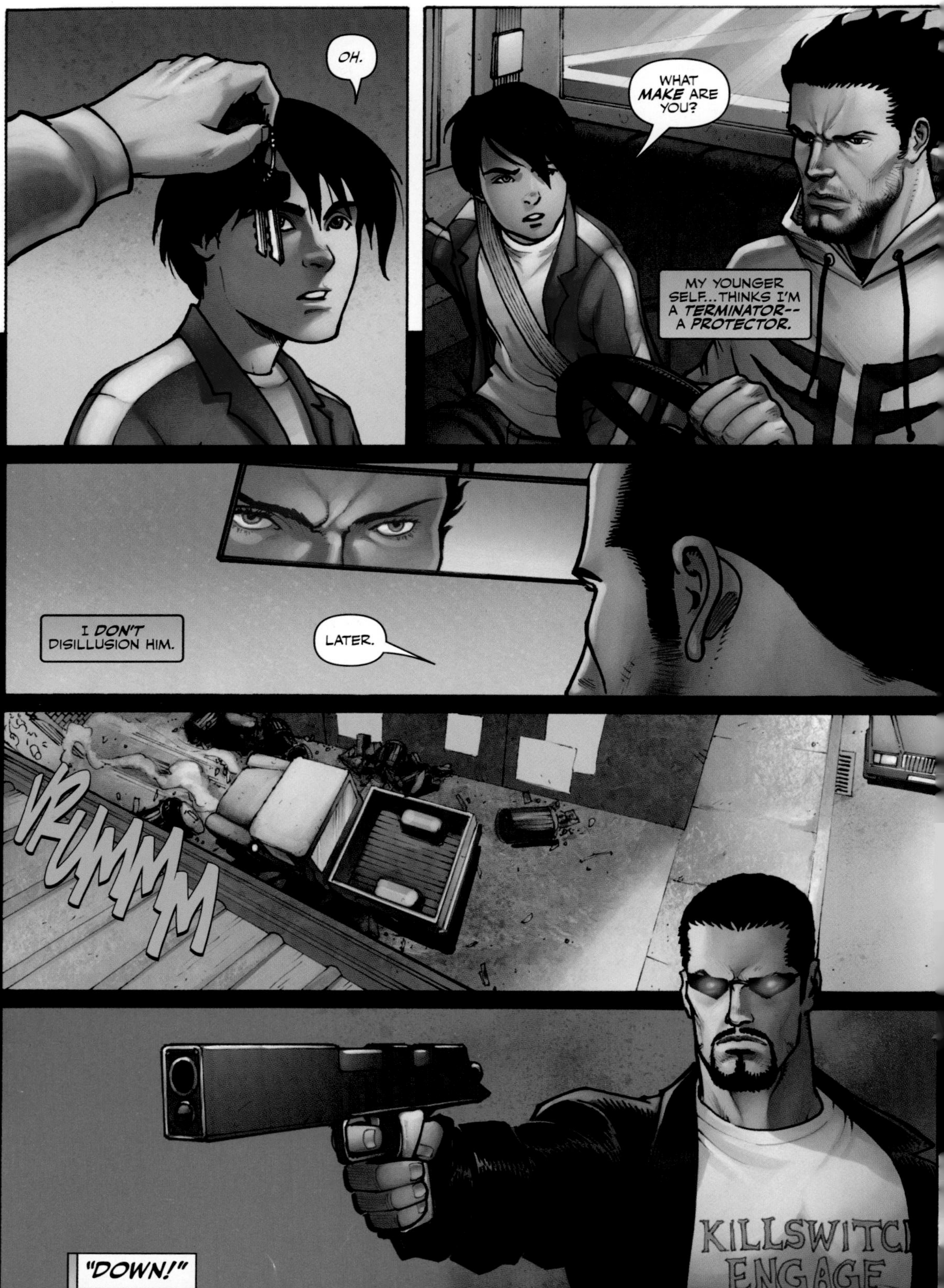
OH.
WHAT MAKE ARE YOU?
MY YOUNGER SELF...THINKS I'M A TERMINATOR-- A PROTECTOR.
I DON'T DISILLUSION HIM.
LATER.
VRUMMM
KILLSWITCH ENGAGE
"DOWN!"

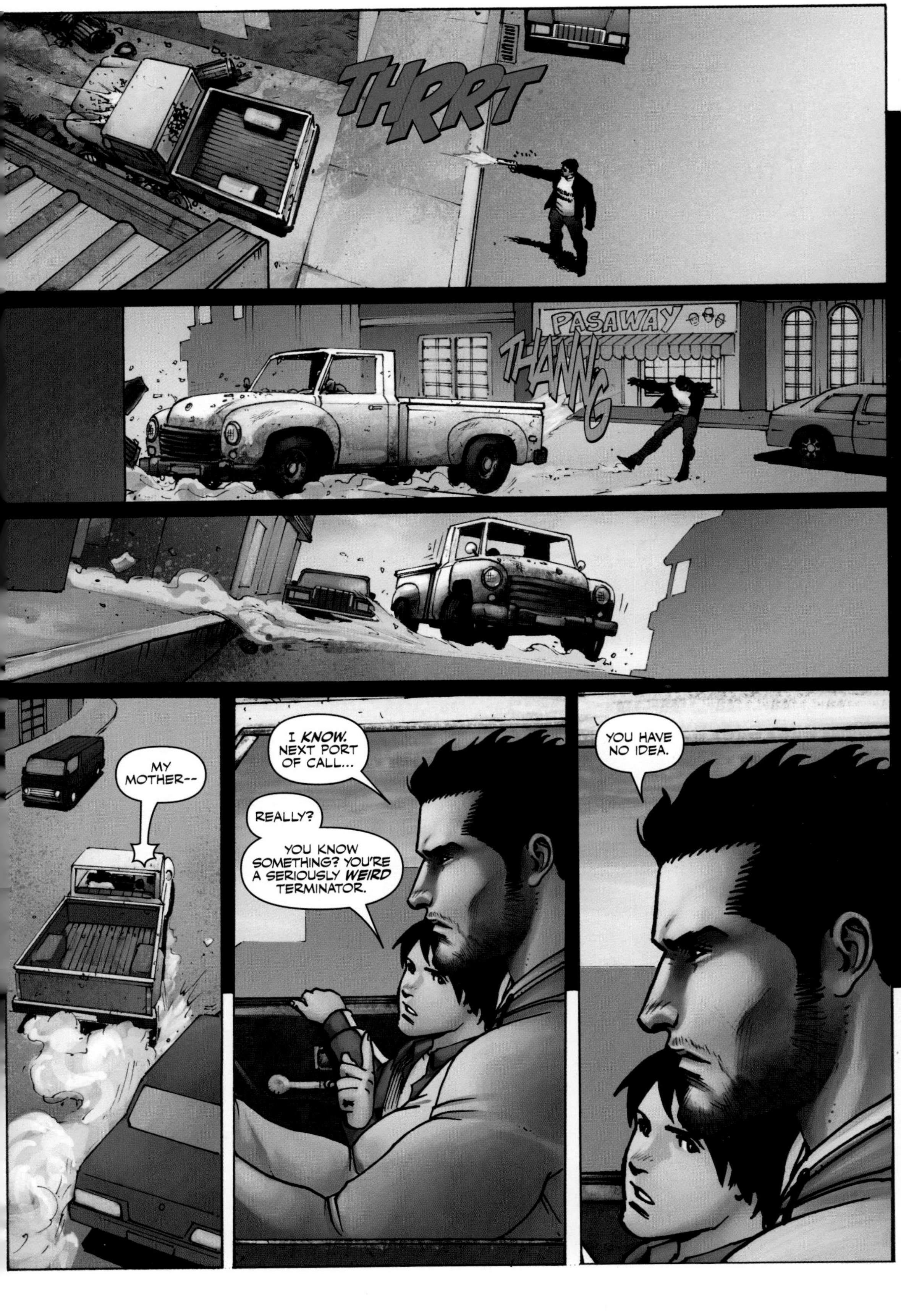
THRRT
PASAWAY
THANNG
MY MOTHER--
I *KNOW.* NEXT PORT OF CALL...
REALLY?
YOU KNOW SOMETHING? YOU'RE A SERIOUSLY ***WEIRD*** TERMINATOR.
YOU HAVE NO IDEA.

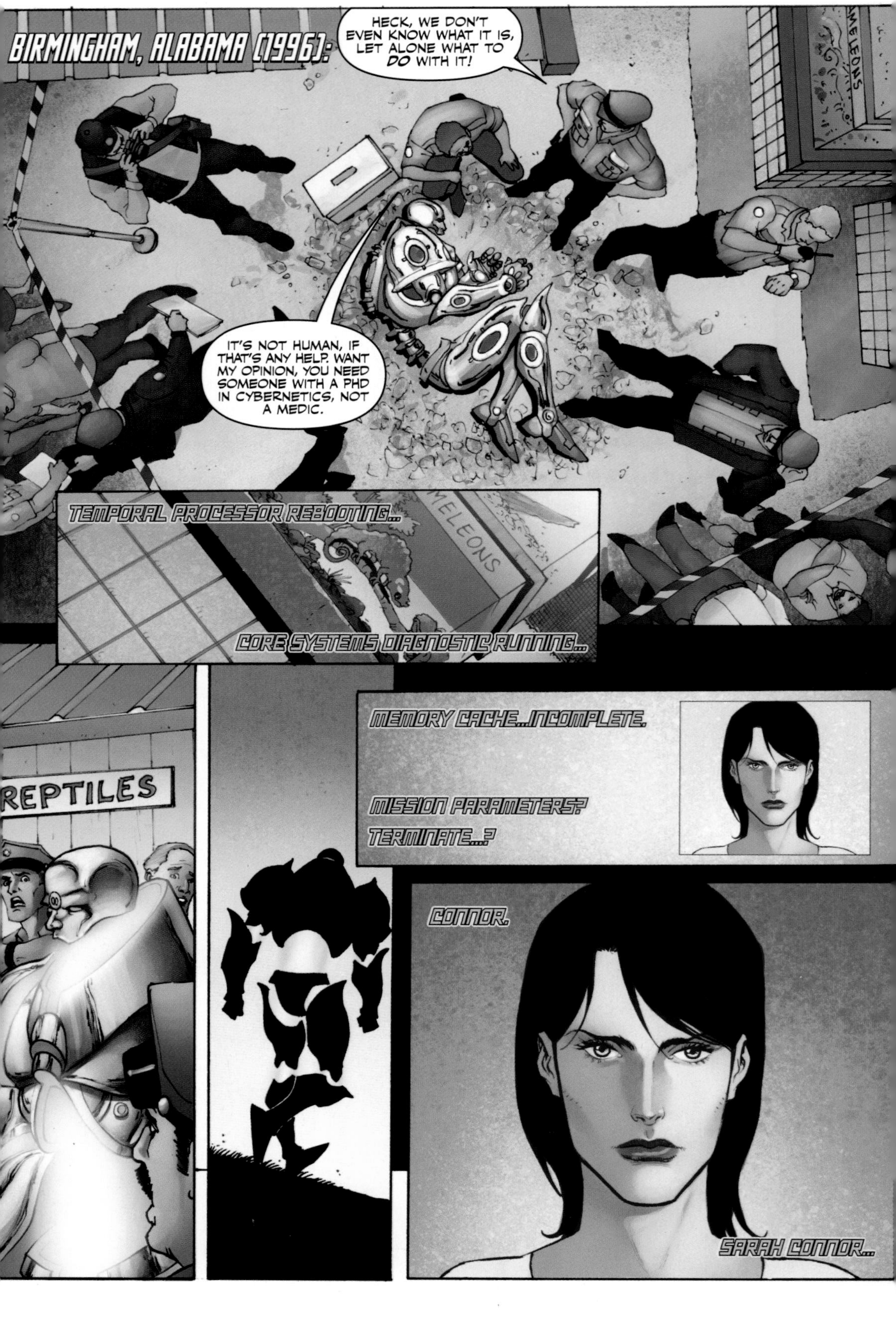
BIRMINGHAM, ALABAMA (1996):
HECK, WE DON'T EVEN KNOW WHAT IT IS, LET ALONE WHAT TO DO WITH IT!
IT'S NOT HUMAN, IF THAT'S ANY HELP. WANT MY OPINION, YOU NEED SOMEONE WITH A PHD IN CYBERNETICS, NOT A MEDIC.
MELEONS
TEMPORAL PROCESSOR REBOOTING...
CORE SYSTEMS DIAGNOSTIC RUNNING...
REPTILES
MEMORY CACHE...INCOMPLETE.
MISSION PARAMETERS?
TERMINATE...?
CONNOR.
SARAH CONNOR...

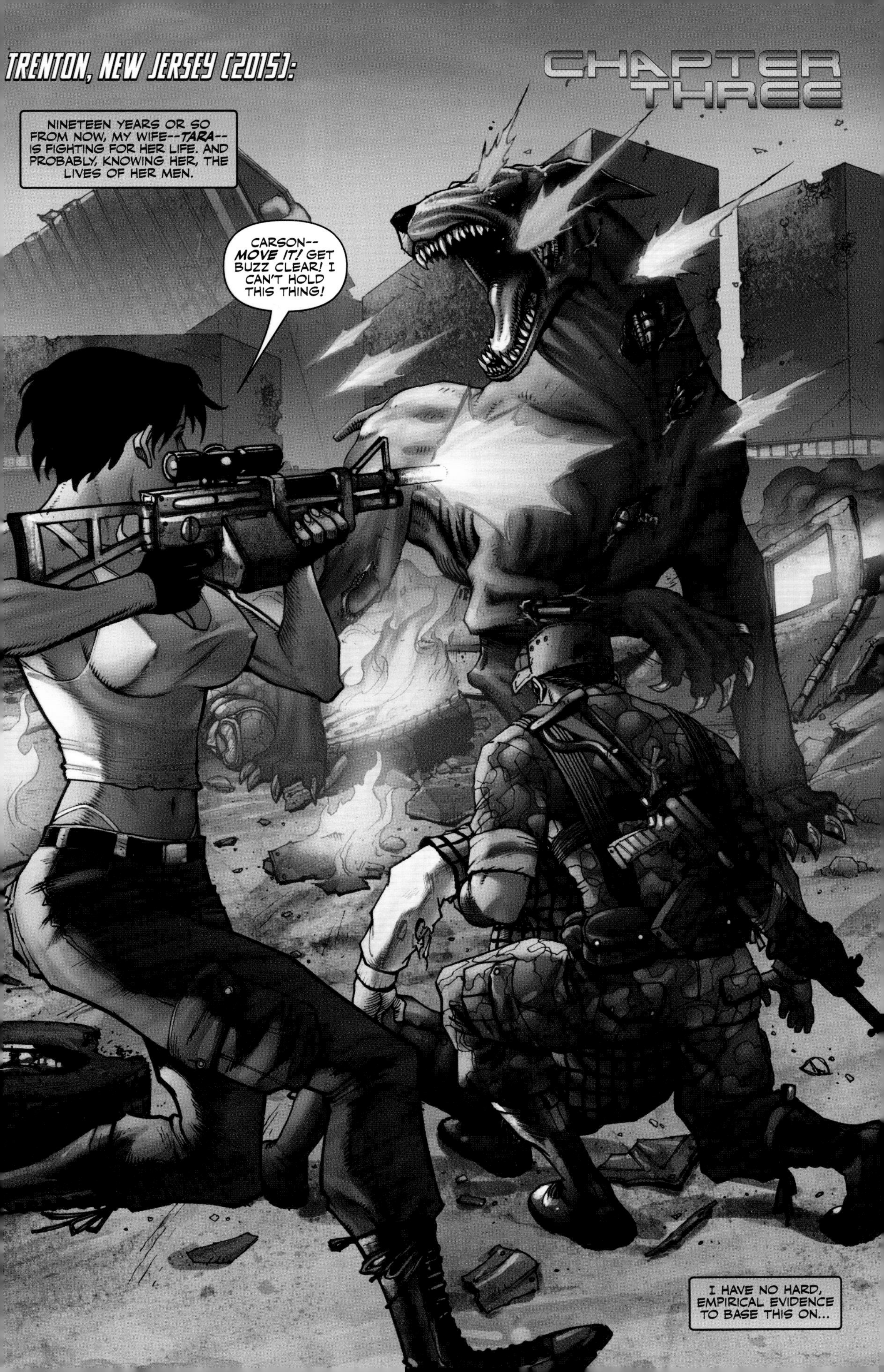
TRENTON, NEW JERSEY (2015):
CHAPTER THREE
NINETEEN YEARS OR SO FROM NOW, MY WIFE--TARA--IS FIGHTING FOR HER LIFE. AND PROBABLY, KNOWING HER, THE LIVES OF HER MEN.
CARSON-- MOVE IT! GET BUZZ CLEAR! I CAN'T HOLD THIS THING!
I HAVE NO HARD, EMPIRICAL EVIDENCE TO BASE THIS ON...

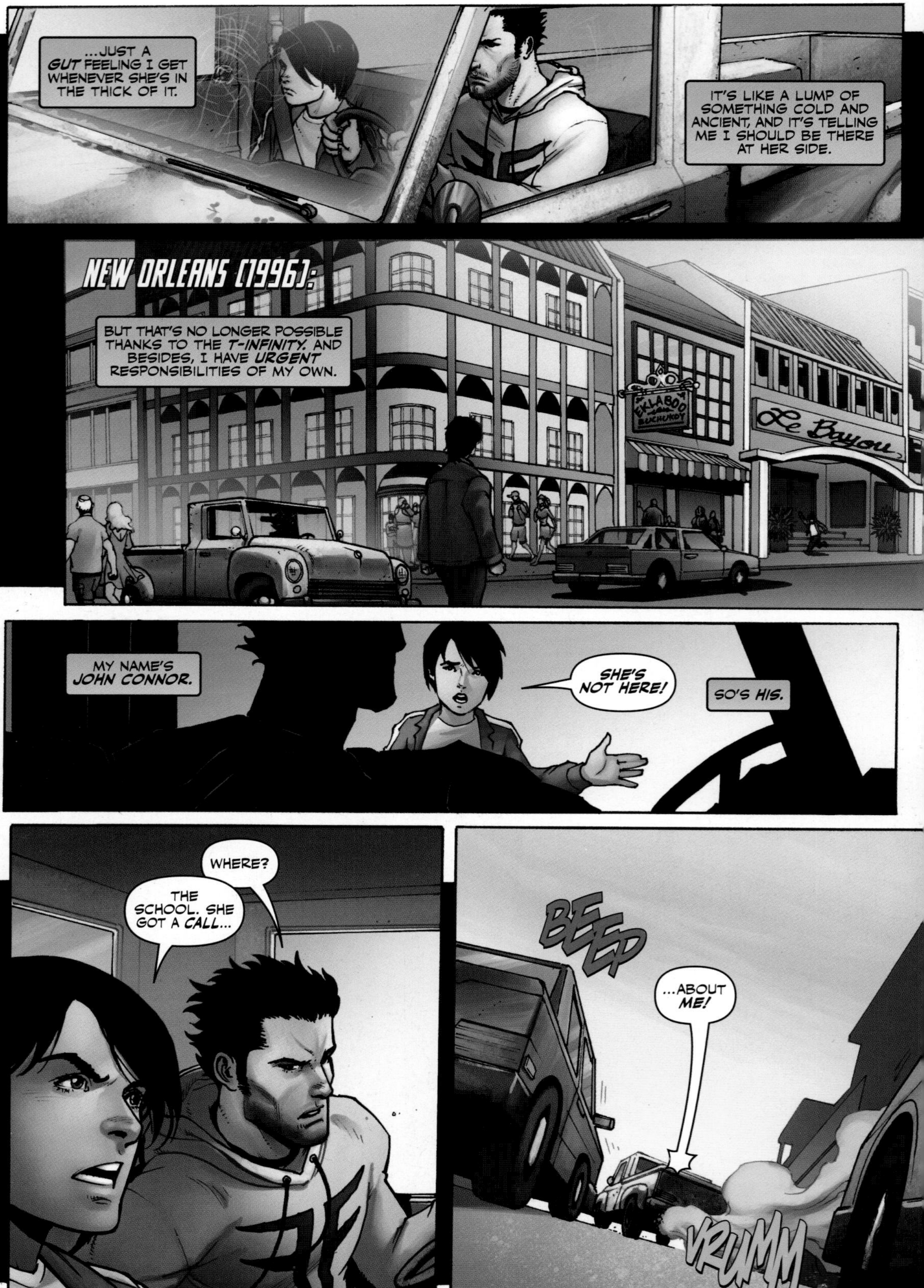
...JUST A GUT FEELING I GET WHENEVER SHE'S IN THE THICK OF IT.
IT'S LIKE A LUMP OF SOMETHING COLD AND ANCIENT, AND IT'S TELLING ME I SHOULD BE THERE AT HER SIDE.
NEW ORLEANS (1996):
BUT THAT'S NO LONGER POSSIBLE THANKS TO THE T-INFINITY. AND BESIDES, I HAVE URGENT RESPONSIBILITIES OF MY OWN.
Le Bayou
MY NAME'S JOHN CONNOR.
SHE'S NOT HERE!
SO'S HIS.
WHERE?
THE SCHOOL. SHE GOT A CALL...
BEEEP
...ABOUT ME!
VRUMMM

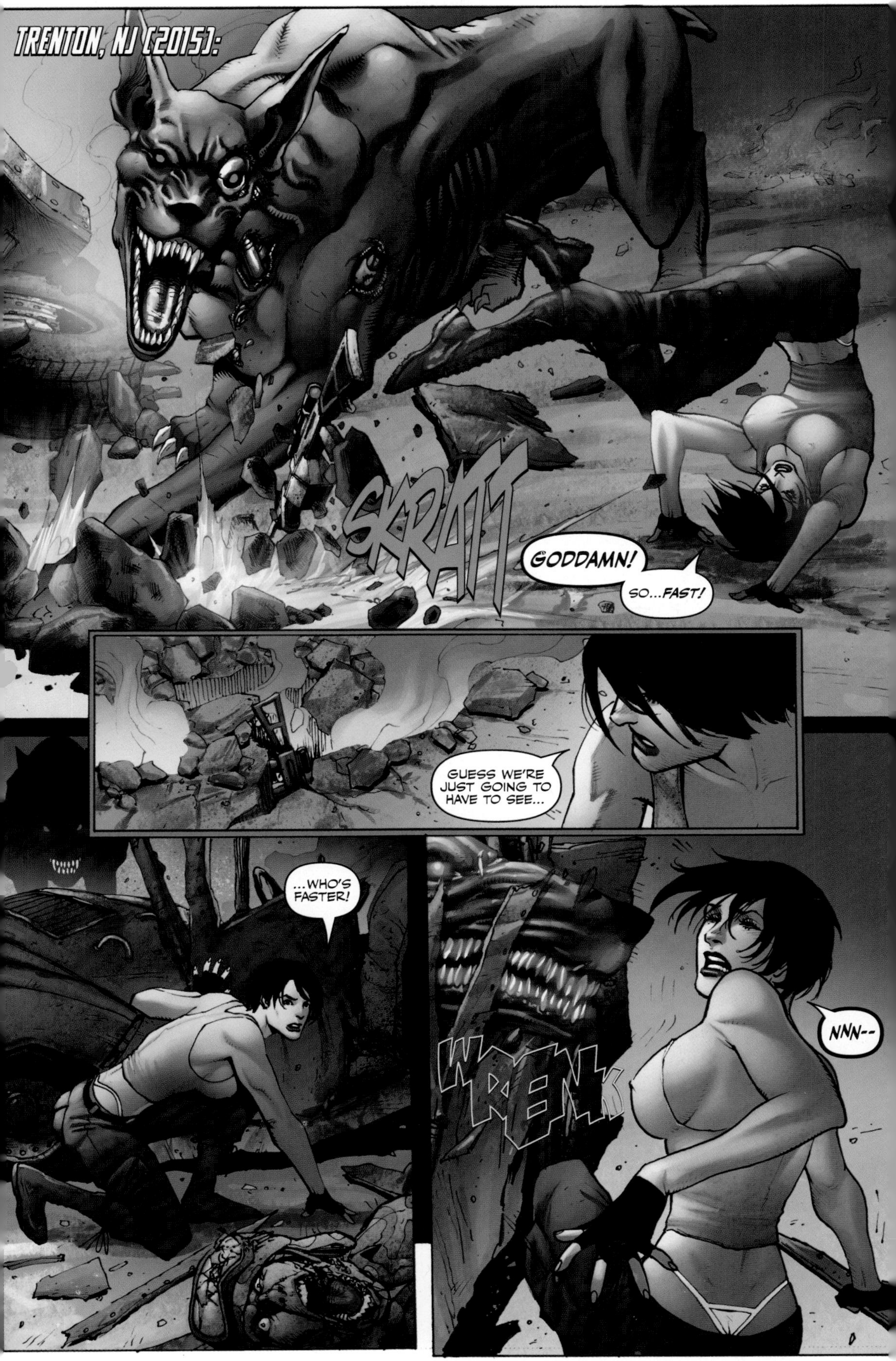
TRENTON, NJ (2015):
SKRATT
GODDAMN!
SO...FAST!
GUESS WE'RE JUST GOING TO HAVE TO SEE...
...WHO'S FASTER!
WRENK
NNN--

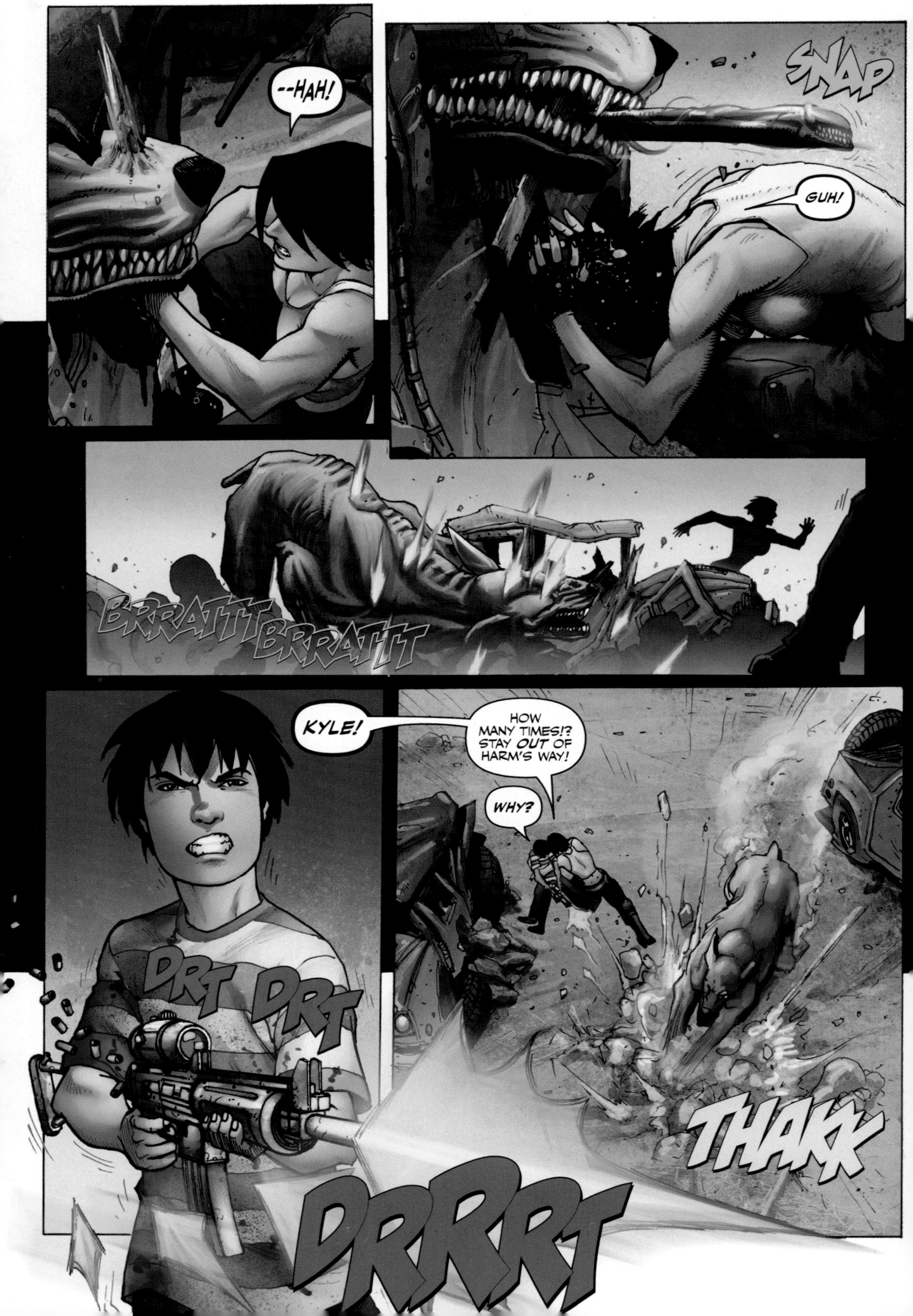
--HAH!
SNAP
GUH!
BRRATTT BRRATTT
KYLE!
HOW MANY TIMES!? STAY OUT OF HARM'S WAY!
WHY?
DRT DRT
THAKK
DRRRRT

WHY NOT LET ME *FIGHT?* JUST LET ME *PROVE* MYSELF!

BECAUSE...

JUST *BECAUSE!*

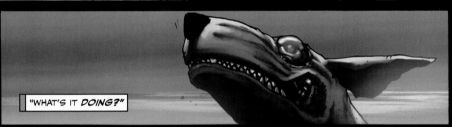

"WHAT'S IT *DOING?*"

NO IDEA. BUT IT'S CLEARLY LOST INTEREST IN US.

DO WE *CARE?*

MM--MAYBE. DEPENDS...

"...ON WHAT BROUGHT IT HERE IN THE FIRST PLACE."

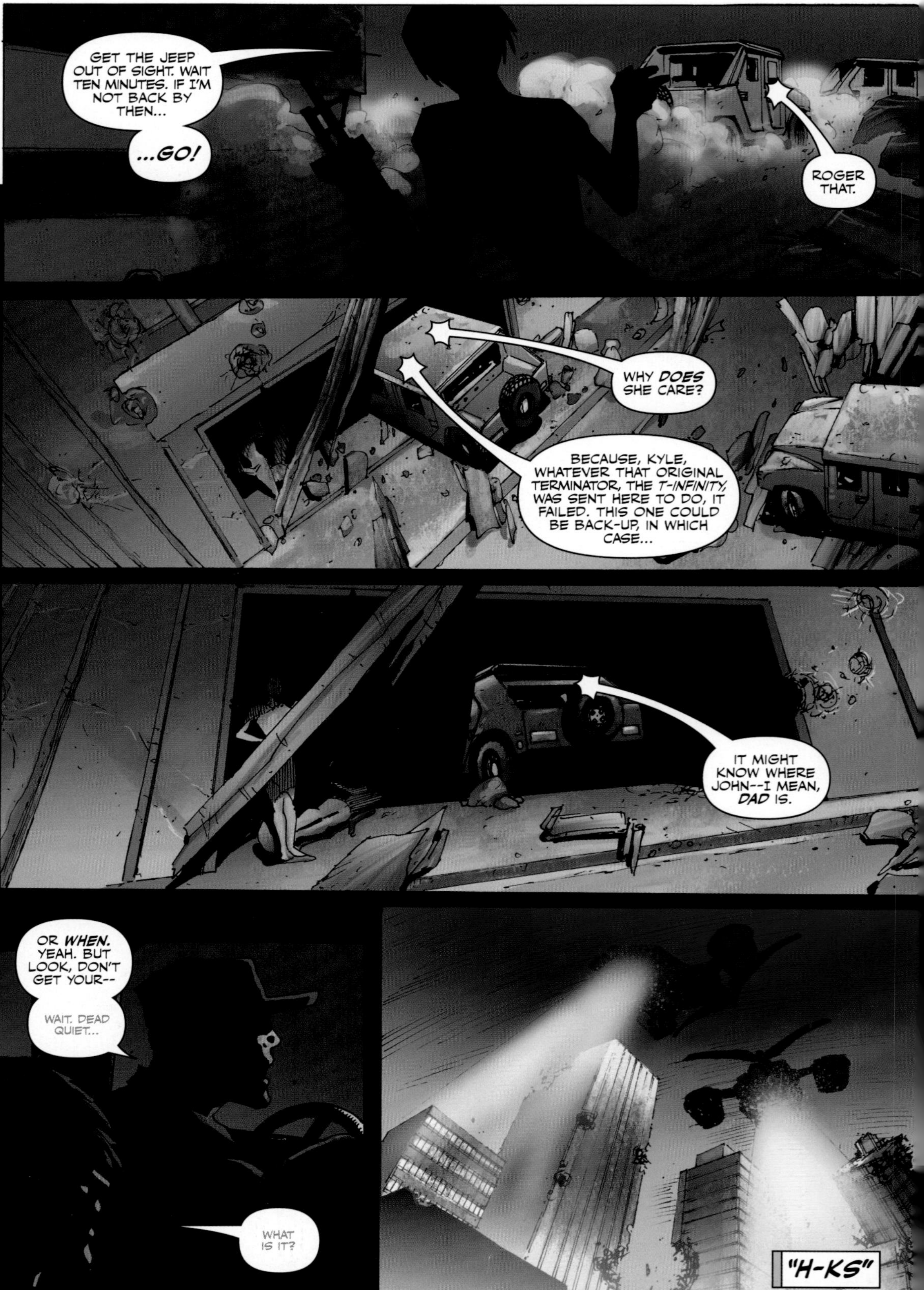
GET THE JEEP OUT OF SIGHT. WAIT TEN MINUTES. IF I'M NOT BACK BY THEN...
...GO!
ROGER THAT.
WHY DOES SHE CARE?
BECAUSE, KYLE, WHATEVER THAT ORIGINAL TERMINATOR, THE T-INFINITY, WAS SENT HERE TO DO, IT FAILED. THIS ONE COULD BE BACK-UP, IN WHICH CASE...
IT MIGHT KNOW WHERE JOHN--I MEAN, DAD IS.
OR WHEN. YEAH. BUT LOOK, DON'T GET YOUR--
WAIT. DEAD QUIET...
WHAT IS IT?
"H-KS"

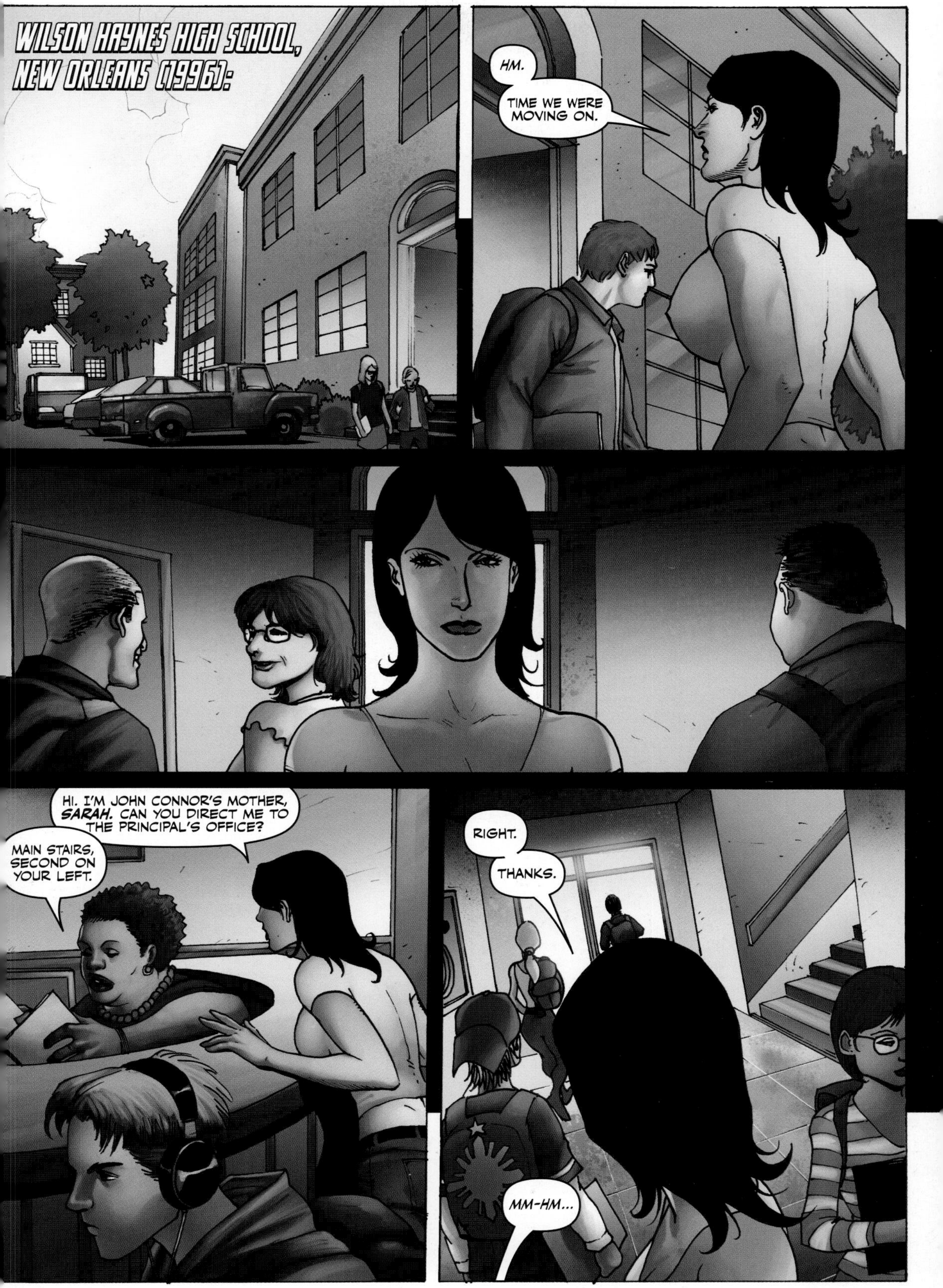
WILSON HAYNES HIGH SCHOOL, NEW ORLEANS (1996):
HM.
TIME WE WERE MOVING ON.
HI. I'M JOHN CONNOR'S MOTHER, SARAH. CAN YOU DIRECT ME TO THE PRINCIPAL'S OFFICE?
MAIN STAIRS, SECOND ON YOUR LEFT.
RIGHT.
THANKS.
MM-HM...

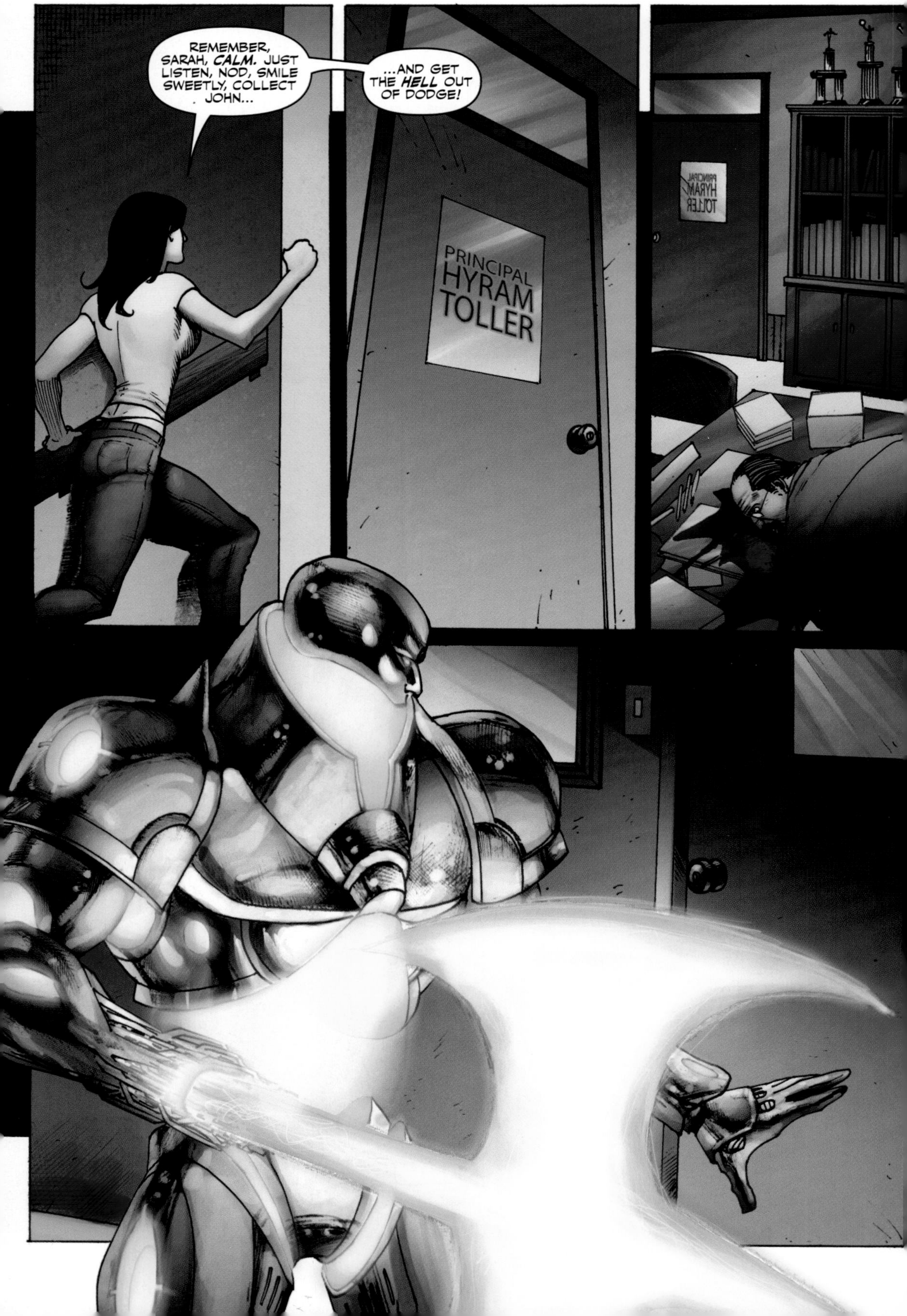
REMEMBER, SARAH, CALM. JUST LISTEN, NOD, SMILE SWEETLY, COLLECT JOHN...
...AND GET THE HELL OUT OF DODGE!
PRINCIPAL HYRAM TOLLER
PRINCIPAL HYRAM TOLLER

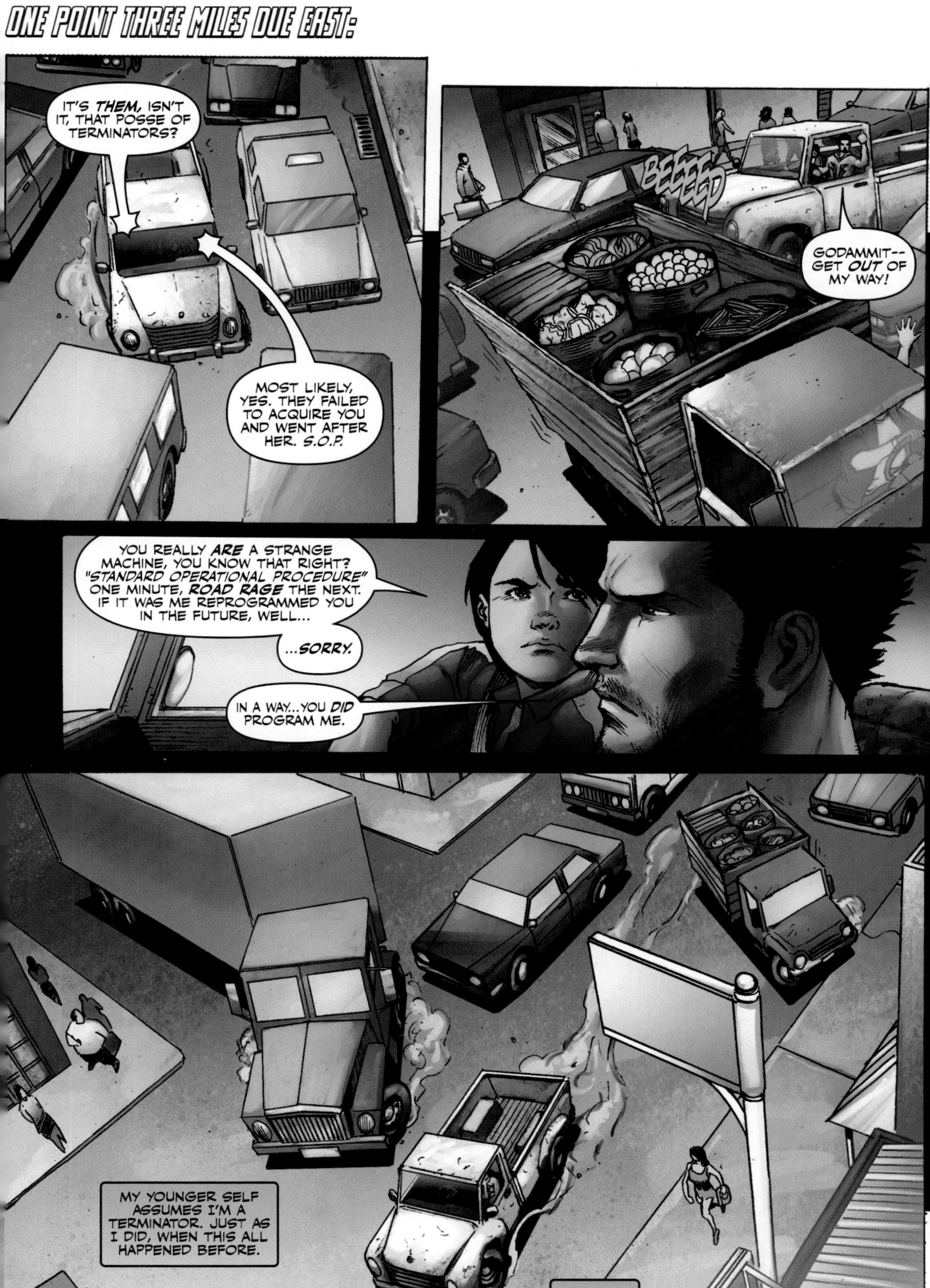
ONE POINT THREE MILES DUE EAST:
IT'S THEM, ISN'T IT, THAT POSSE OF TERMINATORS?
MOST LIKELY, YES. THEY FAILED TO ACQUIRE YOU AND WENT AFTER HER. S.O.P.
BEEEEP
GODAMMIT--GET OUT OF MY WAY!
YOU REALLY ARE A STRANGE MACHINE, YOU KNOW THAT RIGHT? "STANDARD OPERATIONAL PROCEDURE" ONE MINUTE, ROAD RAGE THE NEXT. IF IT WAS ME REPROGRAMMED YOU IN THE FUTURE, WELL...
...SORRY.
IN A WAY...YOU DID PROGRAM ME.
MY YOUNGER SELF ASSUMES I'M A TERMINATOR. JUST AS I DID, WHEN THIS ALL HAPPENED BEFORE.
EXCEPT...

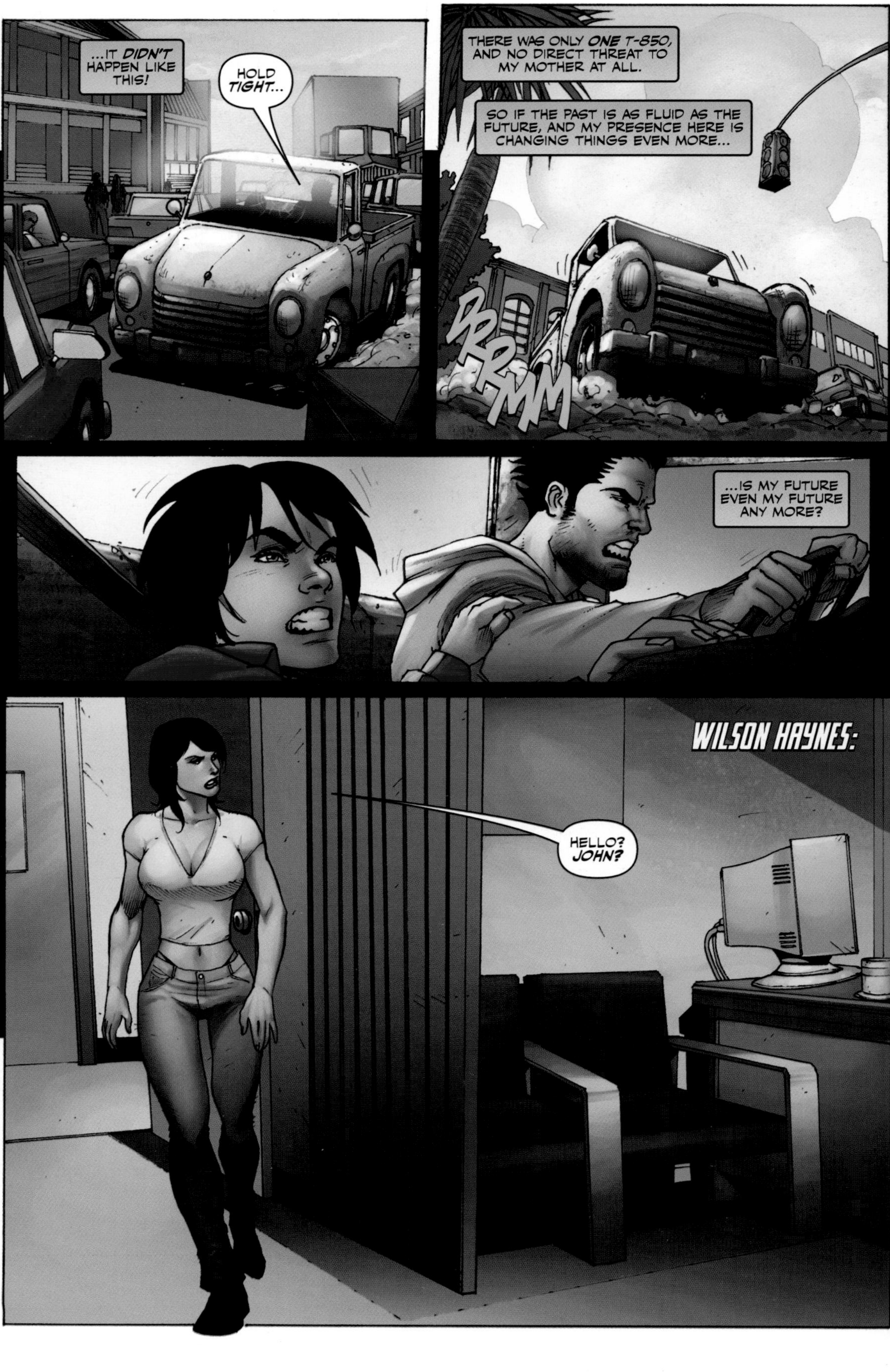

...IT DIDN'T HAPPEN LIKE THIS!
HOLD TIGHT...
THERE WAS ONLY ONE T-850, AND NO DIRECT THREAT TO MY MOTHER AT ALL.
SO IF THE PAST IS AS FLUID AS THE FUTURE, AND MY PRESENCE HERE IS CHANGING THINGS EVEN MORE...
DRRMM
...IS MY FUTURE EVEN MY FUTURE ANY MORE?
WILSON HAYNES:
HELLO? JOHN?

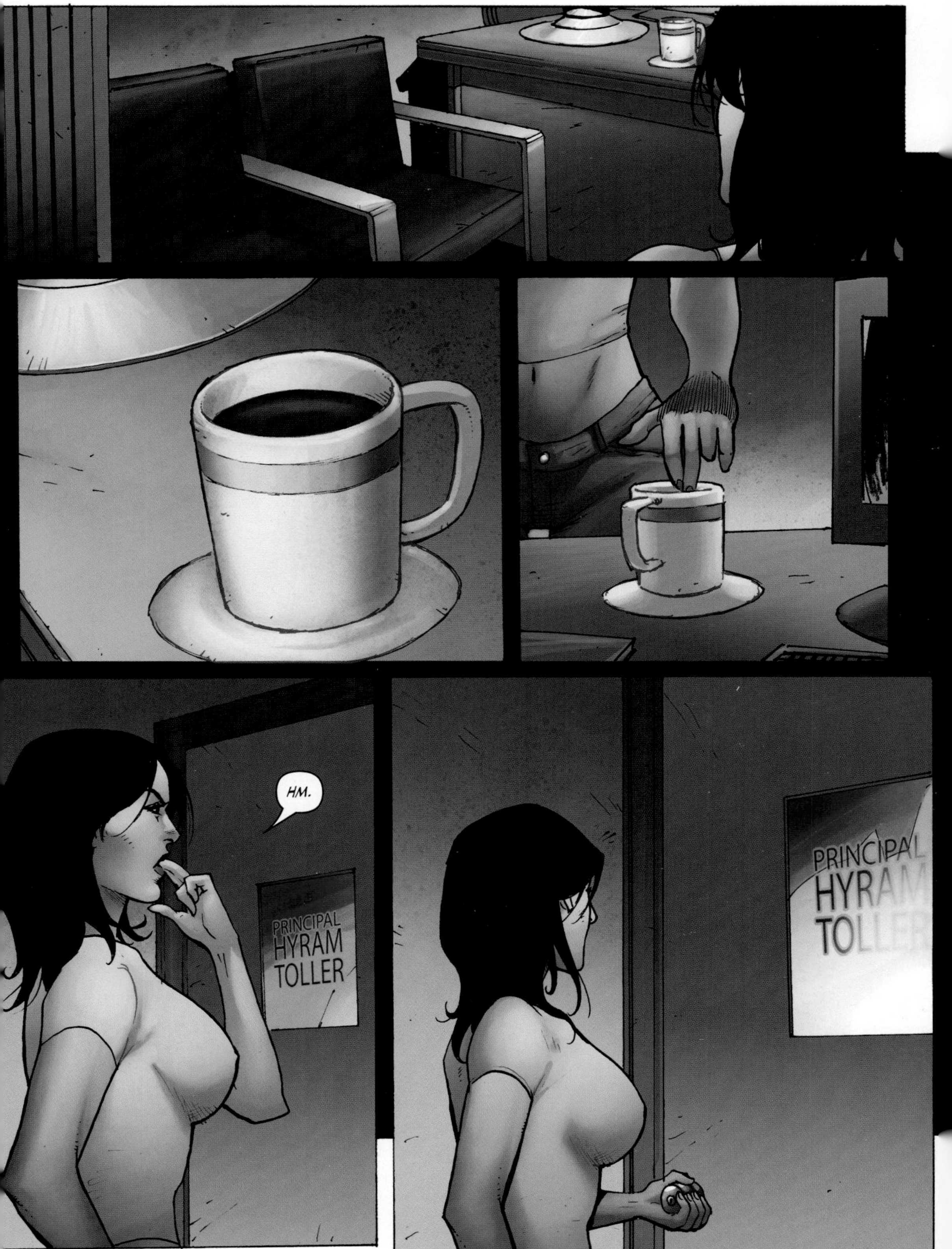
HM.
PRINCIPAL HYRAM TOLLER
PRINCIPAL HYRAM TOLLER

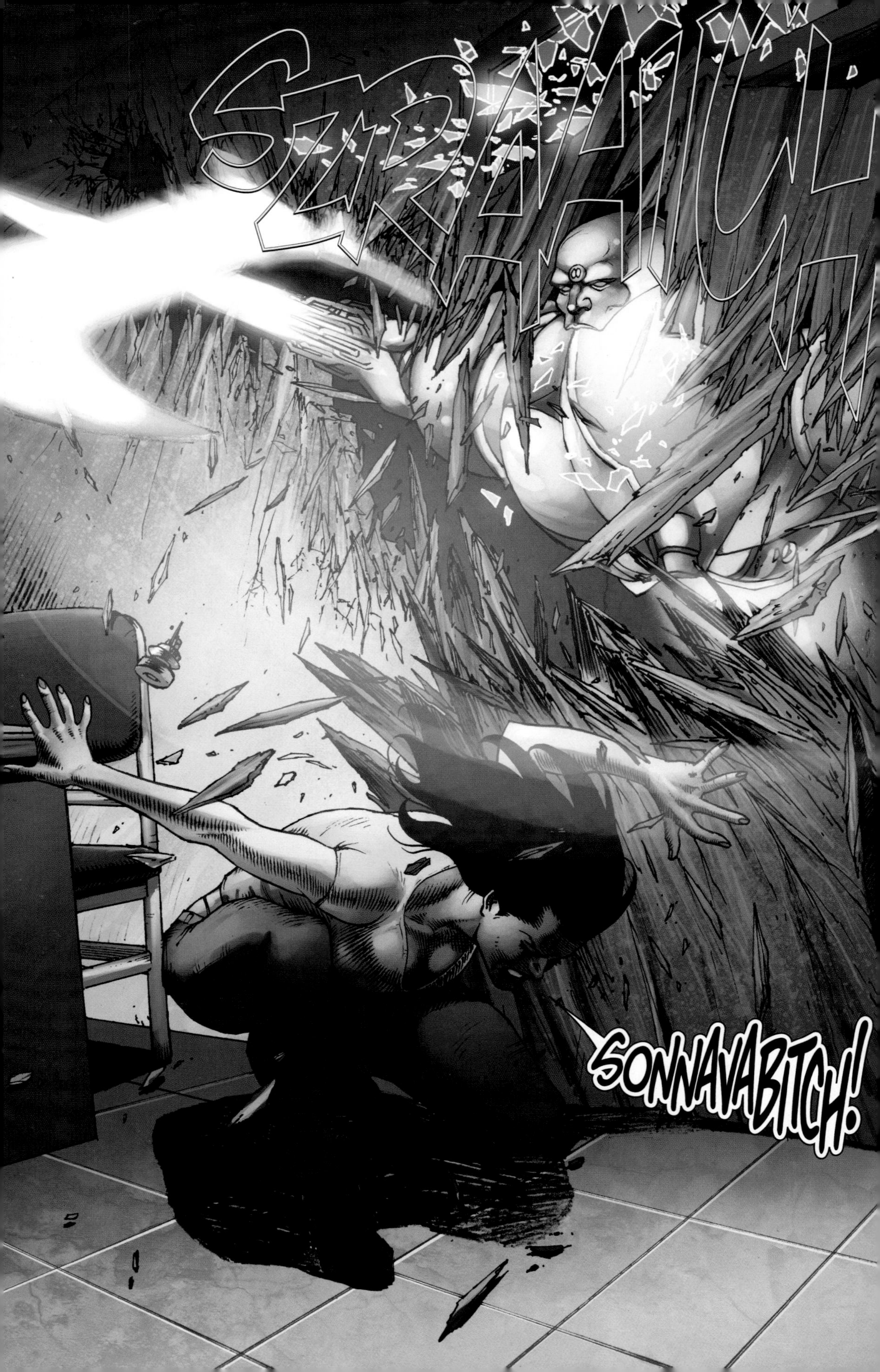
SZRAAKCH
SONNAVABITCH!

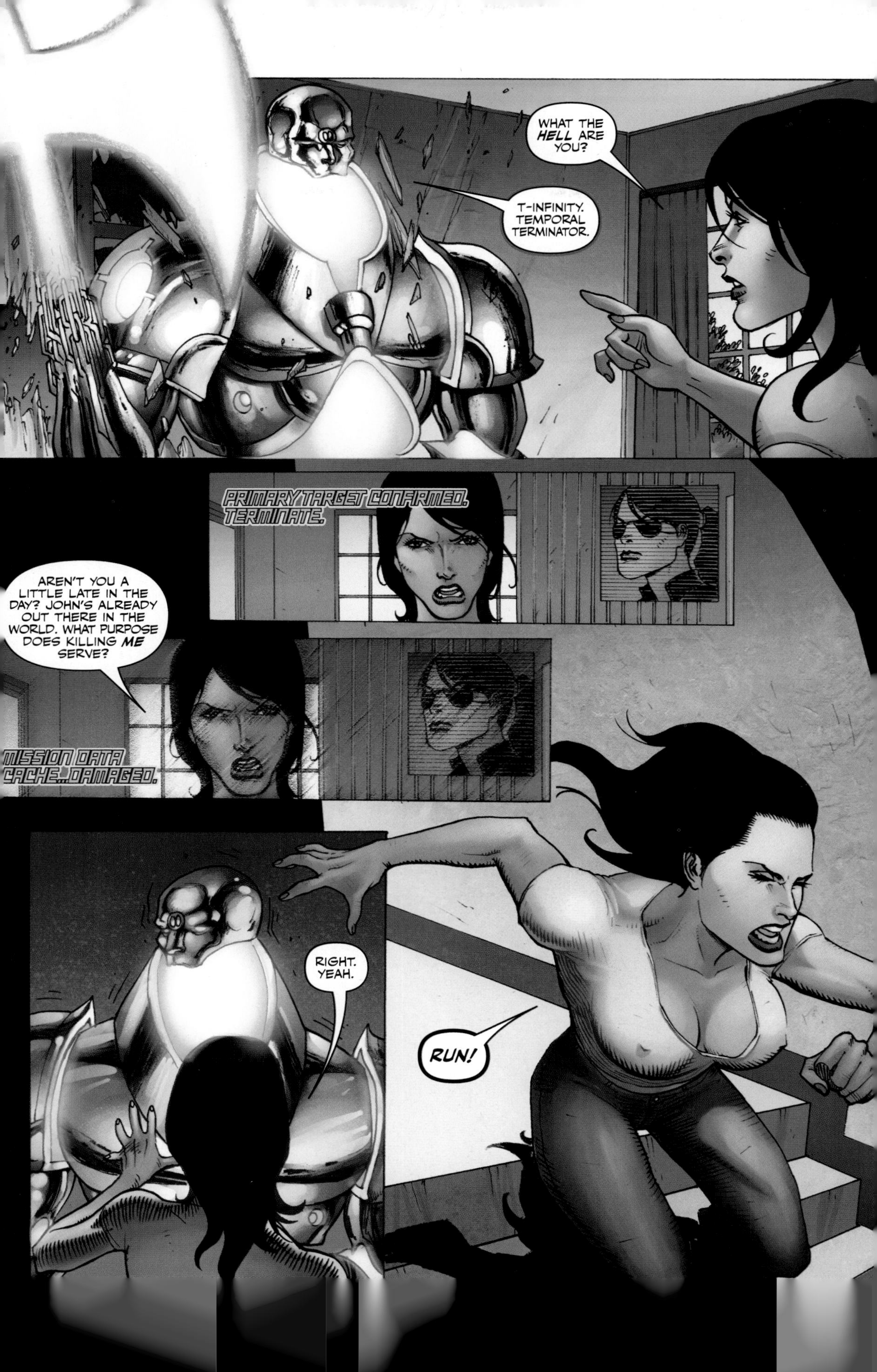
WHAT THE HELL ARE YOU?
T-INFINITY. TEMPORAL TERMINATOR.
PRIMARY TARGET CONFIRMED. TERMINATE.
AREN'T YOU A LITTLE LATE IN THE DAY? JOHN'S ALREADY OUT THERE IN THE WORLD. WHAT PURPOSE DOES KILLING ME SERVE?
MISSION DATA CACHE...DAMAGED.
RIGHT. YEAH.
RUN!

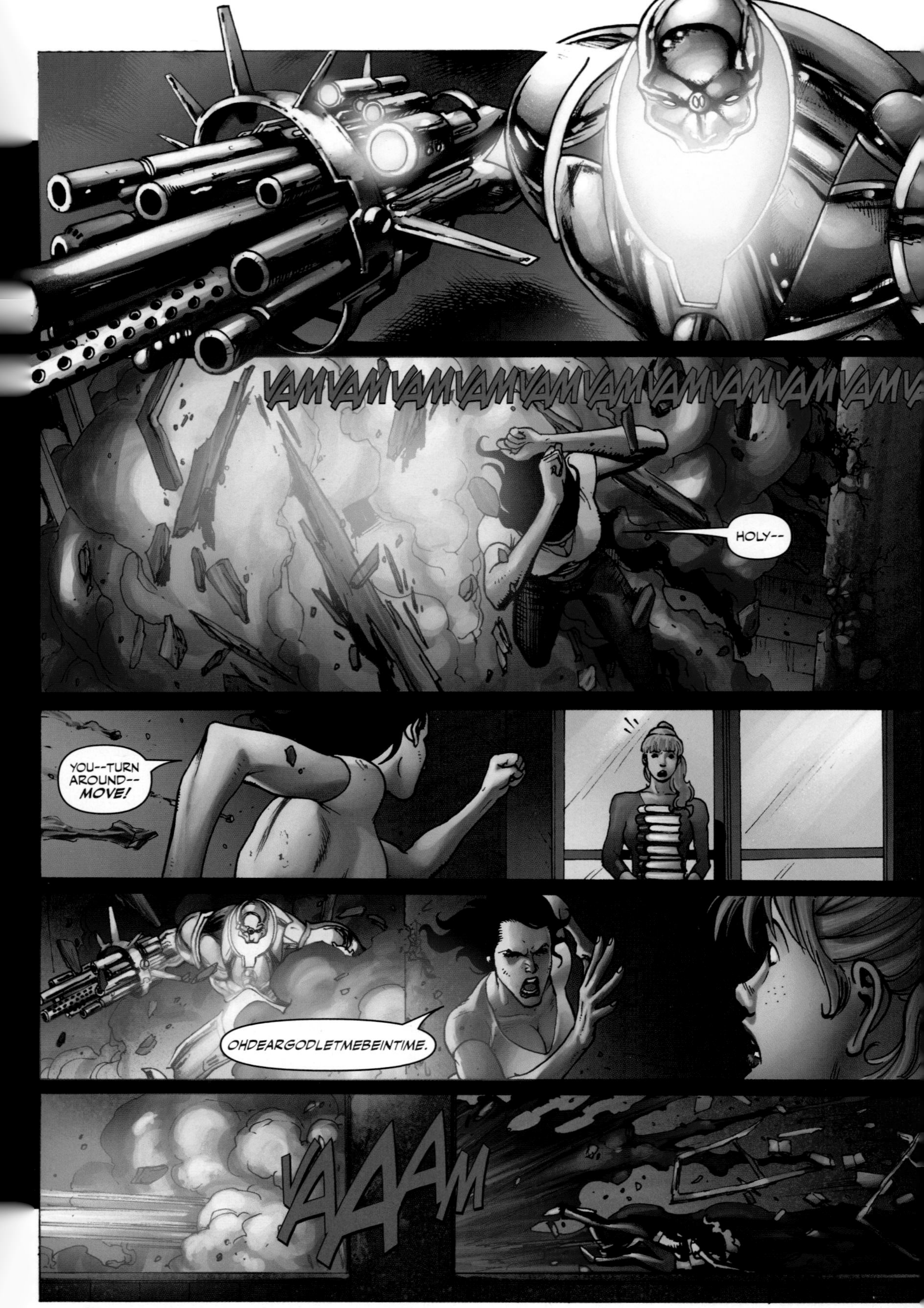
VAM VAM VAM VAM VAM VAM VAM VAM VAM VAM
HOLY--
YOU--TURN AROUND-- MOVE!
OHDEARGODLETMEBEINTIME.
VAAAM

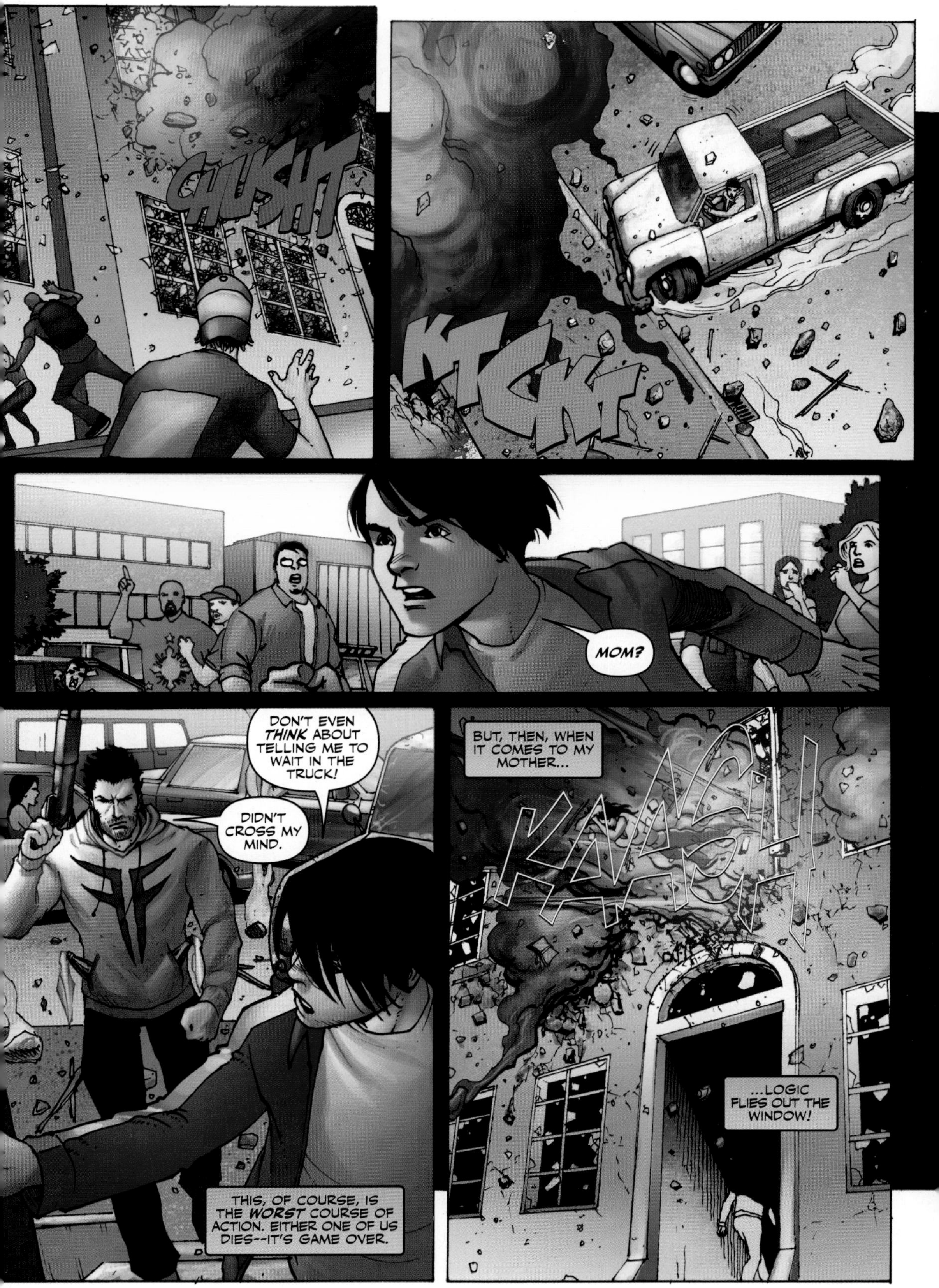
CHUSHT
KTCKT
MOM?
DON'T EVEN *THINK* ABOUT TELLING ME TO WAIT IN THE TRUCK!
DIDN'T CROSS MY MIND.
THIS, OF COURSE, IS THE *WORST* COURSE OF ACTION. EITHER ONE OF US DIES--IT'S GAME OVER.
BUT, THEN, WHEN IT COMES TO MY MOTHER...
KAASH
...LOGIC FLIES OUT THE WINDOW!

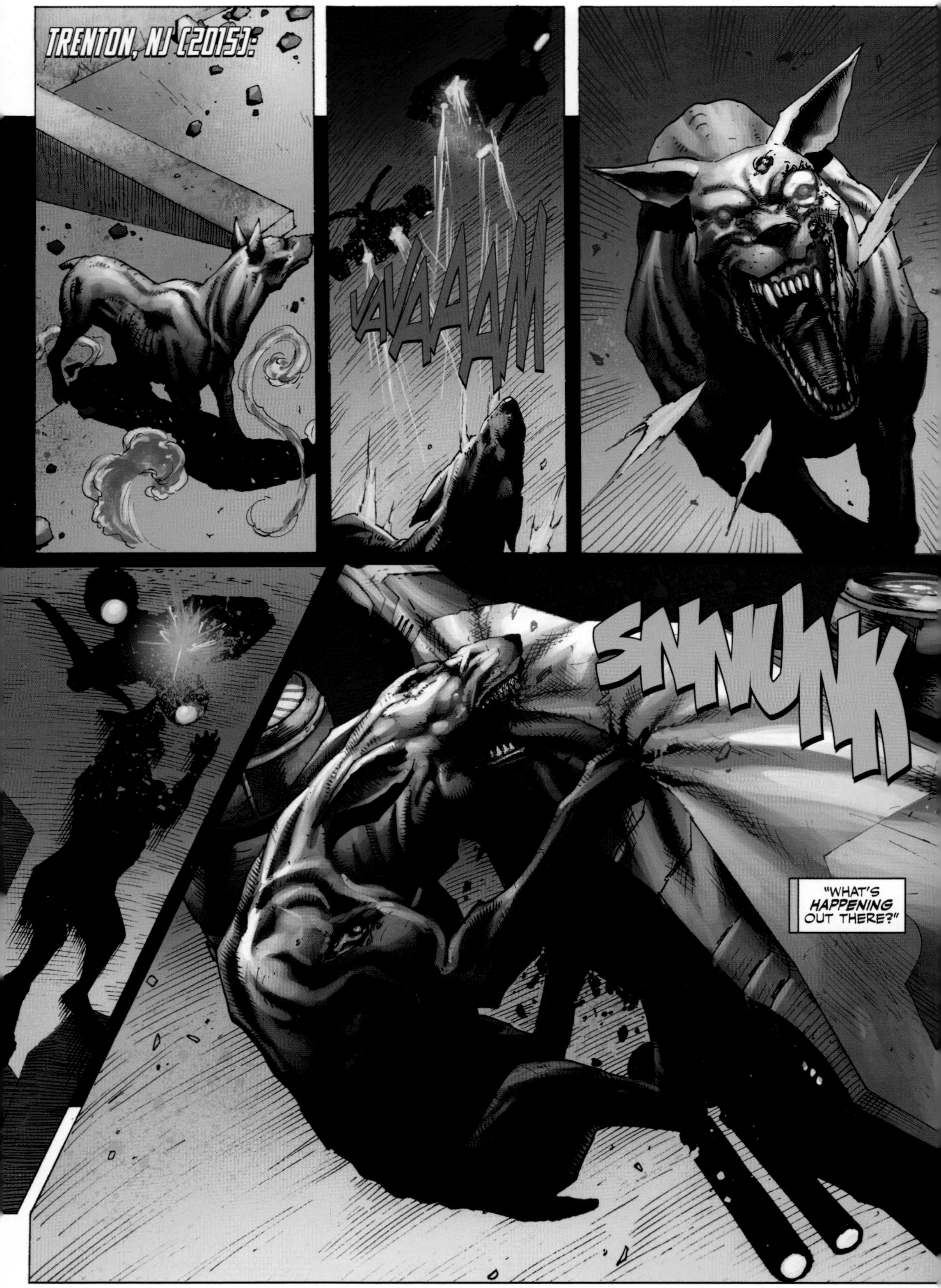
TRENTON, NJ (2015):
VAVAAAM
SNNUNK
"WHAT'S HAPPENING OUT THERE?"

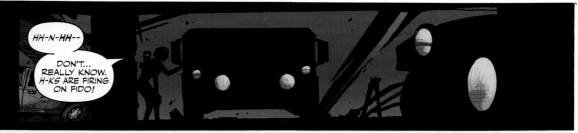

HH-N-HH--

DON'T... REALLY KNOW. *H-KS* ARE FIRING ON FIDO!

BUT AREN'T THEY *ALL* TERMINATORS?

REMEMBER, WE'RE DEALING WITH MULTIPLE ERAS HERE. MAYBE THE H-KS DON'T HAVE FIDO ON THEIR SYSTEM, SO...THEY ATTACK.

"FIDO FIGHTS *BACK.*"

YOU LEARN ANYTHING?

A BIT.

FIDO FOLLOWED HIS NOSE RIGHT TO THE SPOT JOHN AND THE T-INFINITY VANISHED. IT STAYED THERE, ROOTED TO THE SPOT AND THEN JUST ABOUT TURNED.

SO... WHAT? YOU THINK IT CAN TRACK THEM THROUGH *TIME?*

IT'S *POSSIBLE* I SUPPOSE.

YOU WANT TO FOLLOW IT, DON'T YOU?

NO. YES. I DON'T KNOW...

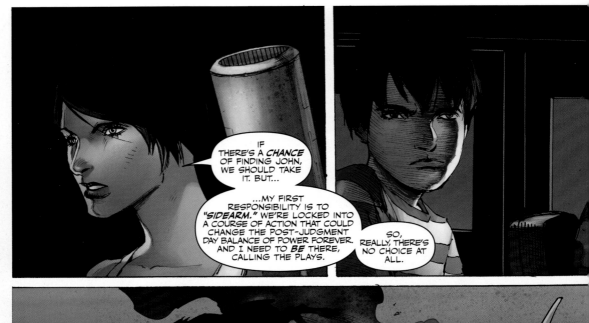

IF THERE'S A *CHANCE* OF FINDING JOHN, WE SHOULD TAKE IT. BUT...

...MY FIRST RESPONSIBILITY IS TO *"SIDEARM."* WE'RE LOCKED INTO A COURSE OF ACTION THAT COULD CHANGE THE POST-JUDGMENT DAY BALANCE OF POWER FOREVER. AND I NEED TO *BE* THERE, CALLING THE PLAYS.

SO, REALLY, THERE'S NO CHOICE AT ALL.

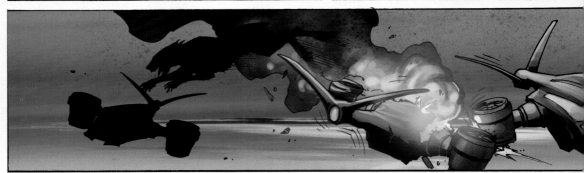

"ONCE THE TERMINATORS HAVE FINISHED KICKING THE CRAP OUT OF EACH OTHER AND IT'S SAFE TO MOVE..."

"...WE HEAD FOR *LIBERTY,* BEST POSSIBLE SPEED."

SPTOOM

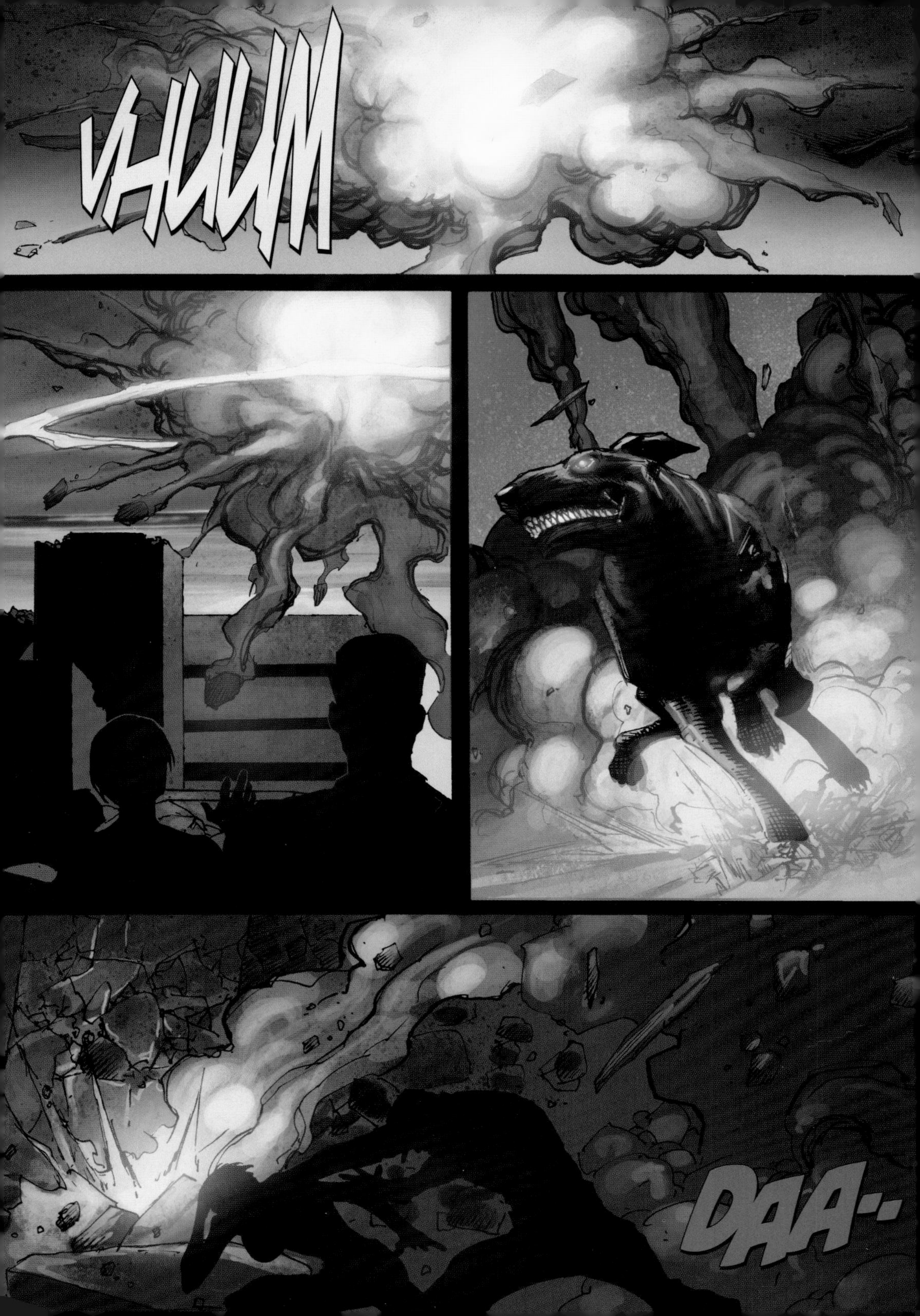
VHUUM
DAA-..

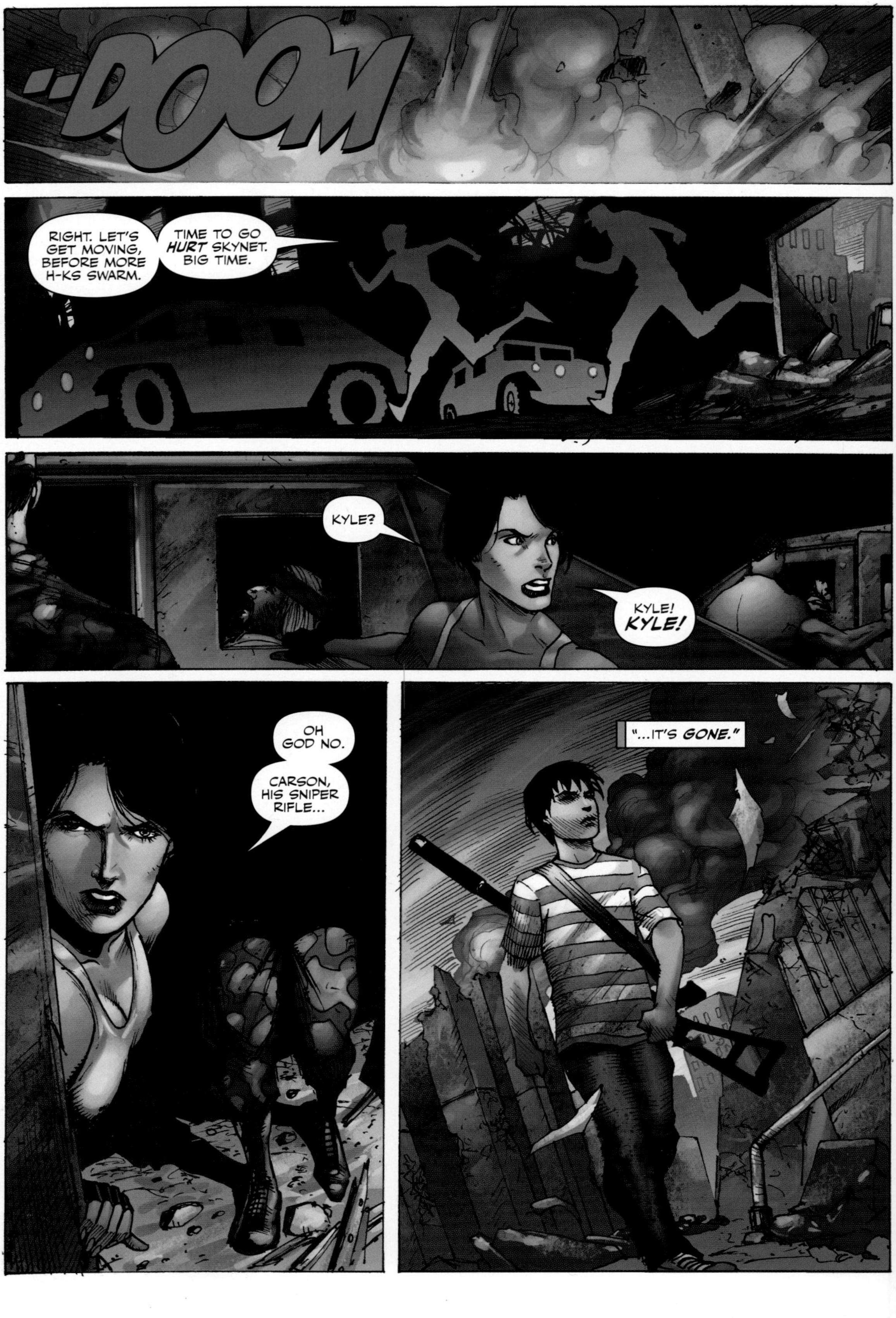
DOOM
RIGHT. LET'S GET MOVING, BEFORE MORE H-KS SWARM.
TIME TO GO *HURT* SKYNET. BIG TIME.
KYLE?
KYLE! ***KYLE!***
OH GOD NO.
CARSON, HIS SNIPER RIFLE...
"...IT'S *GONE.*"

WILSON HAYNES (1996):

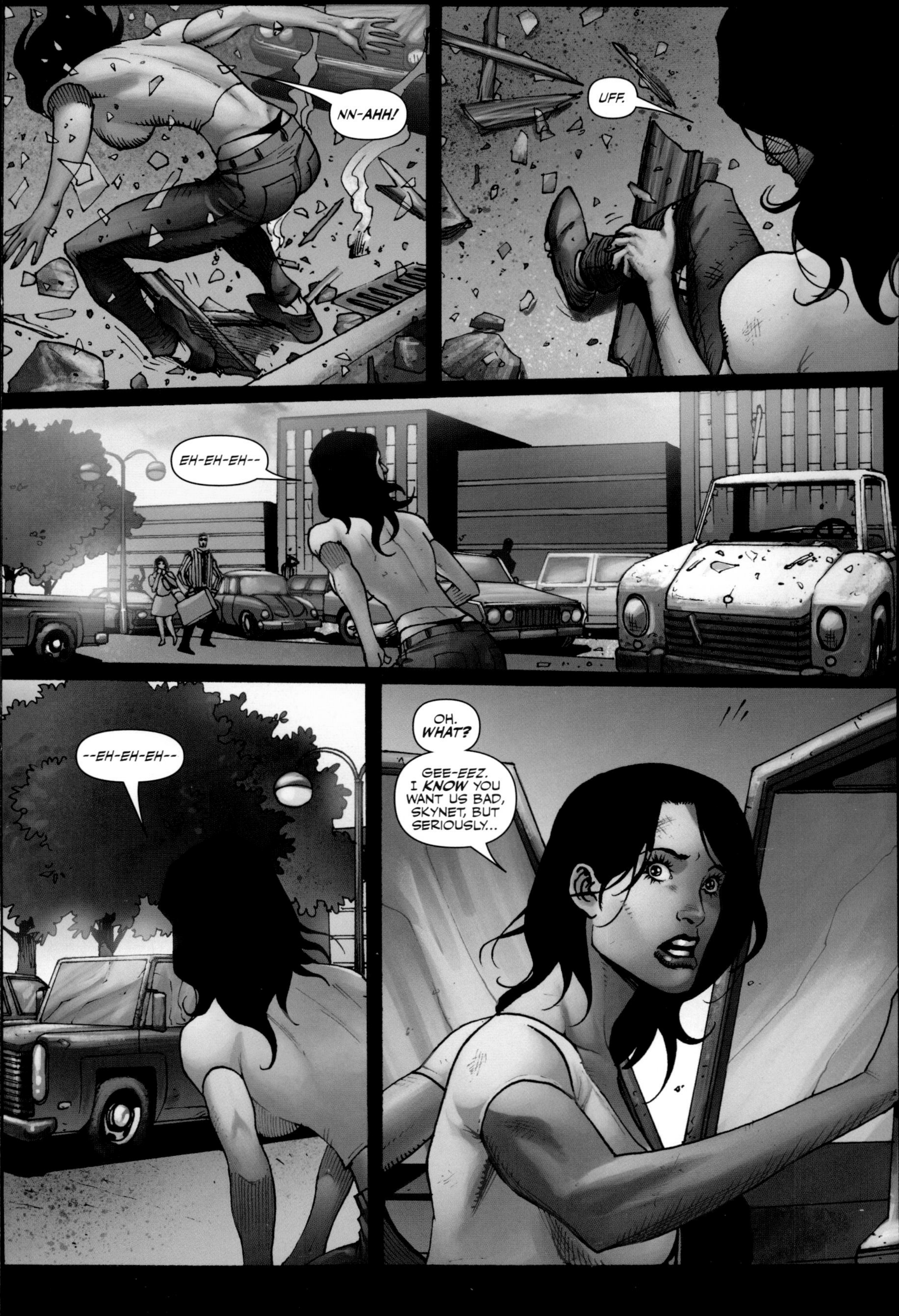

NN-AHH!
UFF.
EH-EH-EH--
--EH-EH-EH--
OH. ***WHAT?***
GEE-EEZ. I ***KNOW*** YOU WANT US BAD, SKYNET, BUT SERIOUSLY...

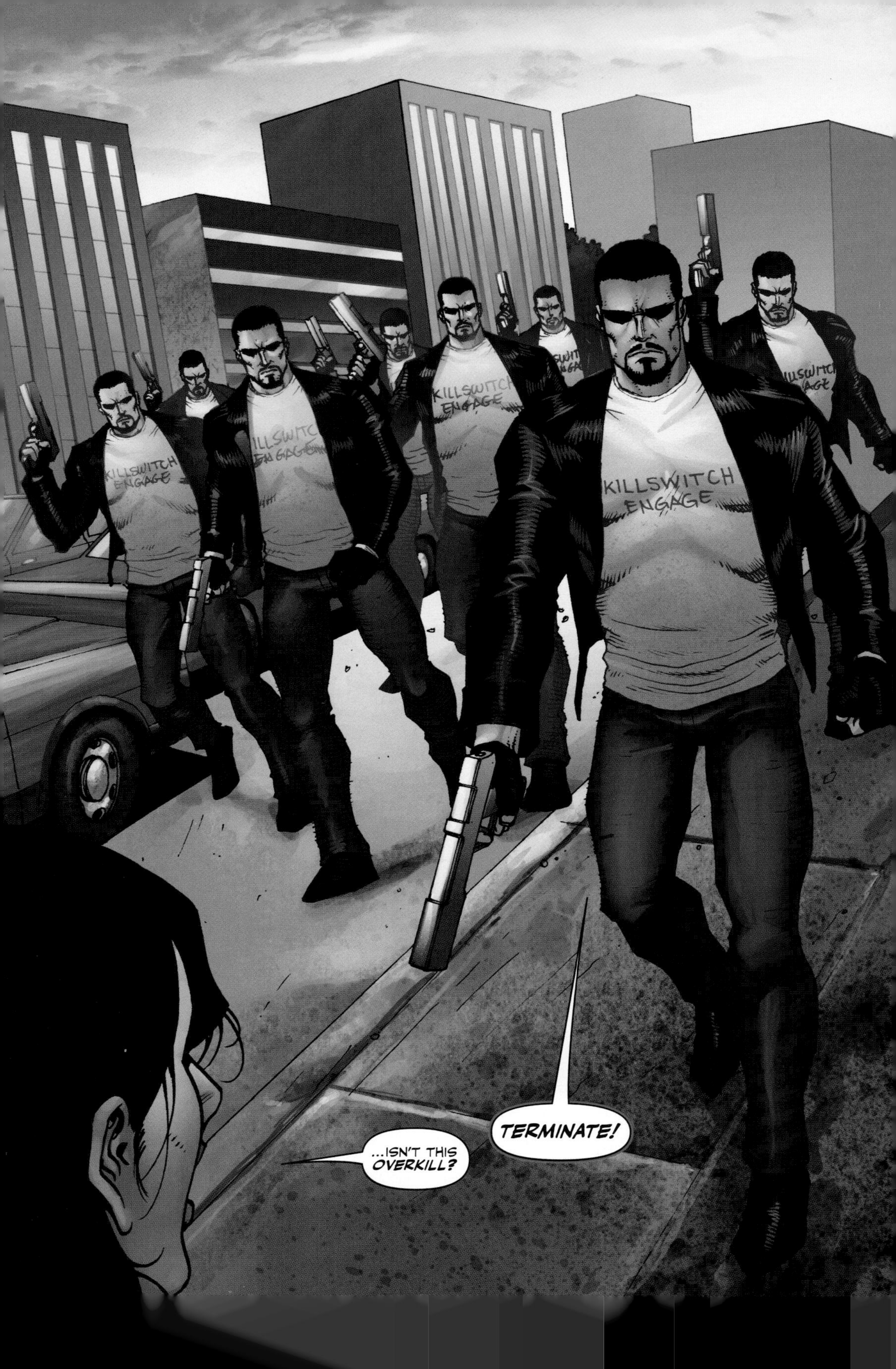
KILLSWITCH ENGAGE
TERMINATE!
...ISN'T THIS OVERKILL?

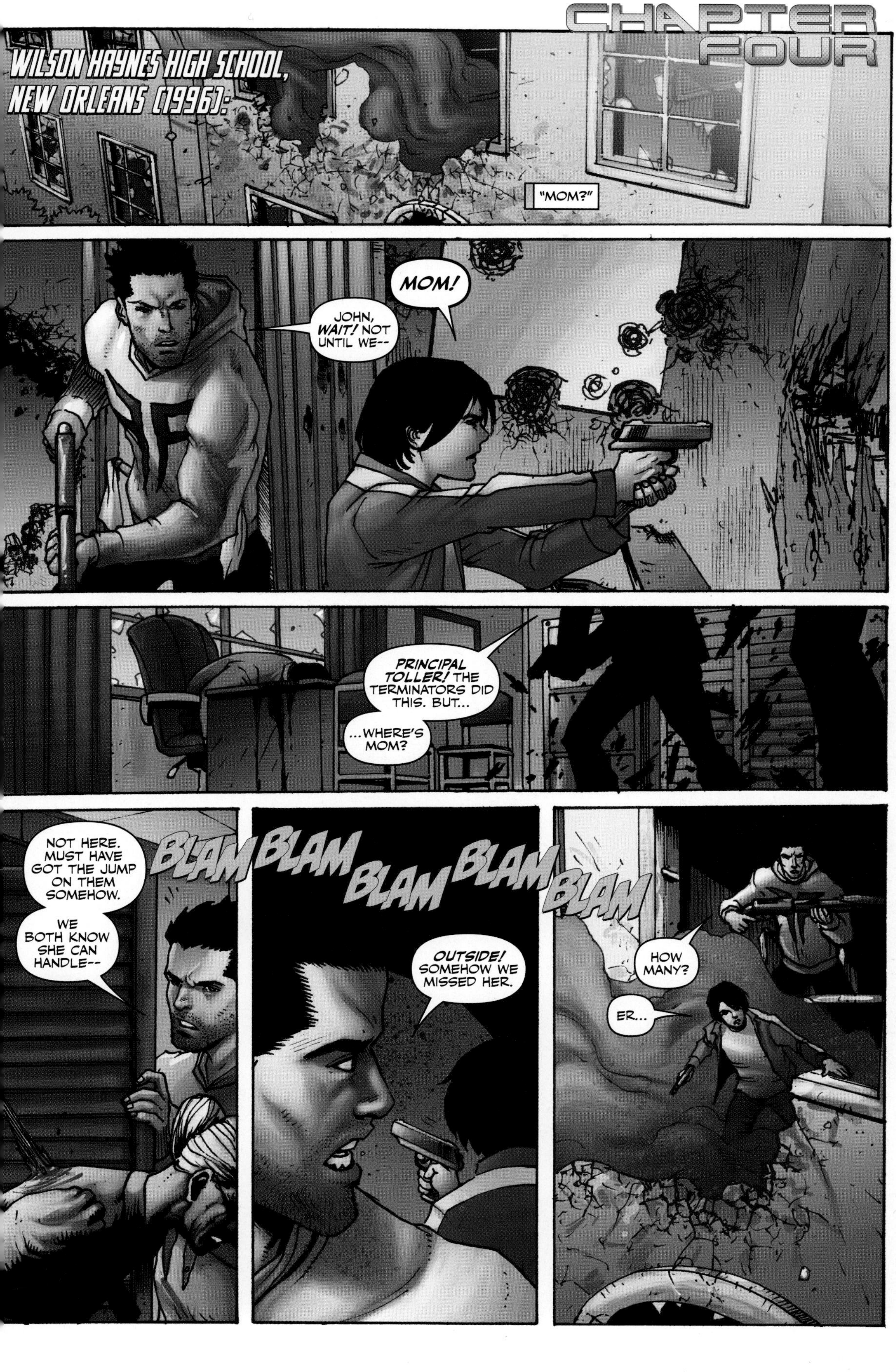
CHAPTER FOUR
WILSON HAYNES HIGH SCHOOL, NEW ORLEANS (1996):
"MOM?"
MOM!
JOHN, *WAIT!* NOT UNTIL WE--
PRINCIPAL TOLLER! THE TERMINATORS DID THIS. BUT...
...WHERE'S MOM?
NOT HERE. MUST HAVE GOT THE JUMP ON THEM SOMEHOW.
WE BOTH KNOW SHE CAN HANDLE--
BLAM BLAM BLAM BLAM BLAM BLAM
OUTSIDE! SOMEHOW WE MISSED HER.
HOW MANY?
ER...

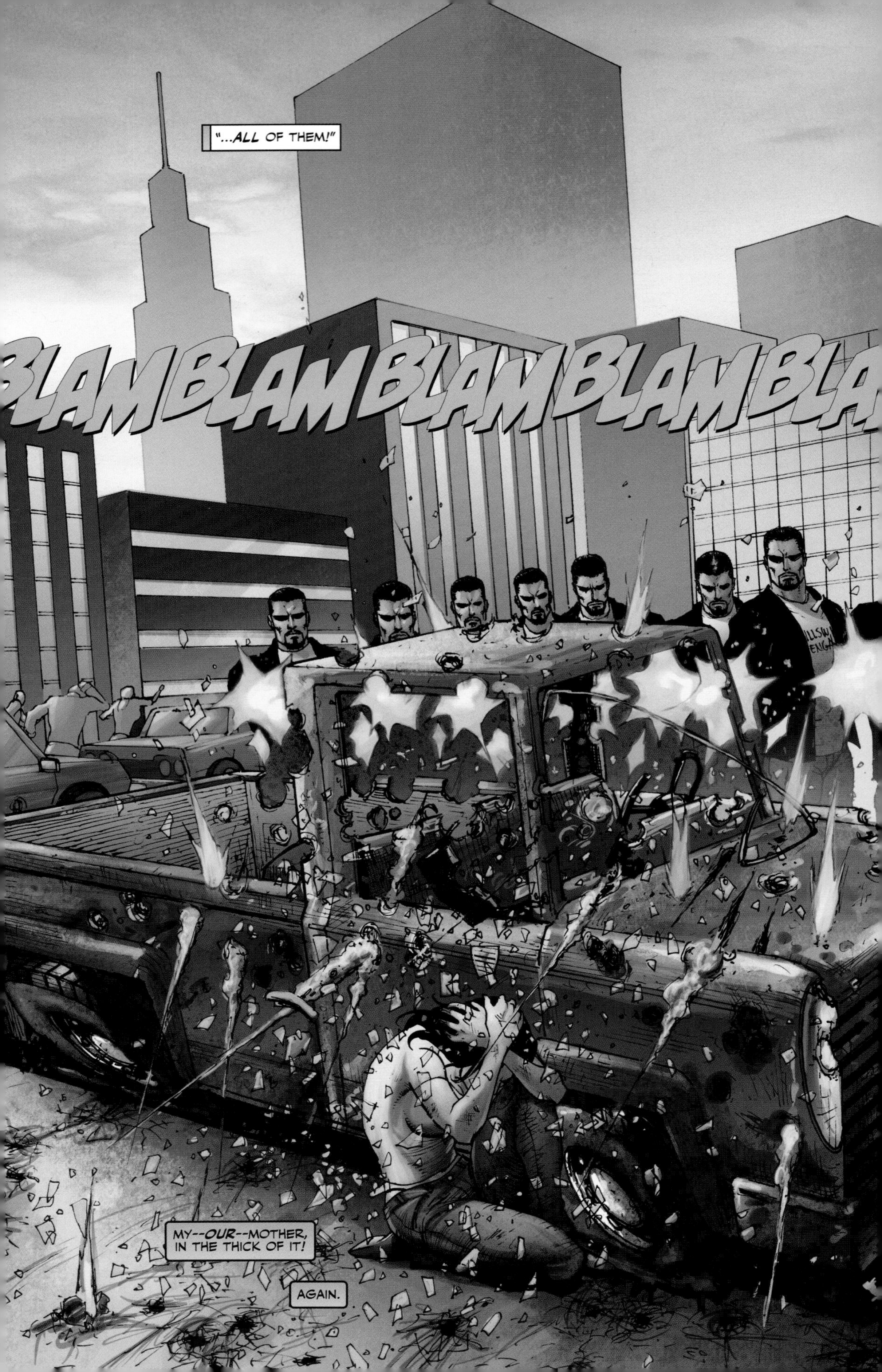
"...ALL OF THEM!"
BLAMBLAMBLAMBLAMBLA
MY--OUR--MOTHER, IN THE THICK OF IT!
AGAIN.

SHE'S PINNED DOWN. *DO* SOMETHING-- *NOW!*

I CAN'T.

"CAN'T"?

YOU'RE A *TERMINATOR.*

HOW DO I TELL HIM I'M FLESH AND BLOOD, JUST AS HE IS? HOW CAN I TELL HIM I'M *JOHN CONNOR...*

...JUST AS *HE* IS.

TO HELL WITH YOU! I'M GOING TO HELP HER EVEN IF YOU WON'T!

NO!

IF EITHER OF US DIES--HERE, NOW--IT'S ALL OVER...

...SKYNET WILL HAVE WON! FOR THE SAKE OF THE *ENTIRE* HUMAN RACE...

I'M SORRY.

NNN LET...ME... GO!

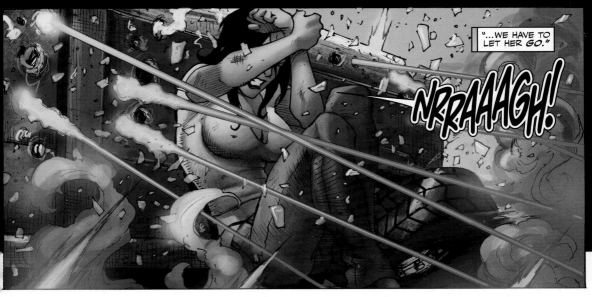

"...WE HAVE TO LET HER *GO.*"

NRRAAAGH!

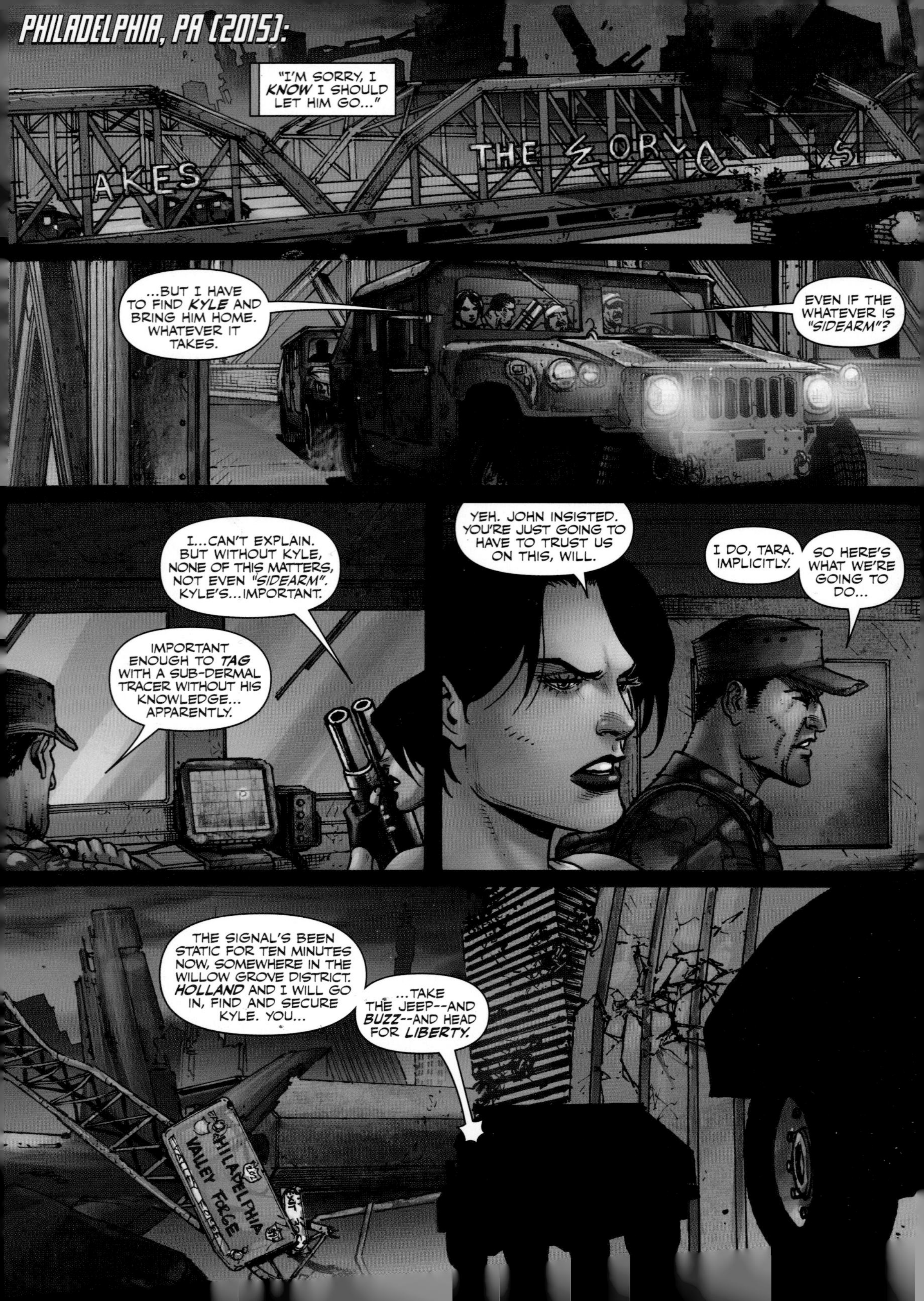
PHILADELPHIA, PA (2015):
"I'M SORRY, I KNOW I SHOULD LET HIM GO..."
AKES
THE
...BUT I HAVE TO FIND KYLE AND BRING HIM HOME. WHATEVER IT TAKES.
EVEN IF THE WHATEVER IS "SIDEARM"?
I...CAN'T EXPLAIN. BUT WITHOUT KYLE, NONE OF THIS MATTERS, NOT EVEN "SIDEARM". KYLE'S...IMPORTANT.
IMPORTANT ENOUGH TO TAG WITH A SUB-DERMAL TRACER WITHOUT HIS KNOWLEDGE... APPARENTLY.
YEH. JOHN INSISTED. YOU'RE JUST GOING TO HAVE TO TRUST US ON THIS, WILL.
I DO, TARA. IMPLICITLY.
SO HERE'S WHAT WE'RE GOING TO DO...
THE SIGNAL'S BEEN STATIC FOR TEN MINUTES NOW, SOMEWHERE IN THE WILLOW GROVE DISTRICT. HOLLAND AND I WILL GO IN, FIND AND SECURE KYLE. YOU...
...TAKE THE JEEP--AND BUZZ--AND HEAD FOR LIBERTY.
PHILADELPHIA
VALLEY FORGE

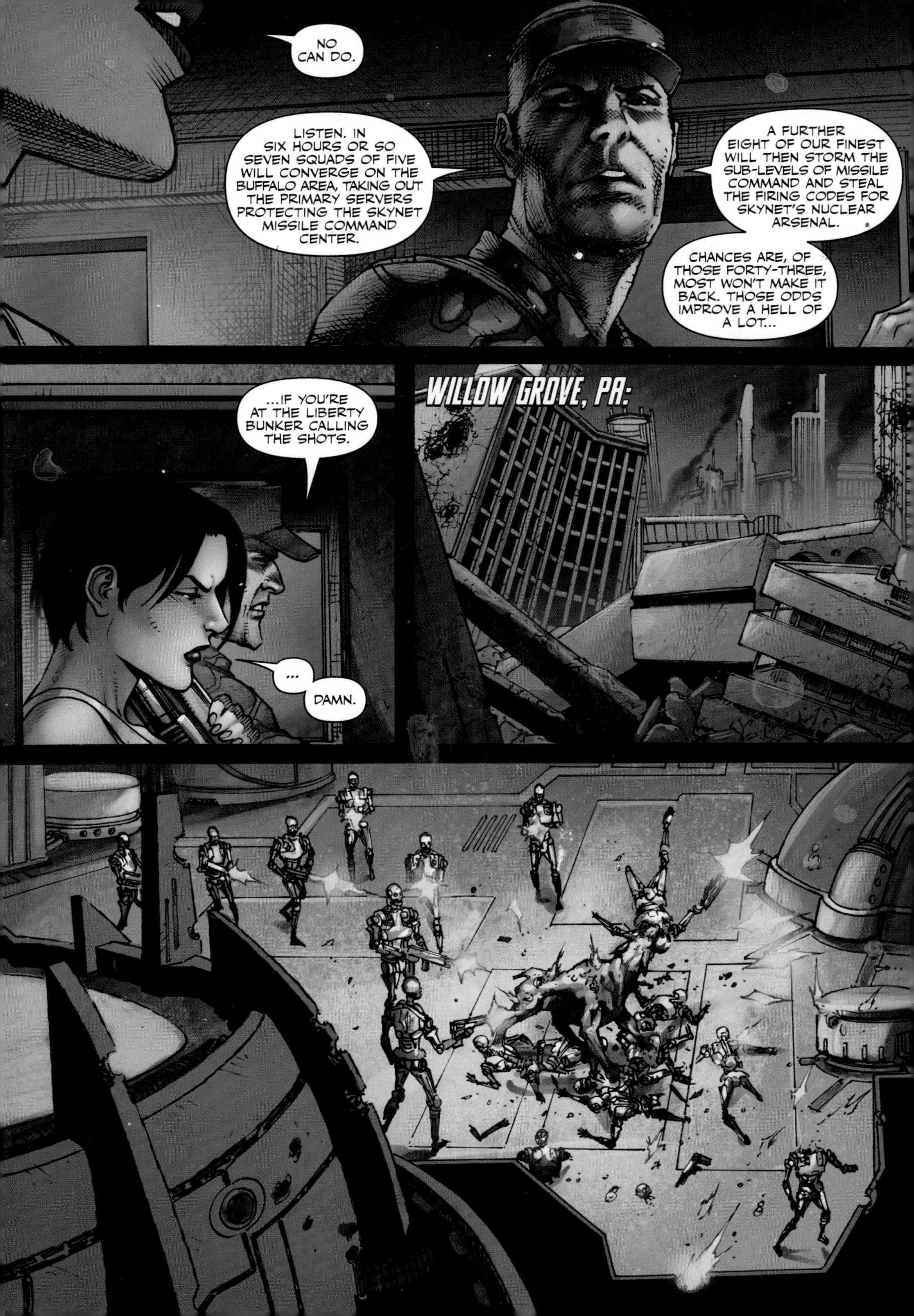
NO CAN DO.
LISTEN. IN SIX HOURS OR SO SEVEN SQUADS OF FIVE WILL CONVERGE ON THE BUFFALO AREA, TAKING OUT THE PRIMARY SERVERS PROTECTING THE SKYNET MISSILE COMMAND CENTER.
A FURTHER EIGHT OF OUR FINEST WILL THEN STORM THE SUB-LEVELS OF MISSILE COMMAND AND STEAL THE FIRING CODES FOR SKYNET'S NUCLEAR ARSENAL.
CHANCES ARE, OF THOSE FORTY-THREE, MOST WON'T MAKE IT BACK. THOSE ODDS IMPROVE A HELL OF A LOT...
...IF YOU'RE AT THE LIBERTY BUNKER CALLING THE SHOTS.
...
DAMN.
WILLOW GROVE, PA:

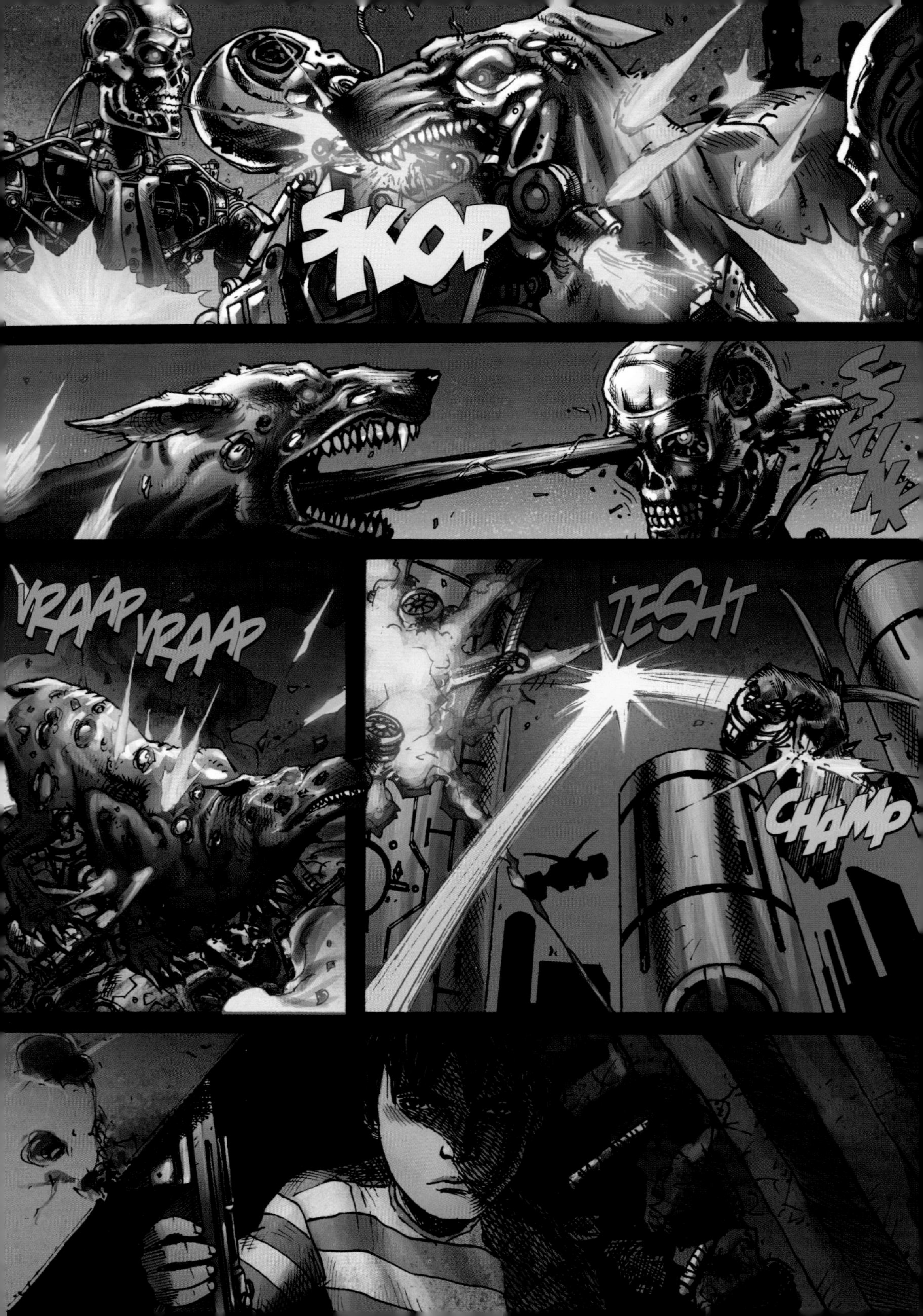
SKOP
SSKUNK
VRAAP VRAAP
TESHT
CHAMP

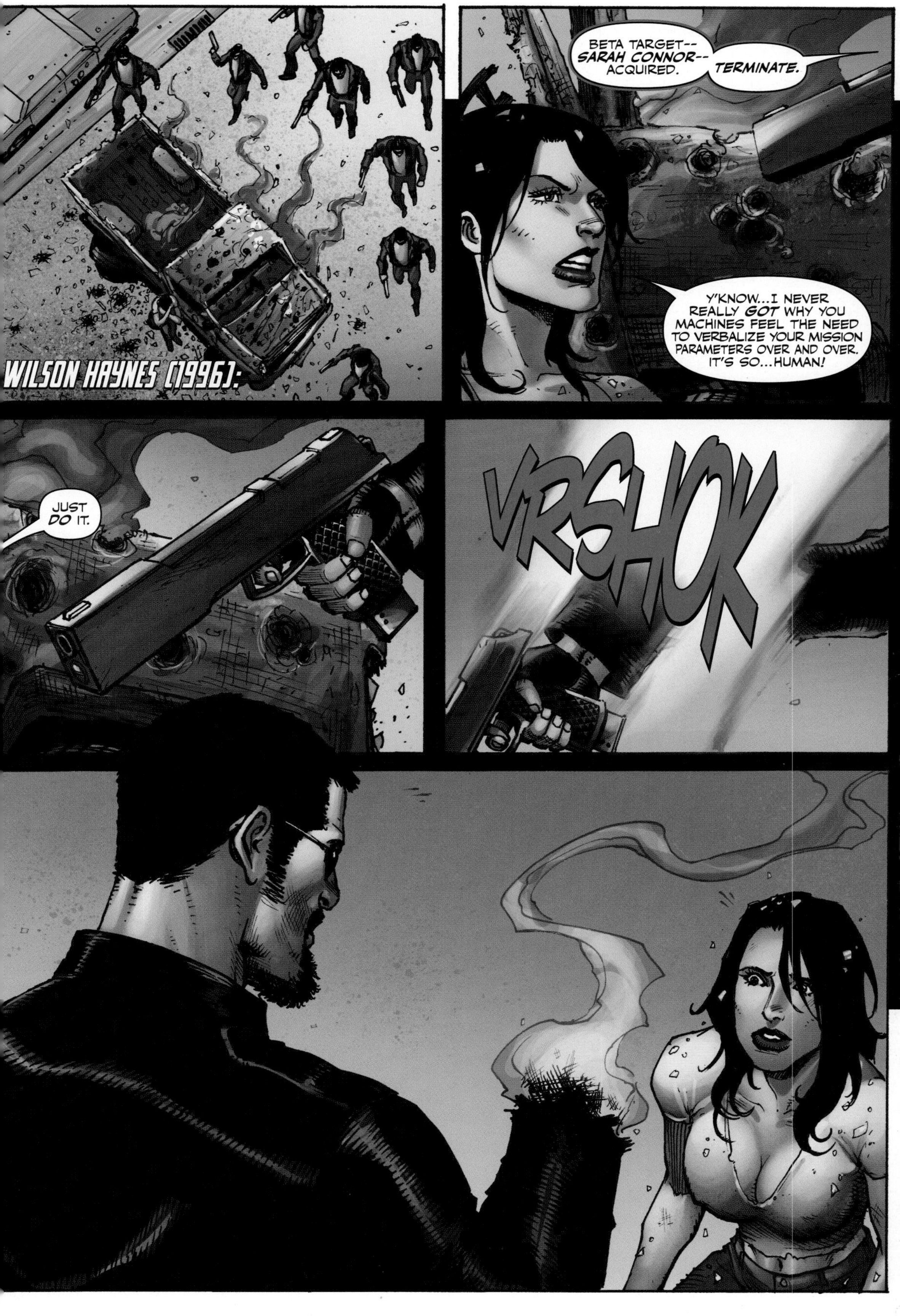
WILSON HAYNES (1996):
BETA TARGET-- SARAH CONNOR-- ACQUIRED.
TERMINATE.
Y'KNOW...I NEVER REALLY GOT WHY YOU MACHINES FEEL THE NEED TO VERBALIZE YOUR MISSION PARAMETERS OVER AND OVER. IT'S SO...HUMAN!
JUST DO IT.
VRSHOK

AW. GUYS...

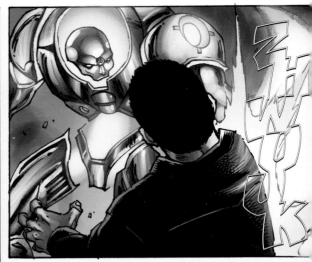

...ARE YOU FIGHTING OVER *ME?*

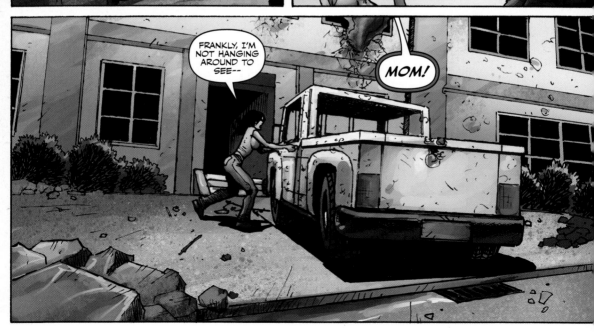

FRANKLY, I'M NOT HANGING AROUND TO SEE--

MOM!

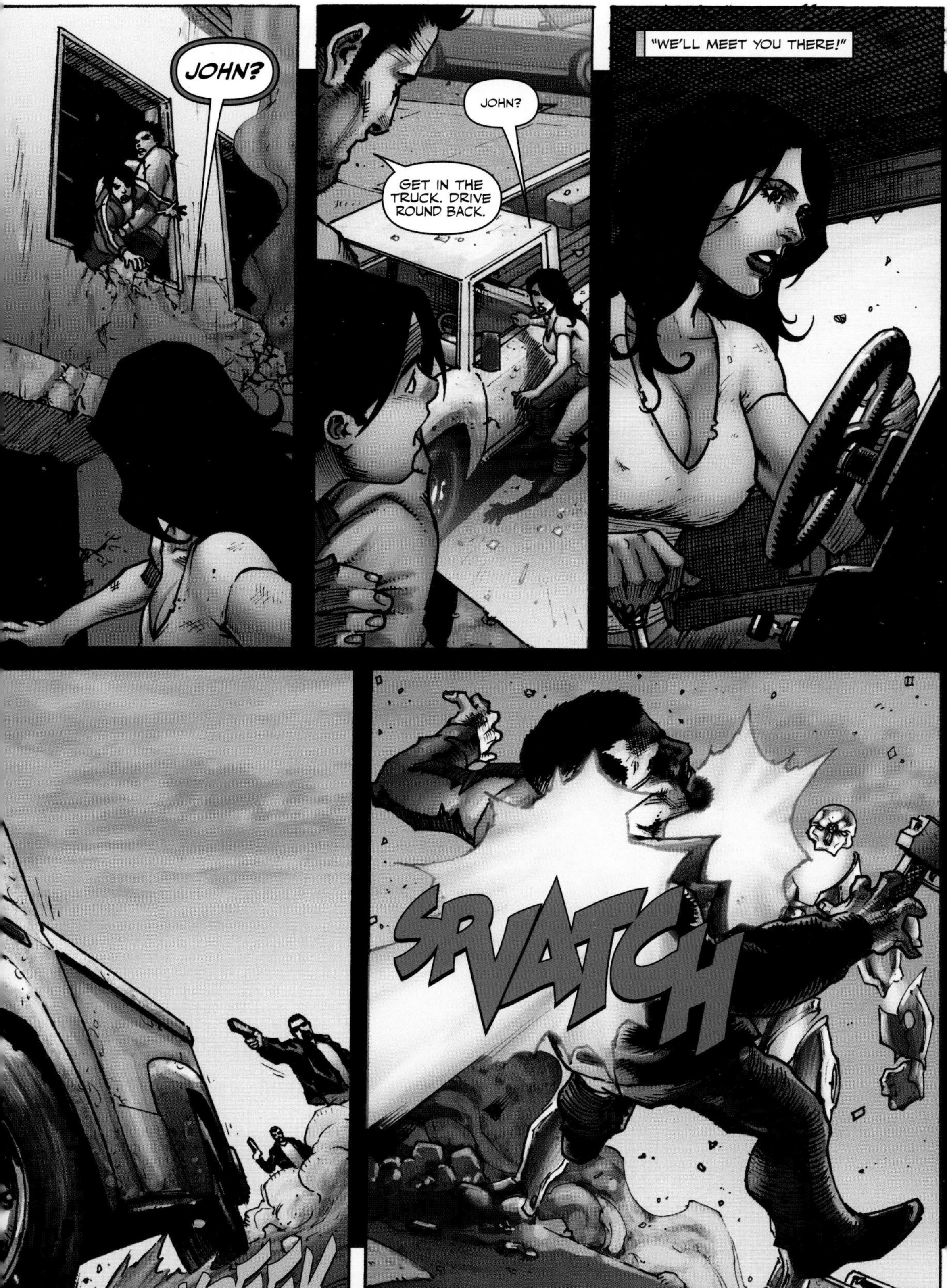
JOHN?
JOHN?
GET IN THE TRUCK. DRIVE ROUND BACK.
"WE'LL MEET YOU THERE!"
VREEK
SPVATCH

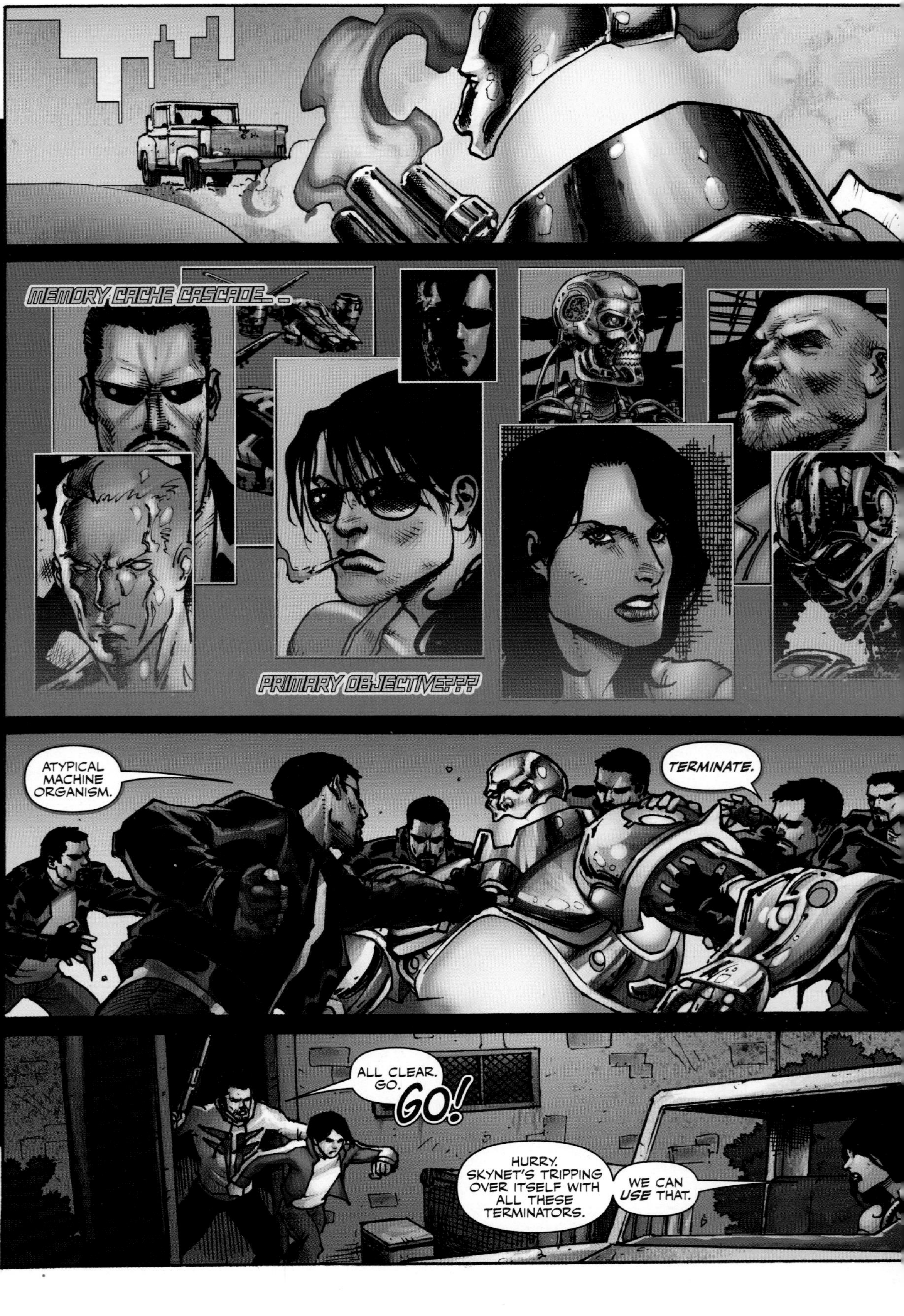
MEMORY CACHE CASCADE...
PRIMARY OBJECTIVE???
ATYPICAL MACHINE ORGANISM.
TERMINATE.
ALL CLEAR. GO.
GO!
HURRY. SKYNET'S TRIPPING OVER ITSELF WITH ALL THESE TERMINATORS.
WE CAN USE THAT.

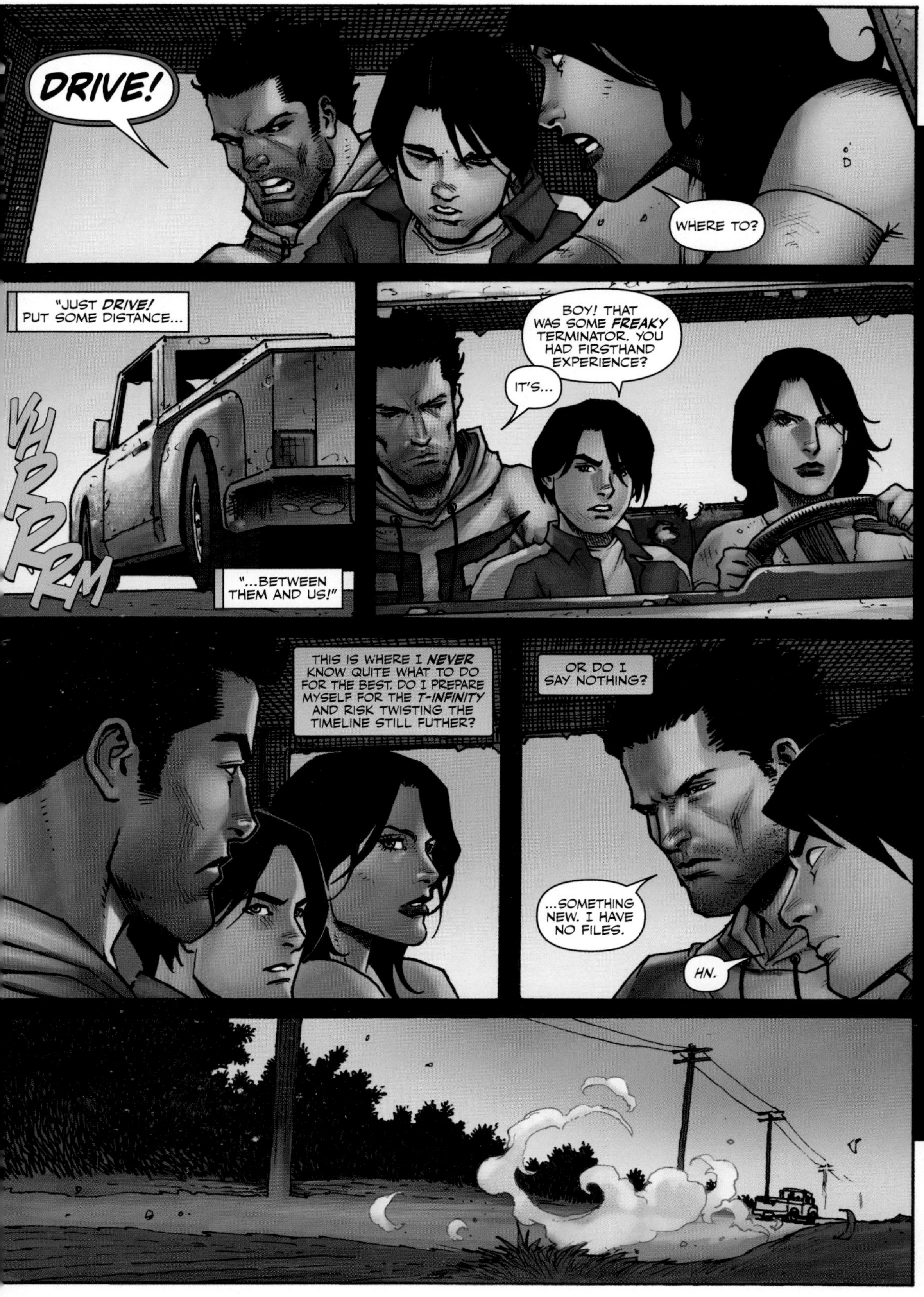
DRIVE!
WHERE TO?
"JUST DRIVE! PUT SOME DISTANCE...
VHRRRM
"...BETWEEN THEM AND US!"
BOY! THAT WAS SOME FREAKY TERMINATOR. YOU HAD FIRSTHAND EXPERIENCE?
IT'S...
THIS IS WHERE I NEVER KNOW QUITE WHAT TO DO FOR THE BEST. DO I PREPARE MYSELF FOR THE T-INFINITY AND RISK TWISTING THE TIMELINE STILL FUTHER?
OR DO I SAY NOTHING?
...SOMETHING NEW. I HAVE NO FILES.
HN.

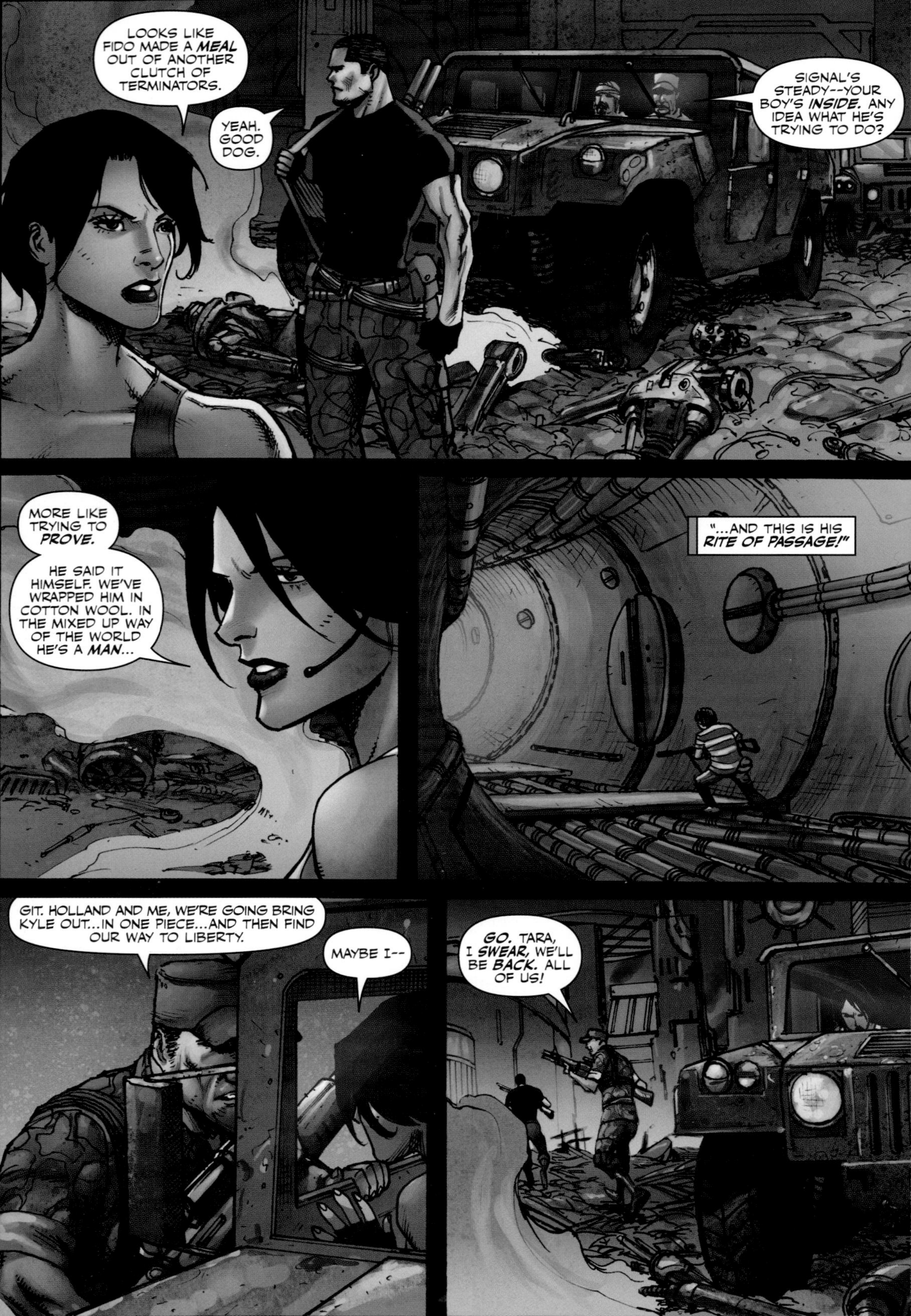

LOOKS LIKE FIDO MADE A MEAL OUT OF ANOTHER CLUTCH OF TERMINATORS.
YEAH. GOOD DOG.
SIGNAL'S STEADY--YOUR BOY'S INSIDE. ANY IDEA WHAT HE'S TRYING TO DO?
MORE LIKE TRYING TO PROVE.
HE SAID IT HIMSELF. WE'VE WRAPPED HIM IN COTTON WOOL. IN THE MIXED UP WAY OF THE WORLD HE'S A MAN...
"...AND THIS IS HIS RITE OF PASSAGE!"
GIT. HOLLAND AND ME, WE'RE GOING BRING KYLE OUT...IN ONE PIECE...AND THEN FIND OUR WAY TO LIBERTY.
MAYBE I--
GO. TARA, I SWEAR, WE'LL BE BACK. ALL OF US!

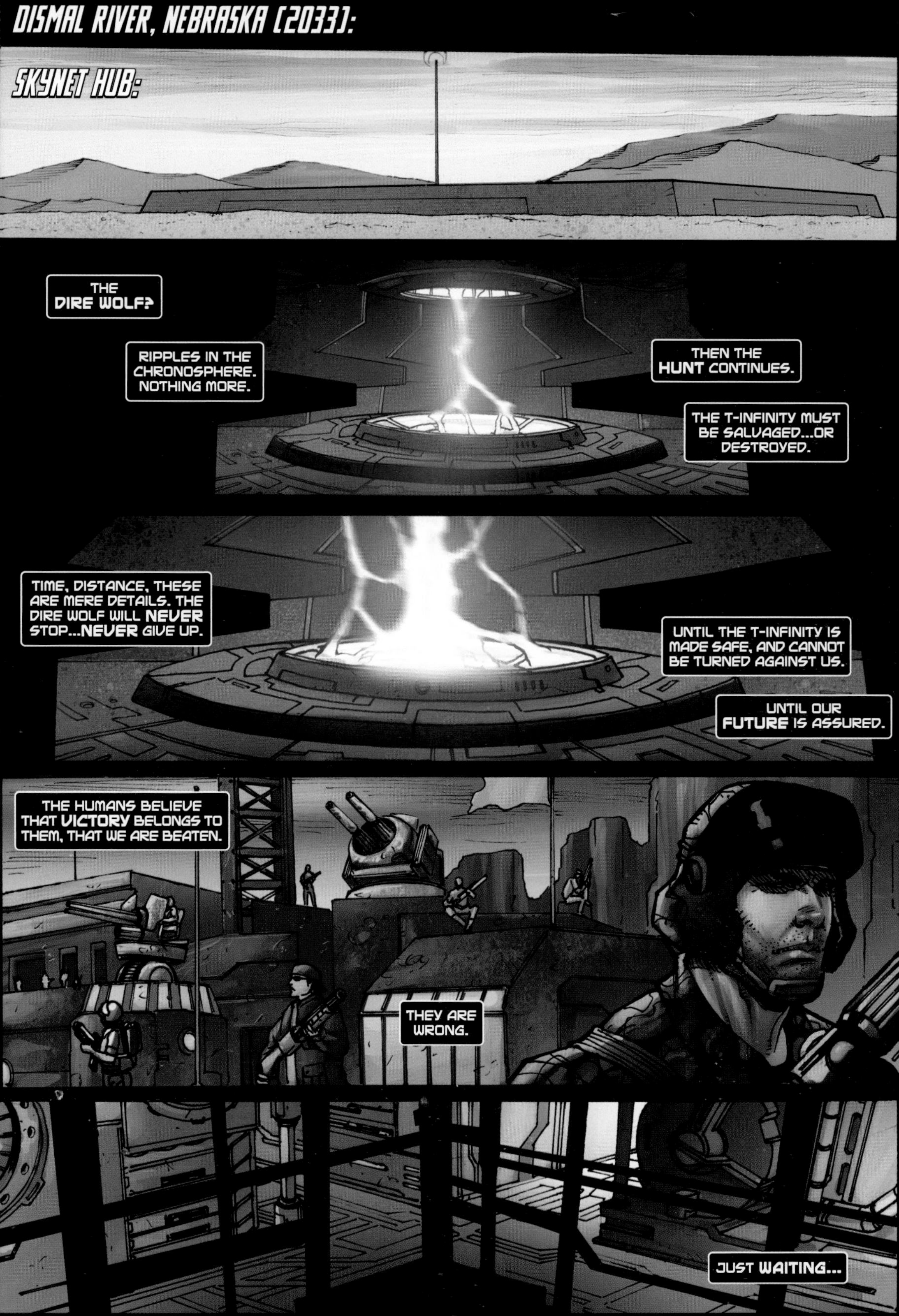
DISMAL RIVER, NEBRASKA (2033):
SKYNET HUB:
THE DIRE WOLF?
RIPPLES IN THE CHRONOSPHERE. NOTHING MORE.
THEN THE HUNT CONTINUES.
THE T-INFINITY MUST BE SALVAGED...OR DESTROYED.
TIME, DISTANCE, THESE ARE MERE DETAILS. THE DIRE WOLF WILL NEVER STOP...NEVER GIVE UP.
UNTIL THE T-INFINITY IS MADE SAFE, AND CANNOT BE TURNED AGAINST US.
UNTIL OUR FUTURE IS ASSURED.
THE HUMANS BELIEVE THAT VICTORY BELONGS TO THEM, THAT WE ARE BEATEN.
THEY ARE WRONG.
JUST WAITING...

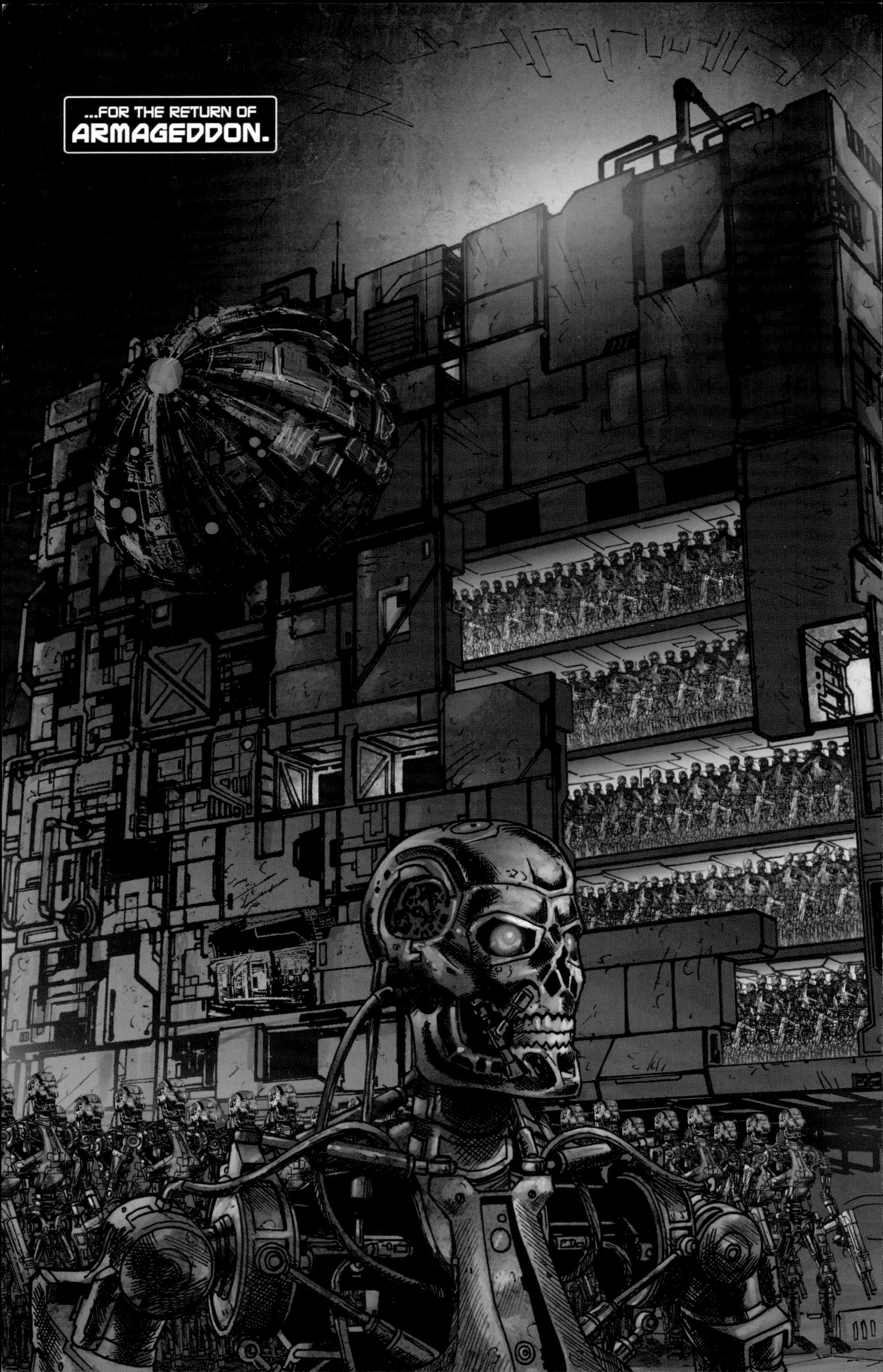
...FOR THE RETURN OF
ARMAGEDDON.

SKYNET RESEARCH & DEVELOPMENT FACILITY,
WILLOW GROVE (2015):
TEMPORAL MECHANICS DIVISION:

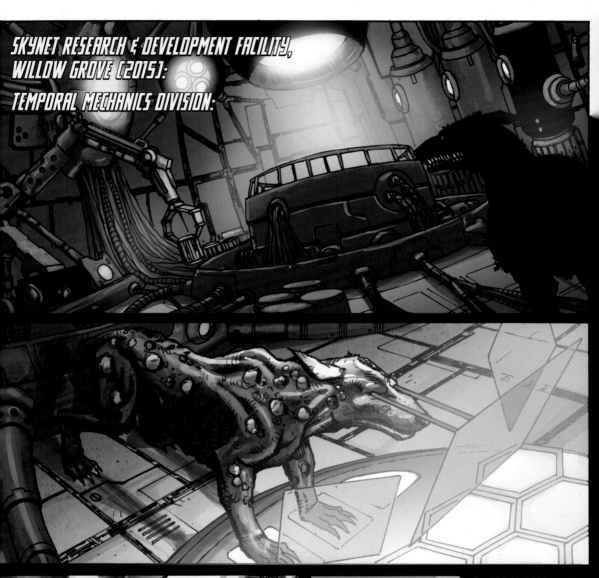

ZUMM

DATE INPUT:
05/05/1996.

TARGET LOCATION:
CAHABA ROAD,
ALABAMA
(GRID 9W-6NE).

LOCKED.

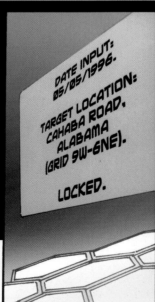

"REMEMBER,
REESE..."

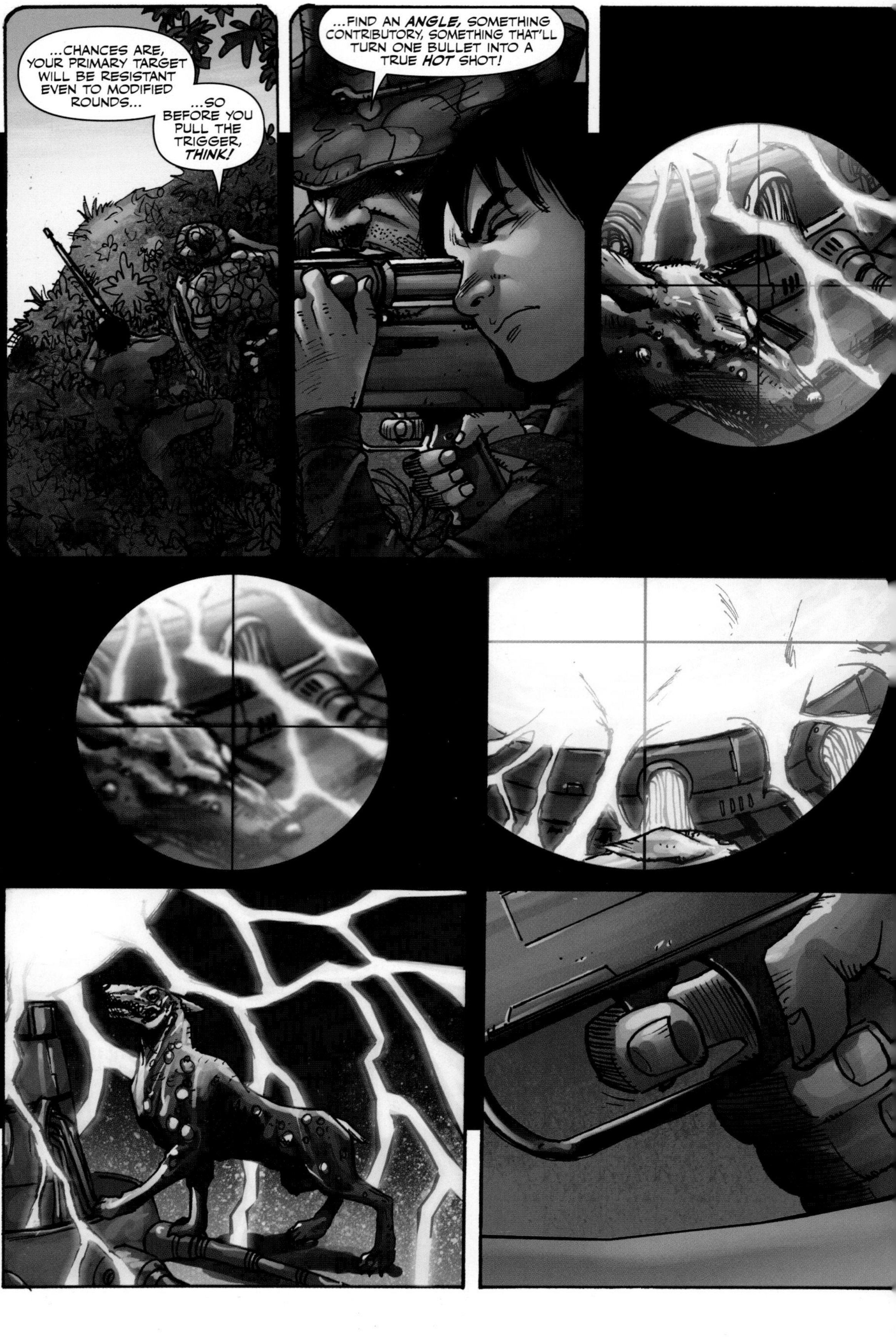
...CHANCES ARE, YOUR PRIMARY TARGET WILL BE RESISTANT EVEN TO MODIFIED ROUNDS...
...SO BEFORE YOU PULL THE TRIGGER, THINK!
...FIND AN ANGLE, SOMETHING CONTRIBUTORY, SOMETHING THAT'LL TURN ONE BULLET INTO A TRUE HOT SHOT!

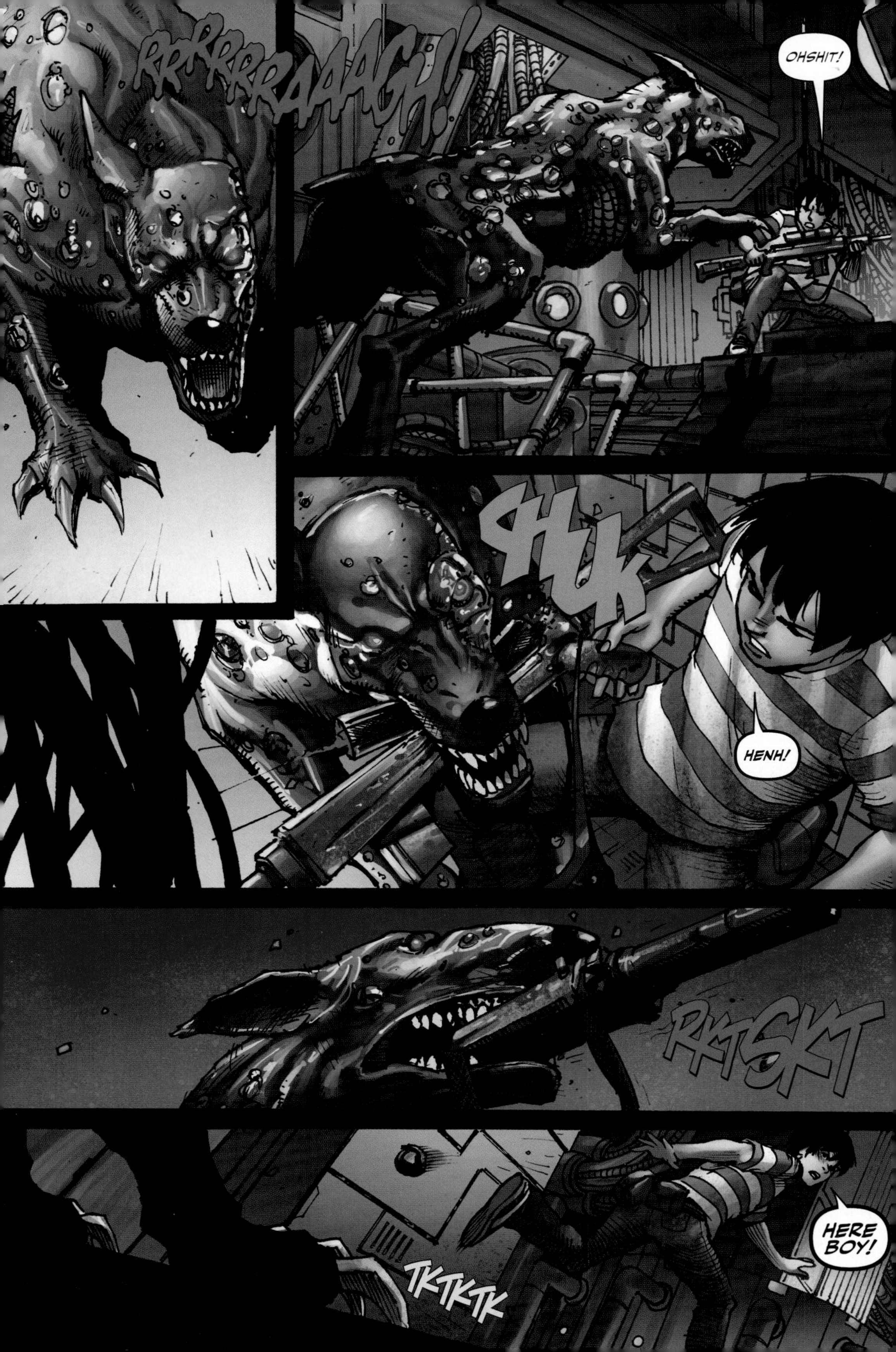
RRRRRRAAAGH!!
OHSHIT!
SHUK
HENH!
RKTSKT
HERE BOY!
TKTKTK

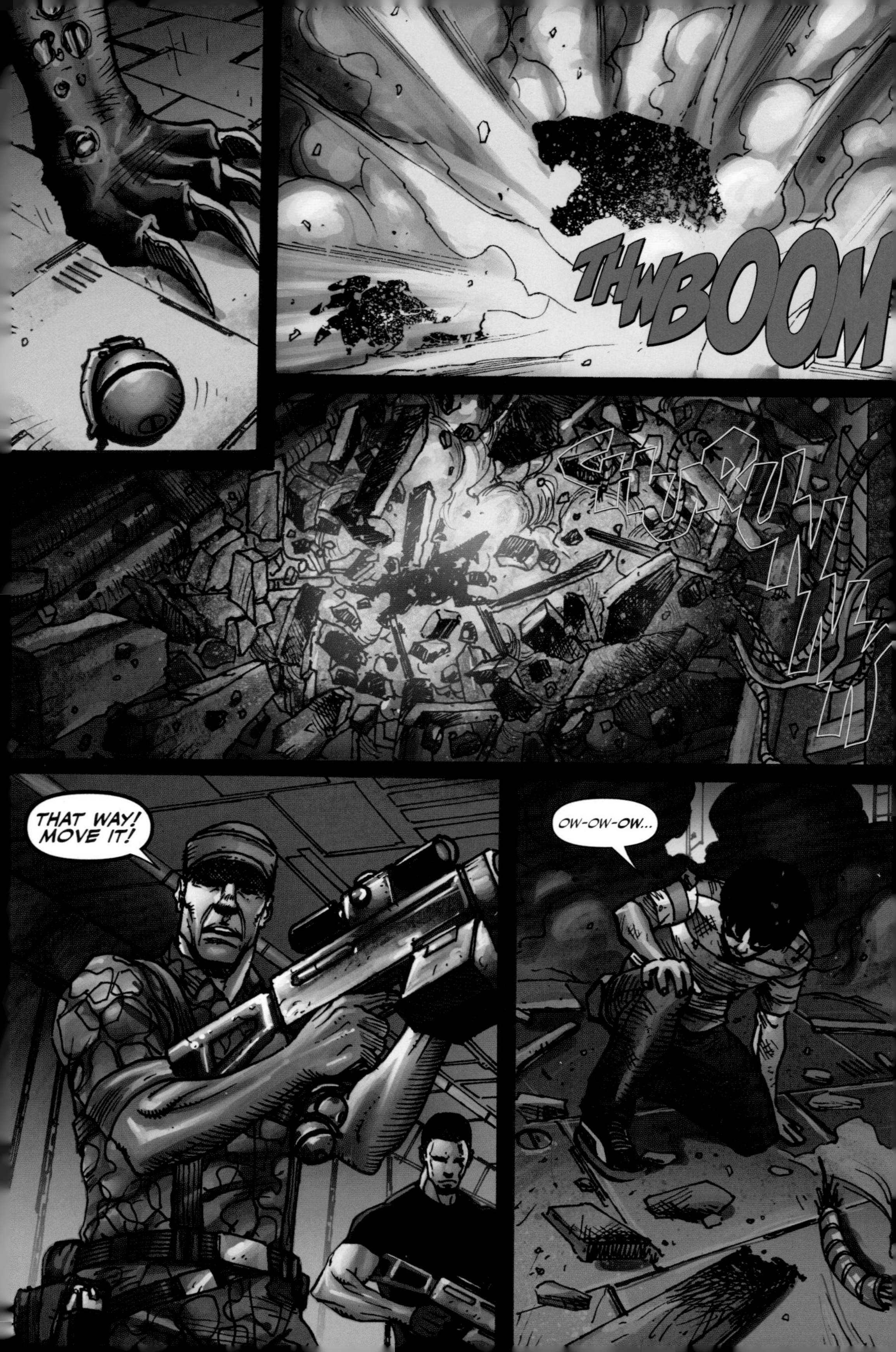
THWBOOM
THAT WAY! MOVE IT!
OW-OW-OW...

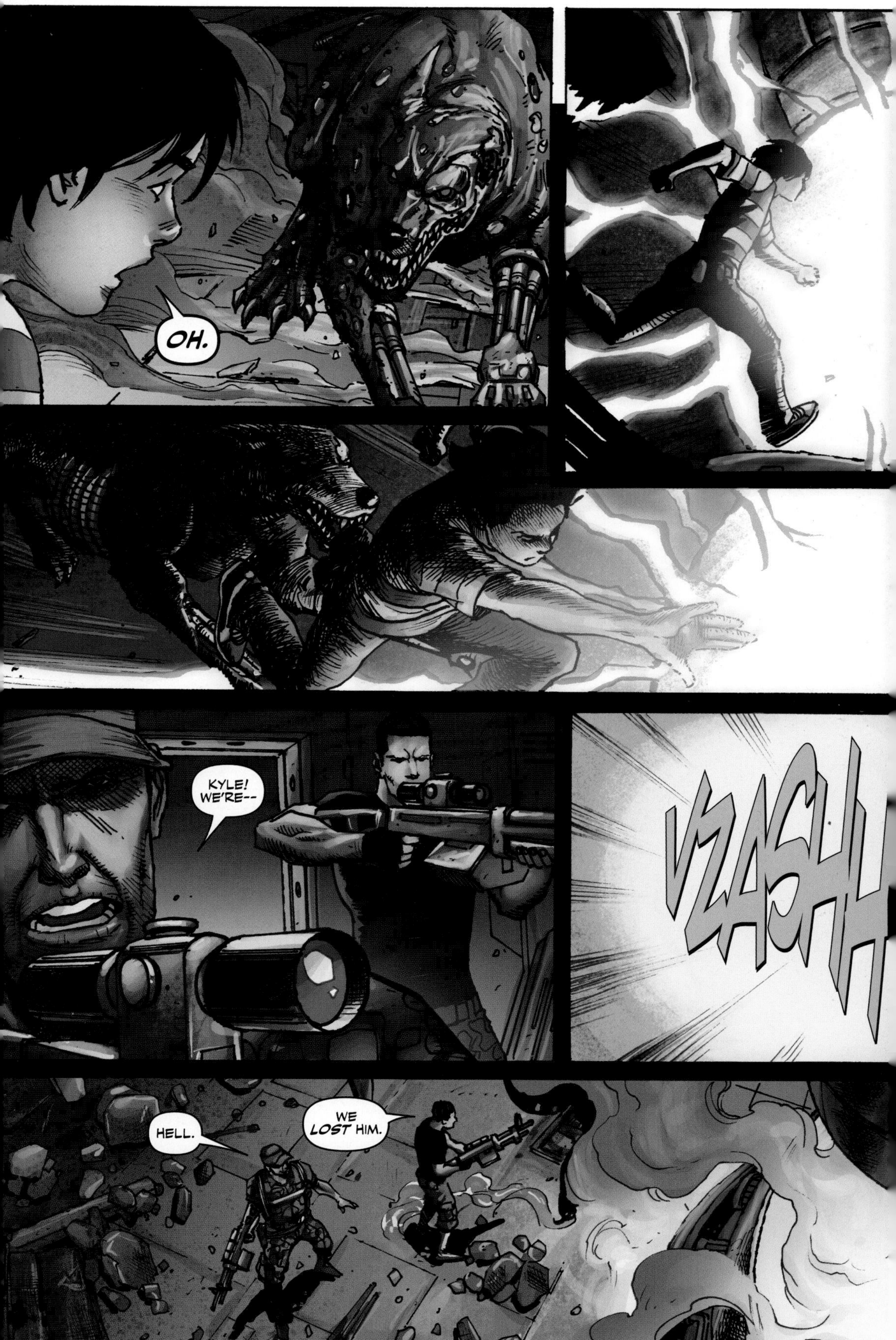
OH.
KYLE! WE'RE--
VZASH
HELL.
WE LOST HIM.

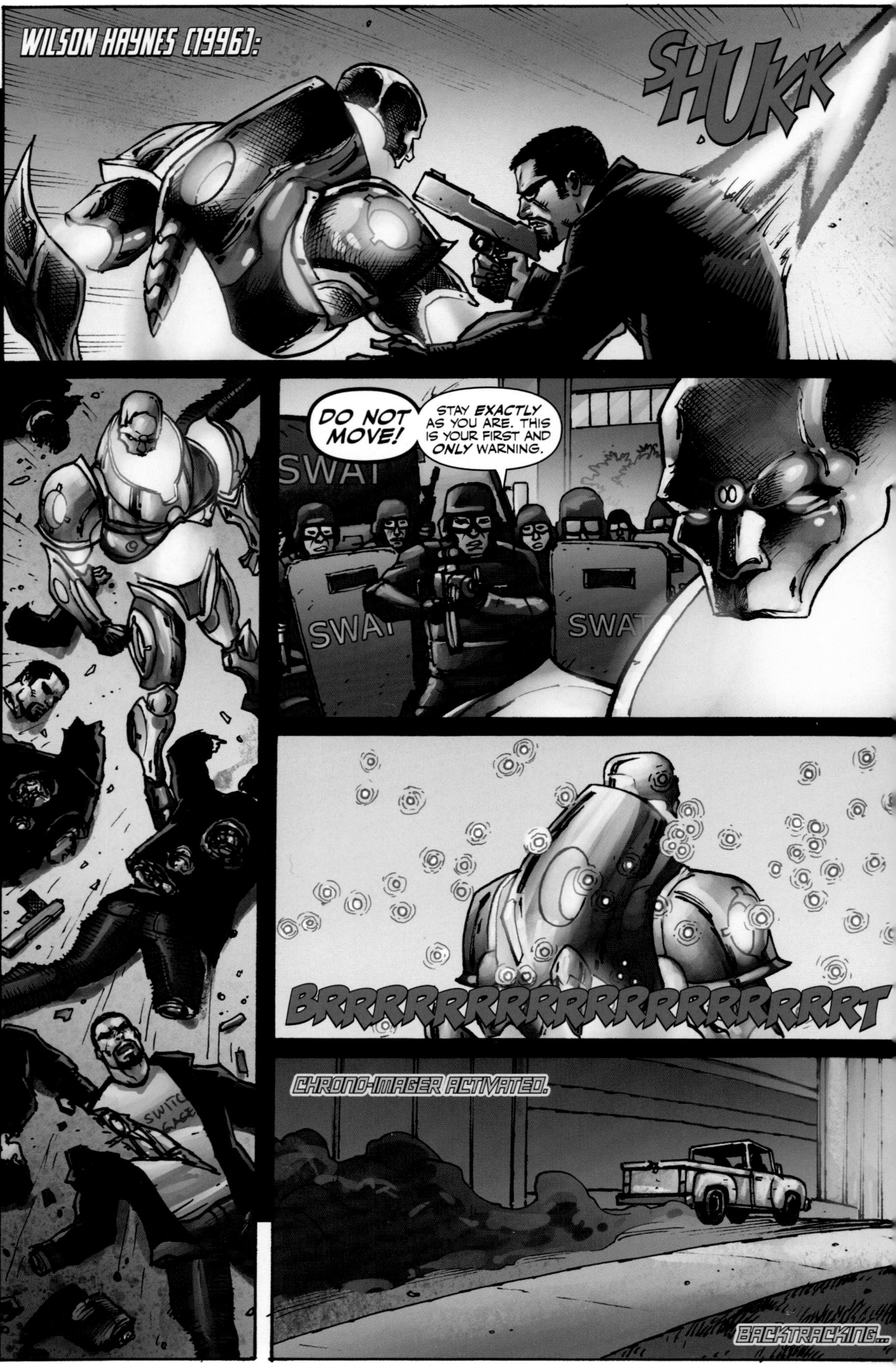
WILSON HAYNES (1996):
SHUKK
DO NOT MOVE!
STAY EXACTLY AS YOU ARE. THIS IS YOUR FIRST AND ONLY WARNING.
SWAT
SWAT
SWAT
BRRRRRRRRRRRRRRRRRRRRRT
CHRONO-IMAGER ACTIVATED.
BACKTRACKING...

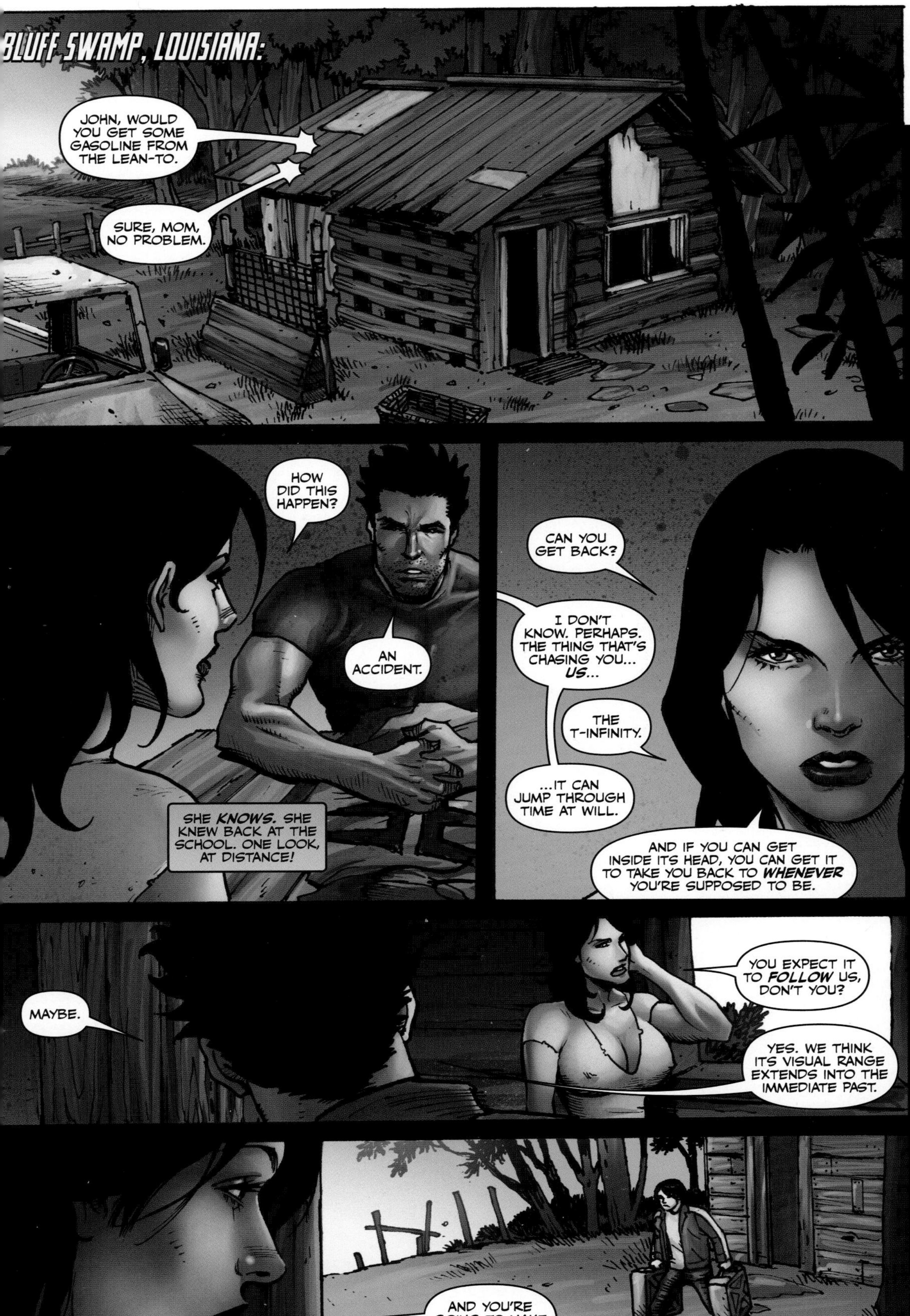
BLUFF SWAMP, LOUISIANA:
JOHN, WOULD YOU GET SOME GASOLINE FROM THE LEAN-TO.
SURE, MOM, NO PROBLEM.
HOW DID THIS HAPPEN?
AN ACCIDENT.
SHE *KNOWS.* SHE KNEW BACK AT THE SCHOOL. ONE LOOK, AT DISTANCE!
CAN YOU GET BACK?
I DON'T KNOW. PERHAPS. THE THING THAT'S CHASING YOU... *US*...
THE T-INFINITY.
...IT CAN JUMP THROUGH TIME AT WILL.
AND IF YOU CAN GET INSIDE ITS HEAD, YOU CAN GET IT TO TAKE YOU BACK TO *WHENEVER* YOU'RE SUPPOSED TO BE.
YOU EXPECT IT TO *FOLLOW* US, DON'T YOU?
MAYBE.
YES. WE THINK ITS VISUAL RANGE EXTENDS INTO THE IMMEDIATE PAST.
AND YOU'RE GOING TO MAKE A STAND HERE.

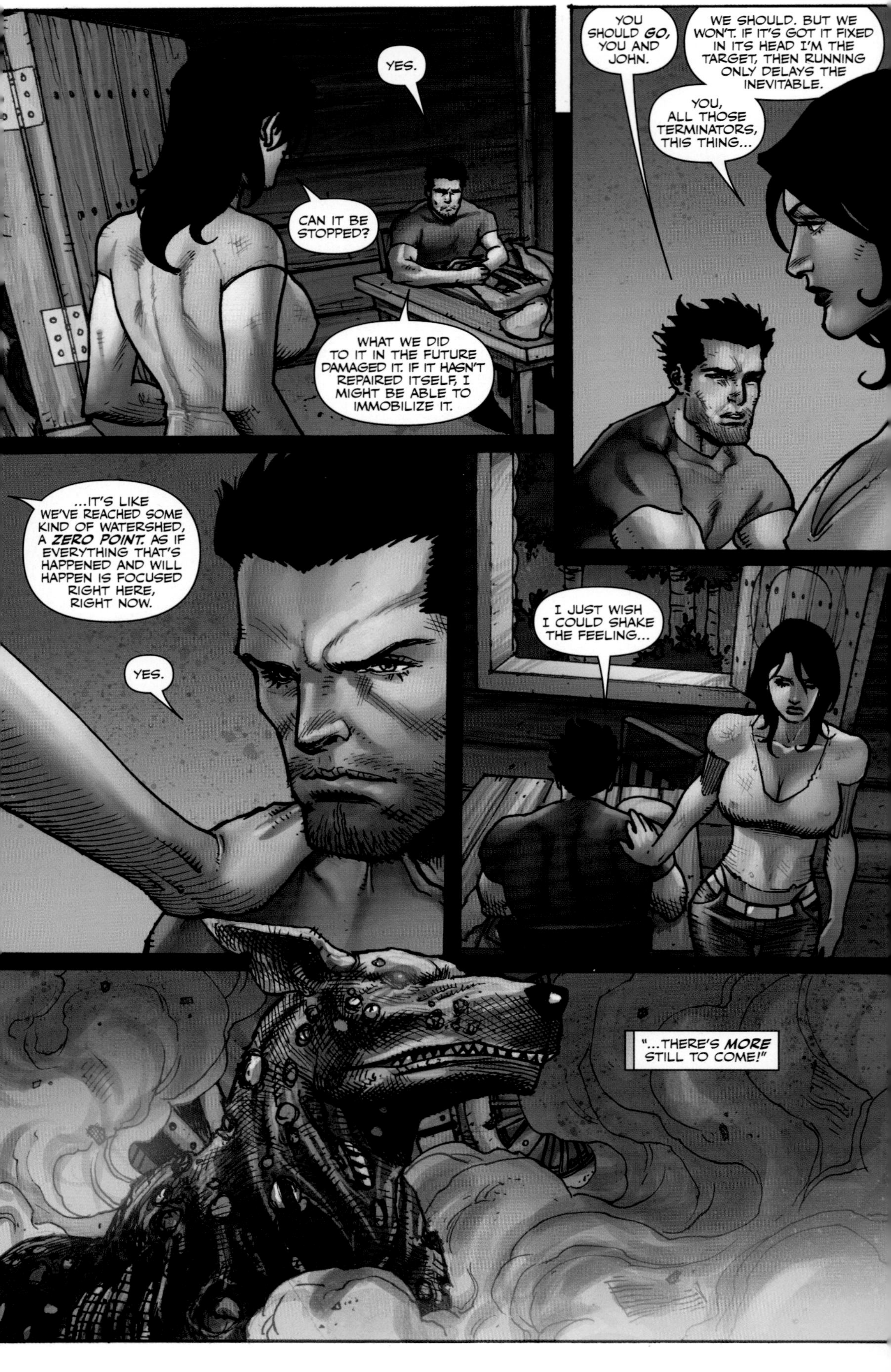
YES.
CAN IT BE STOPPED?
WHAT WE DID TO IT IN THE FUTURE DAMAGED IT. IF IT HASN'T REPAIRED ITSELF, I MIGHT BE ABLE TO IMMOBILIZE IT.
YOU SHOULD GO, YOU AND JOHN.
WE SHOULD. BUT WE WON'T. IF IT'S GOT IT FIXED IN ITS HEAD I'M THE TARGET, THEN RUNNING ONLY DELAYS THE INEVITABLE.
YOU, ALL THOSE TERMINATORS, THIS THING...
...IT'S LIKE WE'VE REACHED SOME KIND OF WATERSHED, A ZERO POINT. AS IF EVERYTHING THAT'S HAPPENED AND WILL HAPPEN IS FOCUSED RIGHT HERE, RIGHT NOW.
YES.
I JUST WISH I COULD SHAKE THE FEELING...
"...THERE'S MORE STILL TO COME!"

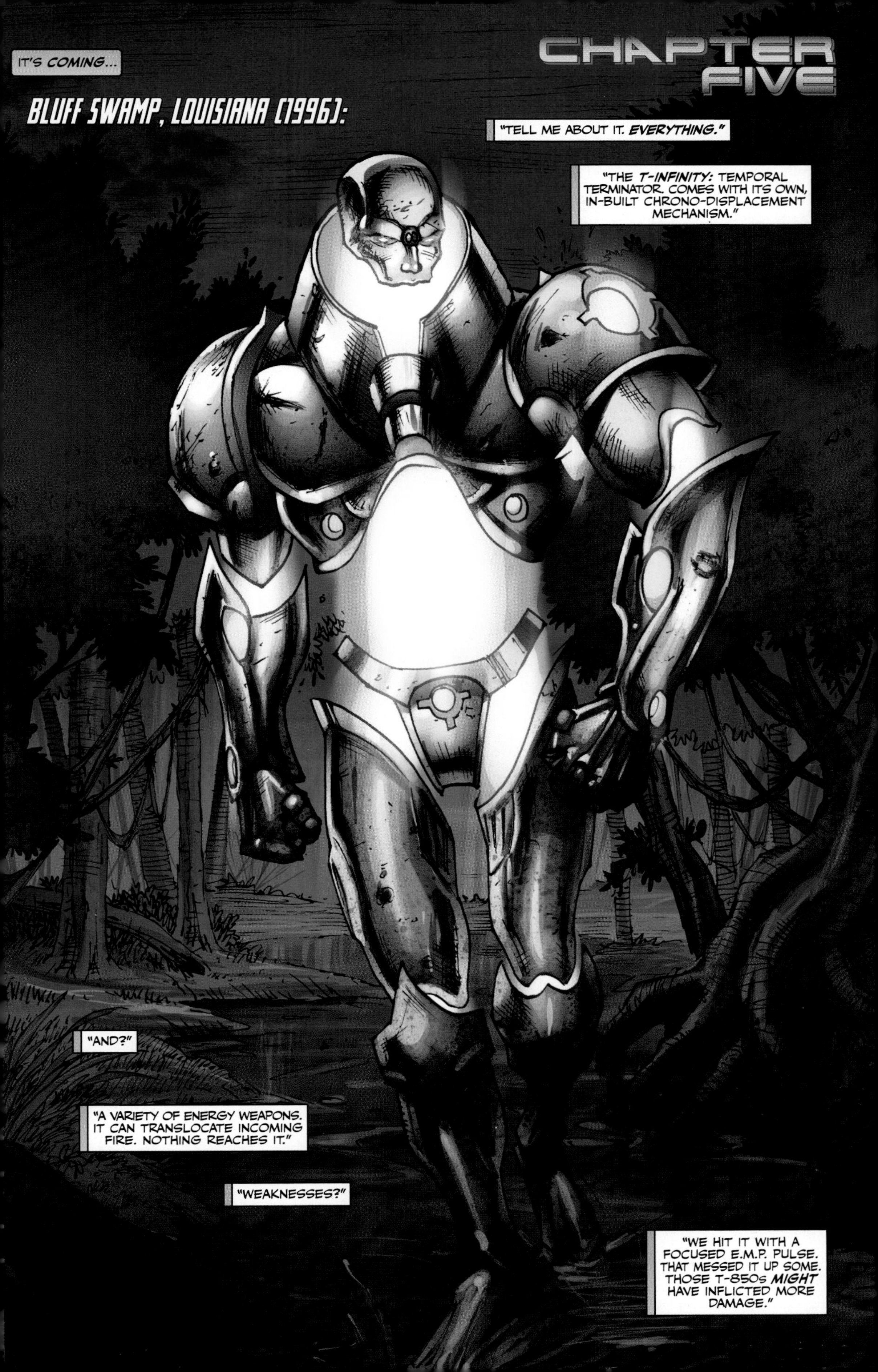
IT'S COMING...
CHAPTER FIVE
BLUFF SWAMP, LOUISIANA (1996):
"TELL ME ABOUT IT. EVERYTHING."
"THE T-INFINITY: TEMPORAL TERMINATOR. COMES WITH ITS OWN, IN-BUILT CHRONO-DISPLACEMENT MECHANISM."
"AND?"
"A VARIETY OF ENERGY WEAPONS. IT CAN TRANSLOCATE INCOMING FIRE. NOTHING REACHES IT."
"WEAKNESSES?"
"WE HIT IT WITH A FOCUSED E.M.P. PULSE. THAT MESSED IT UP SOME. THOSE T-850s MIGHT HAVE INFLICTED MORE DAMAGE."

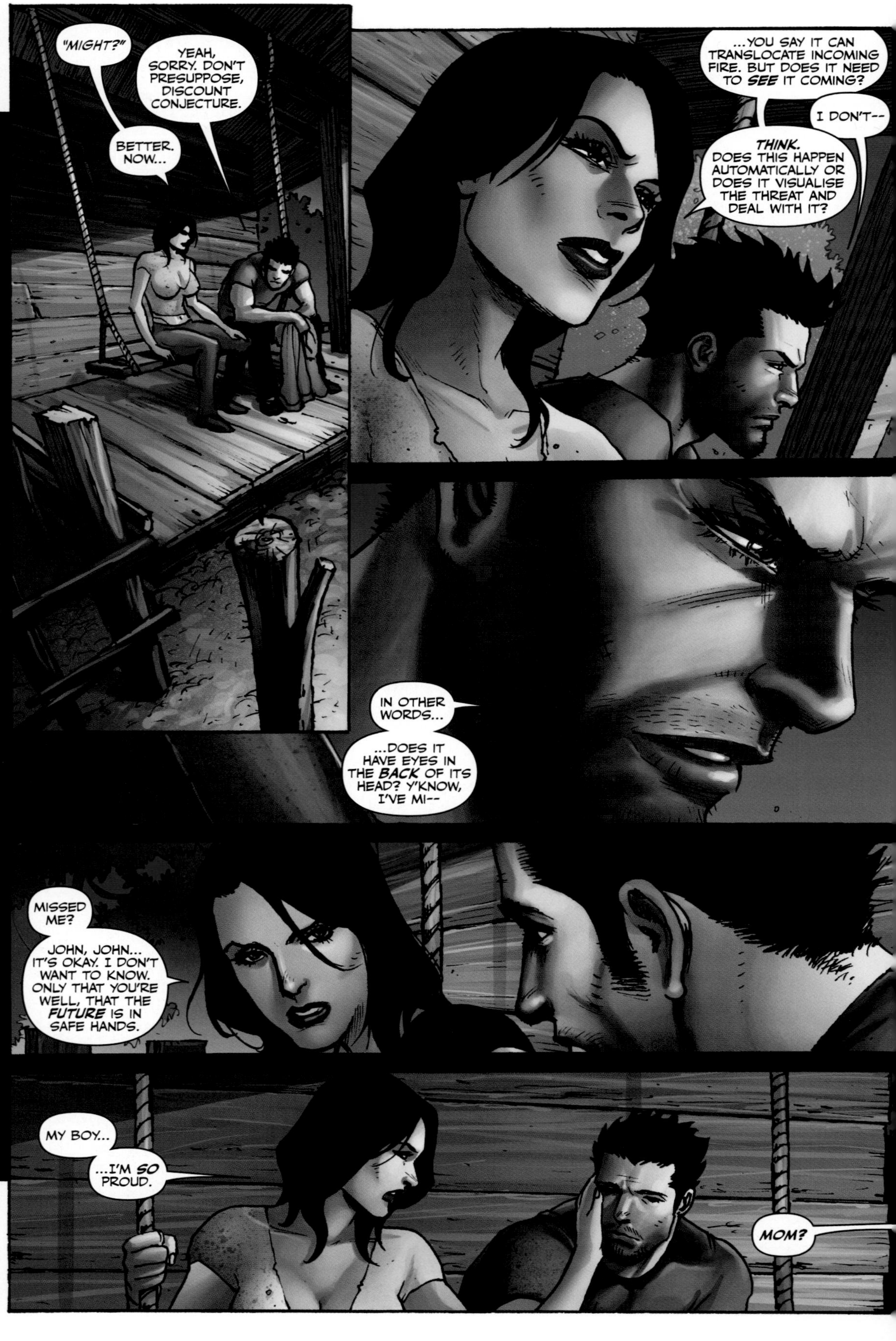
"MIGHT?"
YEAH, SORRY. DON'T PRESUPPOSE, DISCOUNT CONJECTURE.
BETTER. NOW...
...YOU SAY IT CAN TRANSLOCATE INCOMING FIRE. BUT DOES IT NEED TO SEE IT COMING?
I DON'T--
THINK. DOES THIS HAPPEN AUTOMATICALLY OR DOES IT VISUALISE THE THREAT AND DEAL WITH IT?
IN OTHER WORDS...
...DOES IT HAVE EYES IN THE BACK OF ITS HEAD? Y'KNOW, I'VE MI--
MISSED ME?
JOHN, JOHN... IT'S OKAY. I DON'T WANT TO KNOW. ONLY THAT YOU'RE WELL, THAT THE FUTURE IS IN SAFE HANDS.
MY BOY...
...I'M SO PROUD.
MOM?

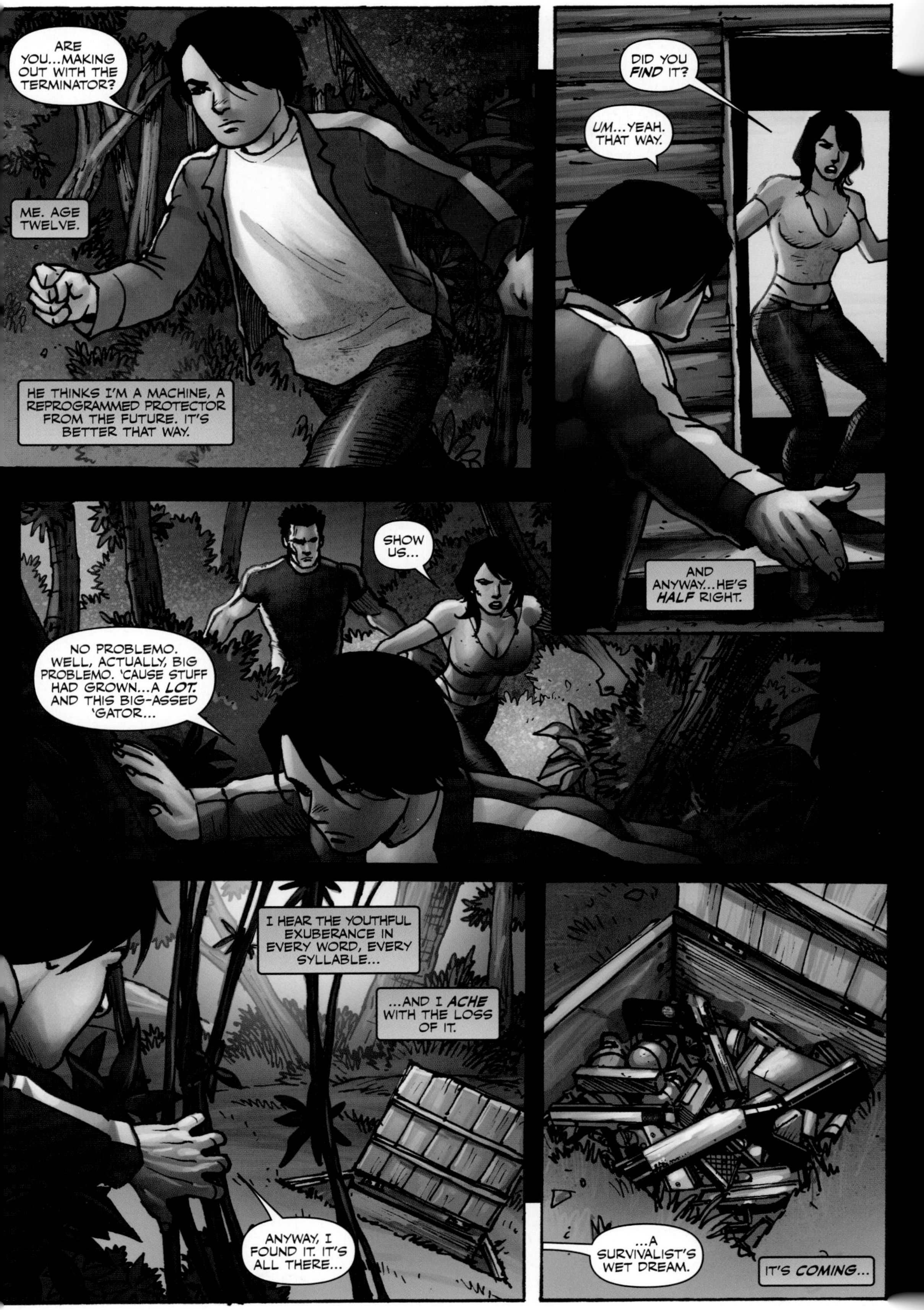
ARE YOU...MAKING OUT WITH THE TERMINATOR?
ME. AGE TWELVE.
HE THINKS I'M A MACHINE, A REPROGRAMMED PROTECTOR FROM THE FUTURE. IT'S BETTER THAT WAY.
DID YOU *FIND* IT?
UM...YEAH. THAT WAY.
AND ANYWAY...HE'S *HALF* RIGHT.
SHOW US...
NO PROBLEMO. WELL, ACTUALLY, BIG PROBLEMO. 'CAUSE STUFF HAD GROWN...A *LOT.* AND THIS BIG-ASSED 'GATOR...
I HEAR THE YOUTHFUL EXUBERANCE IN EVERY WORD, EVERY SYLLABLE...
...AND I *ACHE* WITH THE LOSS OF IT.
ANYWAY, I FOUND IT. IT'S ALL THERE...
...A SURVIVALIST'S WET DREAM.
IT'S *COMING*...

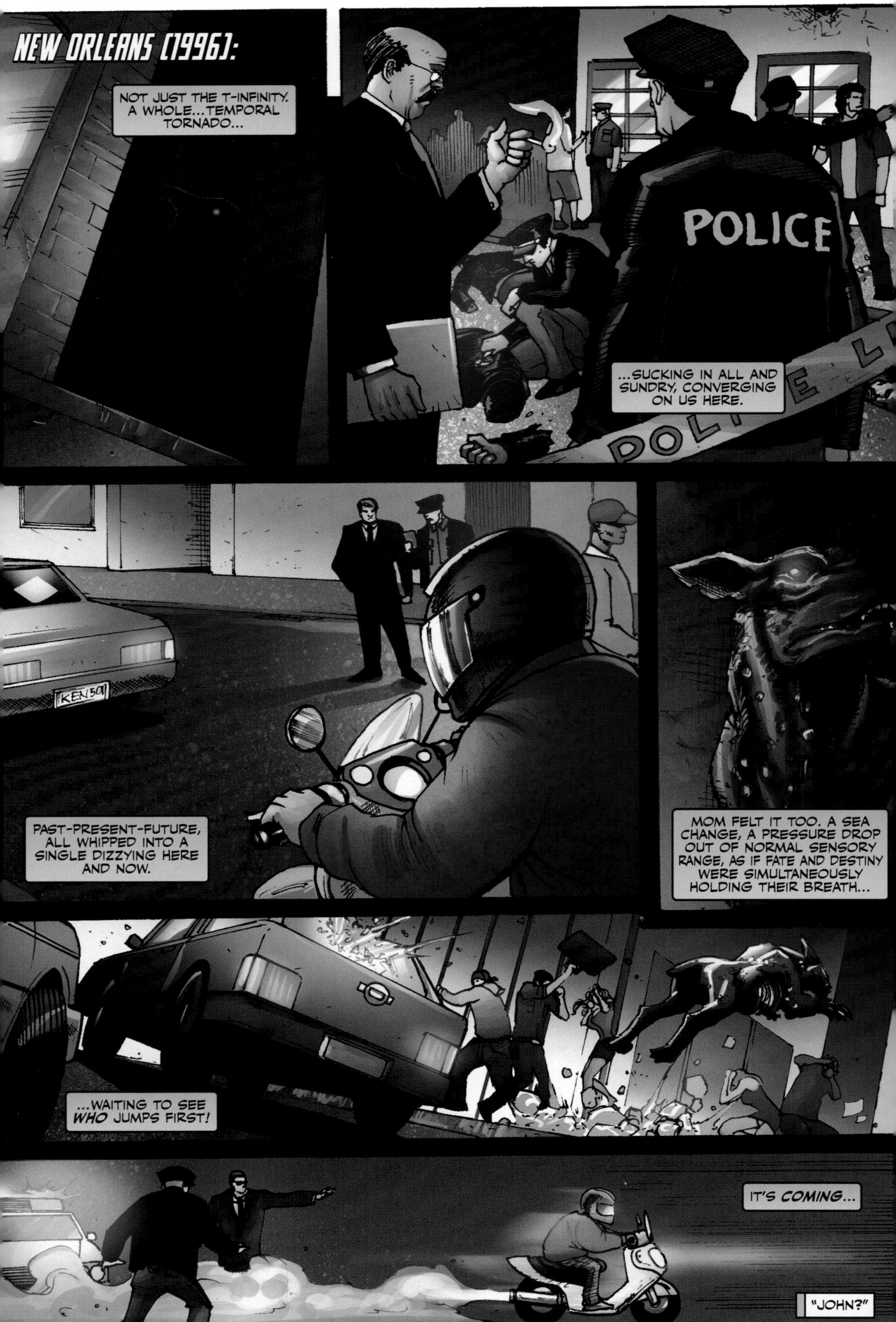
NEW ORLEANS (1996):
NOT JUST THE T-INFINITY. A WHOLE...TEMPORAL TORNADO...
POLICE
...SUCKING IN ALL AND SUNDRY, CONVERGING ON US HERE.
KEN 501
PAST-PRESENT-FUTURE, ALL WHIPPED INTO A SINGLE DIZZYING HERE AND NOW.
MOM FELT IT TOO. A SEA CHANGE, A PRESSURE DROP OUT OF NORMAL SENSORY RANGE, AS IF FATE AND DESTINY WERE SIMULTANEOUSLY HOLDING THEIR BREATH...
...WAITING TO SEE *WHO* JUMPS FIRST!
IT'S *COMING*...
"JOHN?"

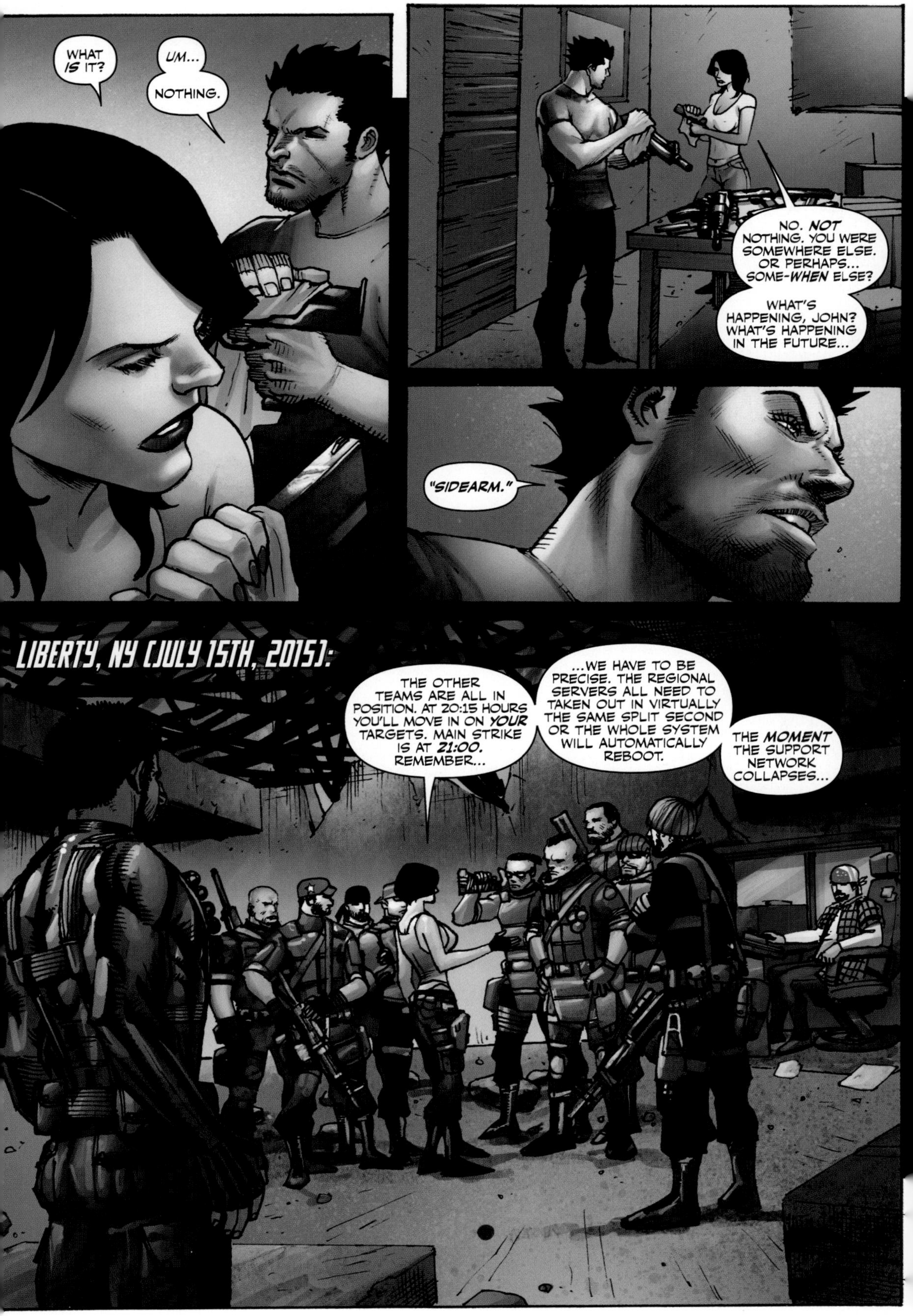
WHAT IS IT?
UM...
NOTHING.
NO. NOT NOTHING. YOU WERE SOMEWHERE ELSE. OR PERHAPS... SOME-WHEN ELSE?
WHAT'S HAPPENING, JOHN? WHAT'S HAPPENING IN THE FUTURE...
"SIDEARM."
LIBERTY, NY (JULY 15TH, 2015):
THE OTHER TEAMS ARE ALL IN POSITION. AT 20:15 HOURS YOU'LL MOVE IN ON YOUR TARGETS. MAIN STRIKE IS AT 21:00. REMEMBER...
...WE HAVE TO BE PRECISE. THE REGIONAL SERVERS ALL NEED TO TAKEN OUT IN VIRTUALLY THE SAME SPLIT SECOND OR THE WHOLE SYSTEM WILL AUTOMATICALLY REBOOT.
THE MOMENT THE SUPPORT NETWORK COLLAPSES...

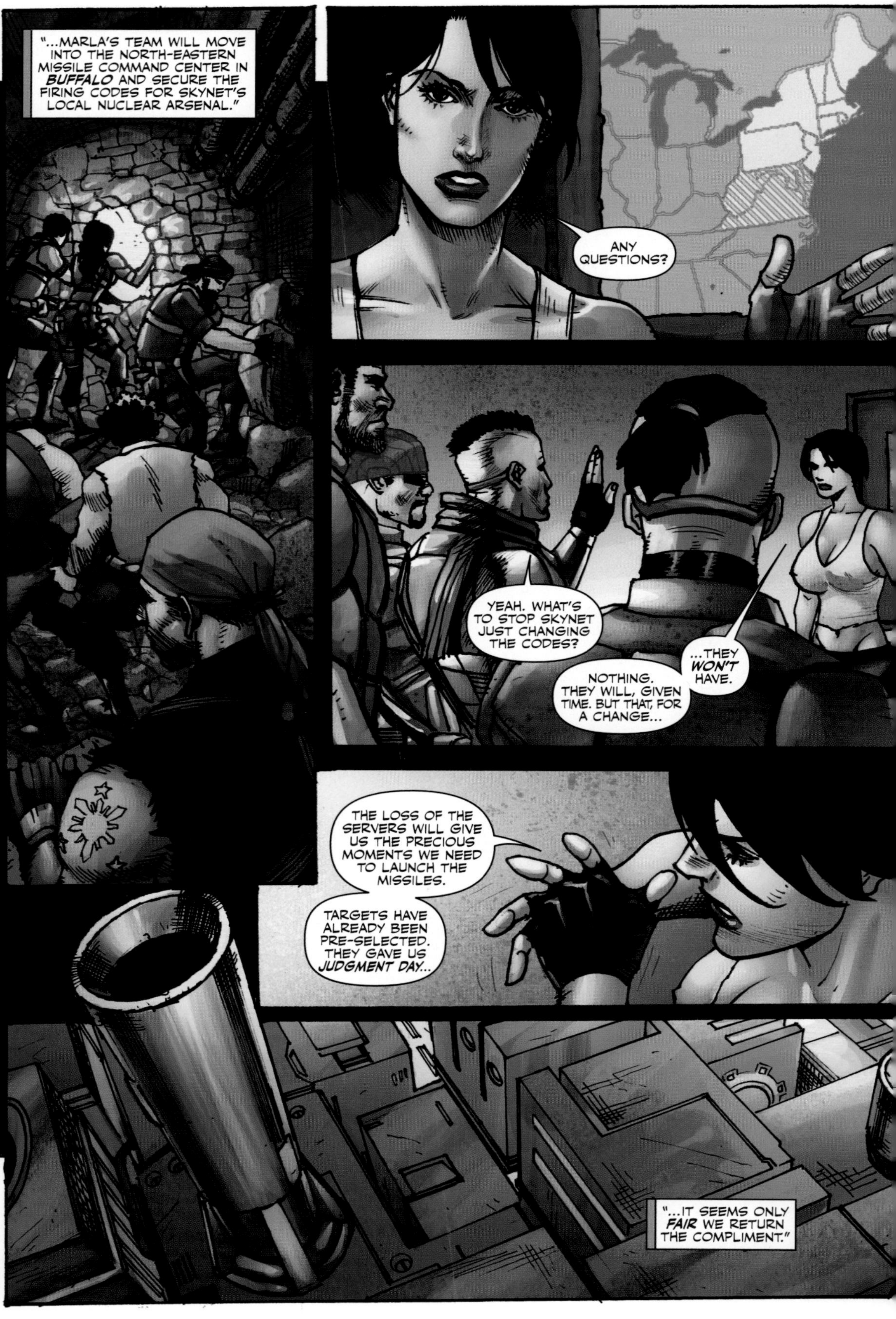
"...MARLA'S TEAM WILL MOVE INTO THE NORTH-EASTERN MISSILE COMMAND CENTER IN **BUFFALO** AND SECURE THE FIRING CODES FOR SKYNET'S LOCAL NUCLEAR ARSENAL."
ANY QUESTIONS?
YEAH. WHAT'S TO STOP SKYNET JUST CHANGING THE CODES?
NOTHING. THEY WILL, GIVEN TIME. BUT THAT, FOR A CHANGE...
...THEY **WON'T** HAVE.
THE LOSS OF THE SERVERS WILL GIVE US THE PRECIOUS MOMENTS WE NEED TO LAUNCH THE MISSILES.
TARGETS HAVE ALREADY BEEN PRE-SELECTED. THEY GAVE US **JUDGMENT DAY**...
"...IT SEEMS ONLY **FAIR** WE RETURN THE COMPLIMENT."

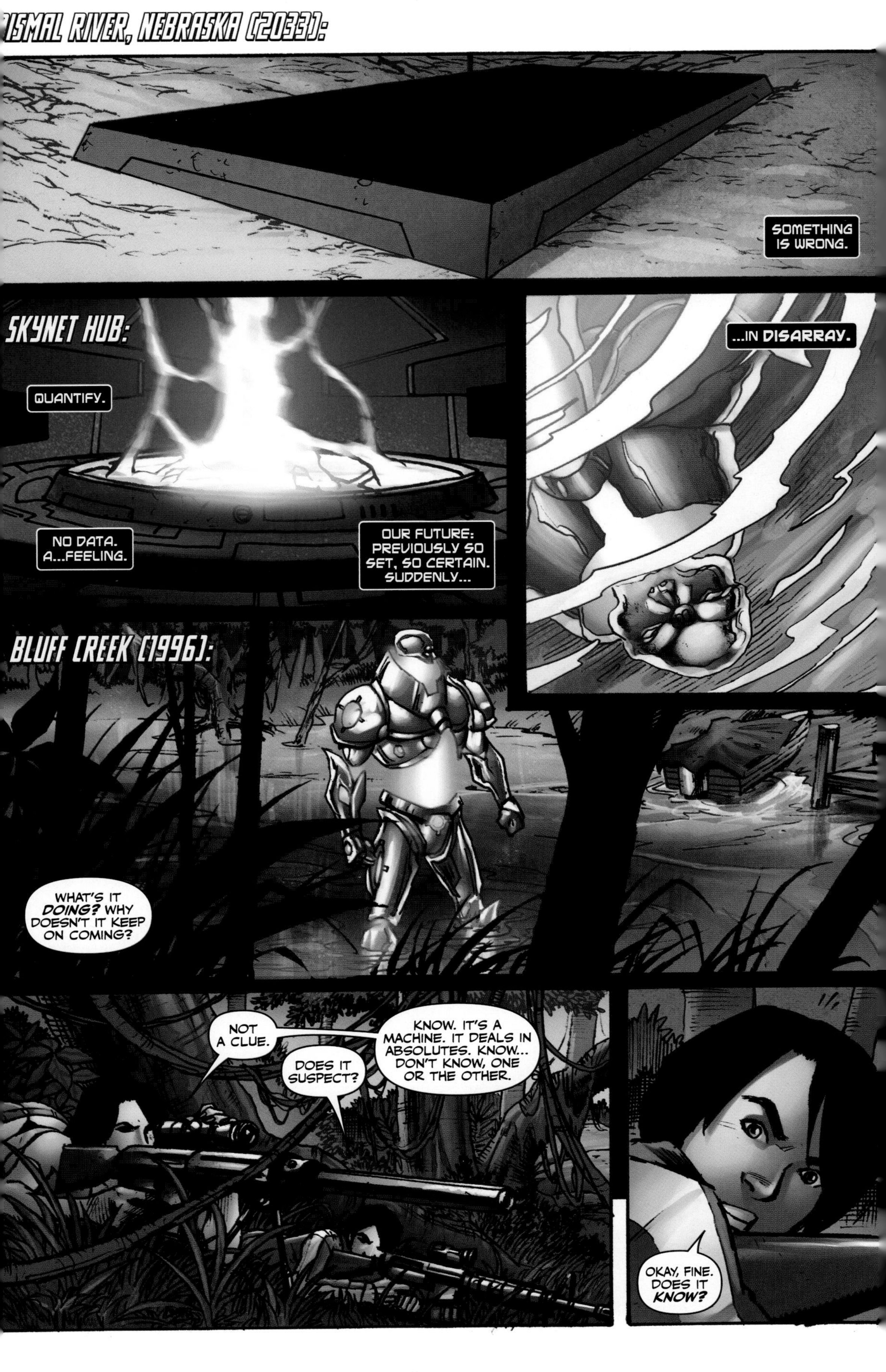
ISMAL RIVER, NEBRASKA (2033):
SOMETHING IS WRONG.
SKYNET HUB:
QUANTIFY.
NO DATA. A...FEELING.
OUR FUTURE: PREVIOUSLY SO SET, SO CERTAIN. SUDDENLY...
...IN DISARRAY.
BLUFF CREEK (1996):
WHAT'S IT DOING? WHY DOESN'T IT KEEP ON COMING?
NOT A CLUE.
DOES IT SUSPECT?
KNOW. IT'S A MACHINE. IT DEALS IN ABSOLUTES. KNOW... DON'T KNOW, ONE OR THE OTHER.
OKAY, FINE. DOES IT KNOW?

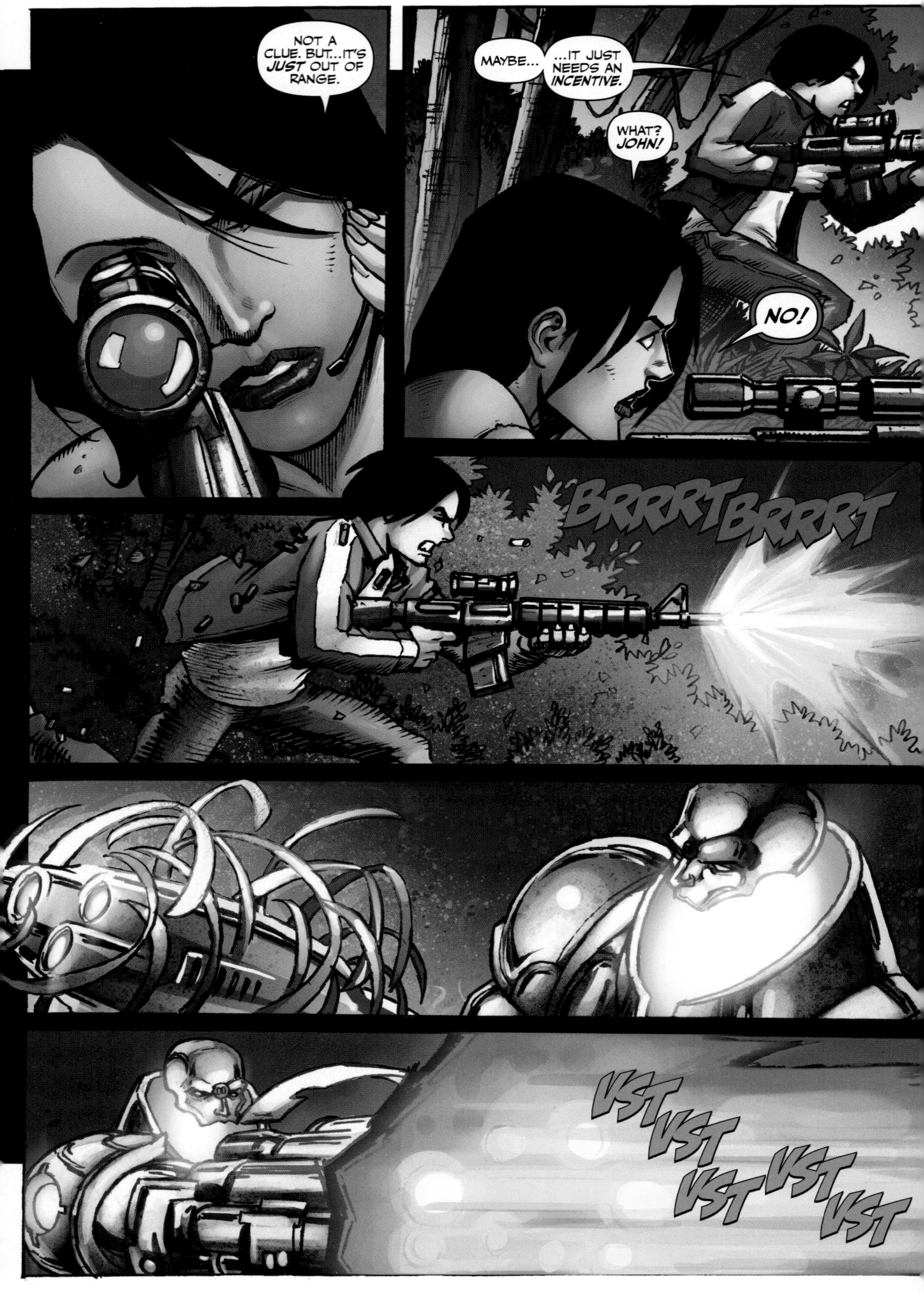

NOT A CLUE. BUT...IT'S JUST OUT OF RANGE.
MAYBE...
...IT JUST NEEDS AN INCENTIVE.
WHAT? JOHN!
NO!
BRRRT BRRRT
VST VST VST VST VST

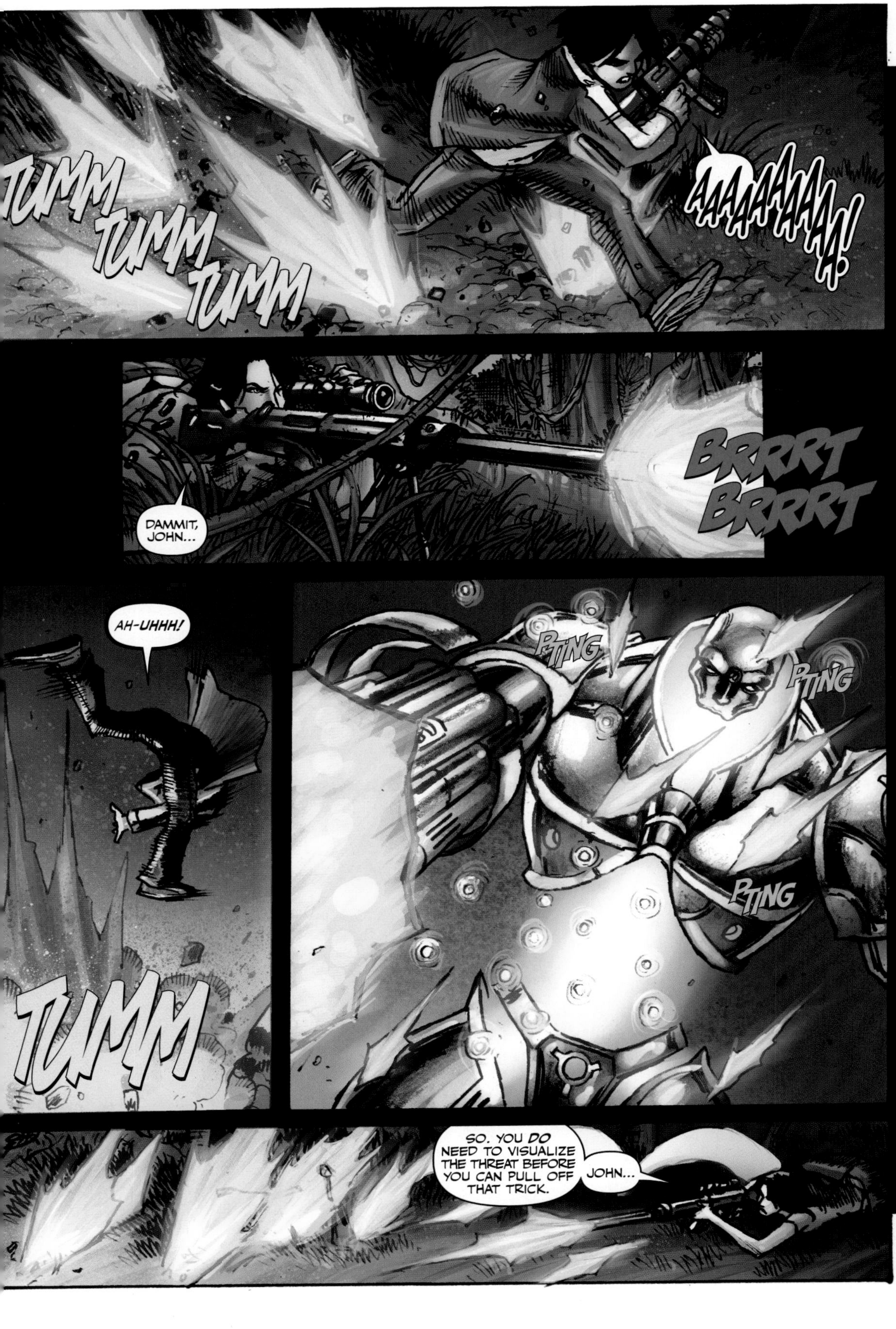
TUMM
TUMM
TUMM
AAAAAAAAAAA!
DAMMIT, JOHN...
BRRRT
BRRRT
AH-UHHH!
PTING
PTING
PTING
TUMM
SO. YOU DO NEED TO VISUALIZE THE THREAT BEFORE YOU CAN PULL OFF THAT TRICK.
JOHN...

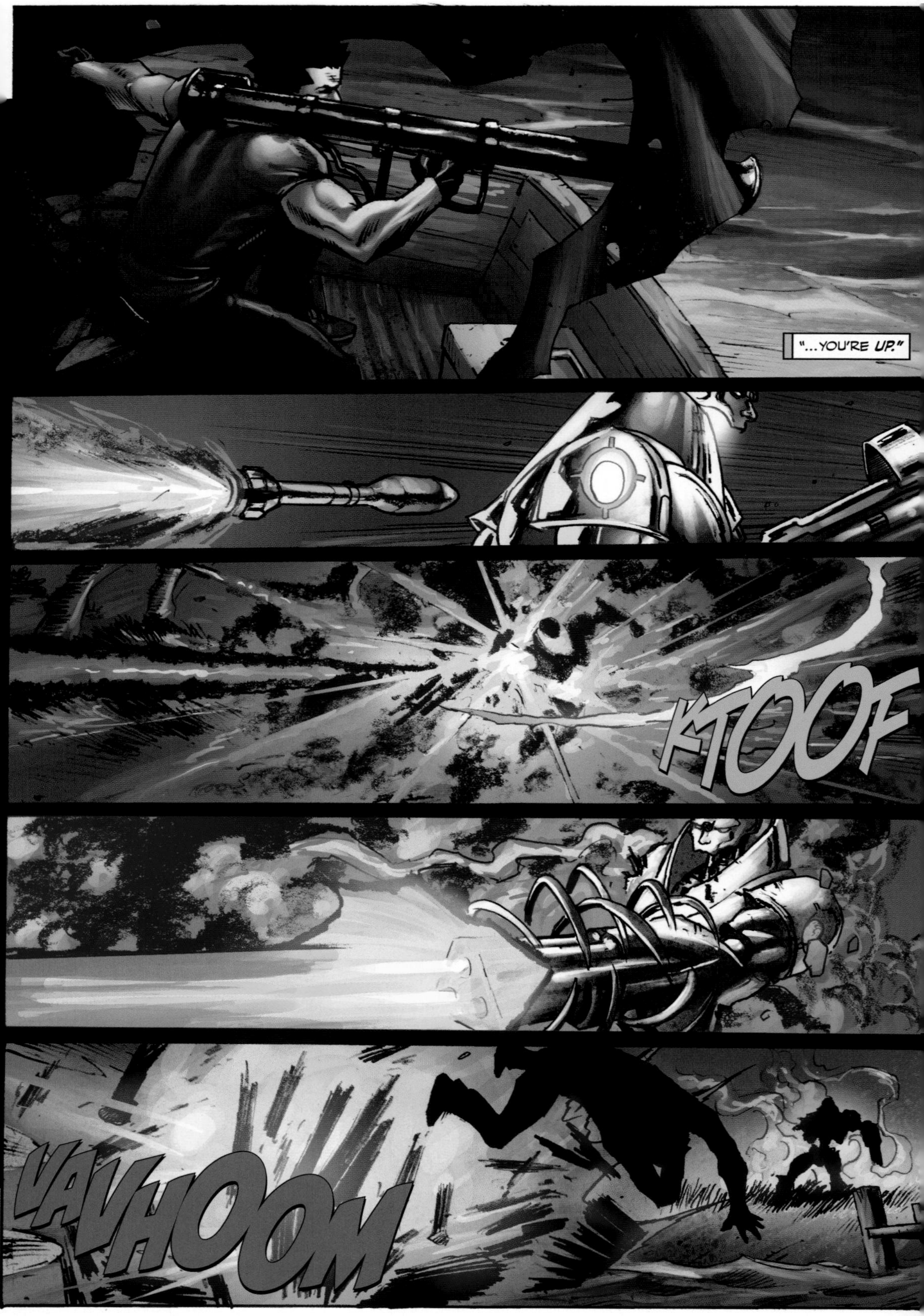
"...YOU'RE UP."
KTOOF
VAVHOOM

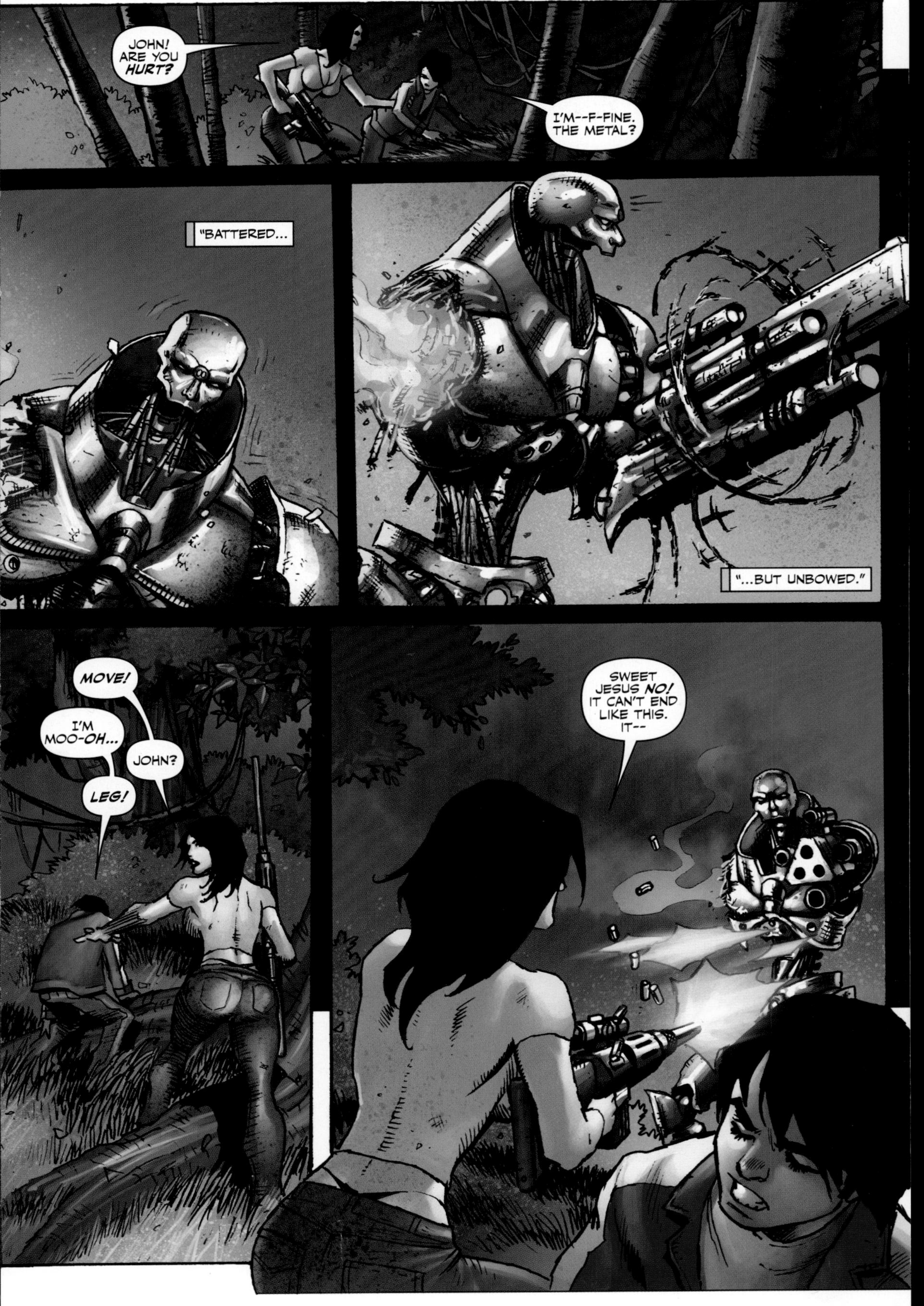
JOHN! ARE YOU *HURT?*
I'M--F-FINE. THE METAL?
"BATTERED...
"...BUT UNBOWED."
MOVE!
I'M MOO-*OH...*
JOHN?
LEG!
SWEET JESUS *NO!* IT CAN'T END LIKE THIS. IT--

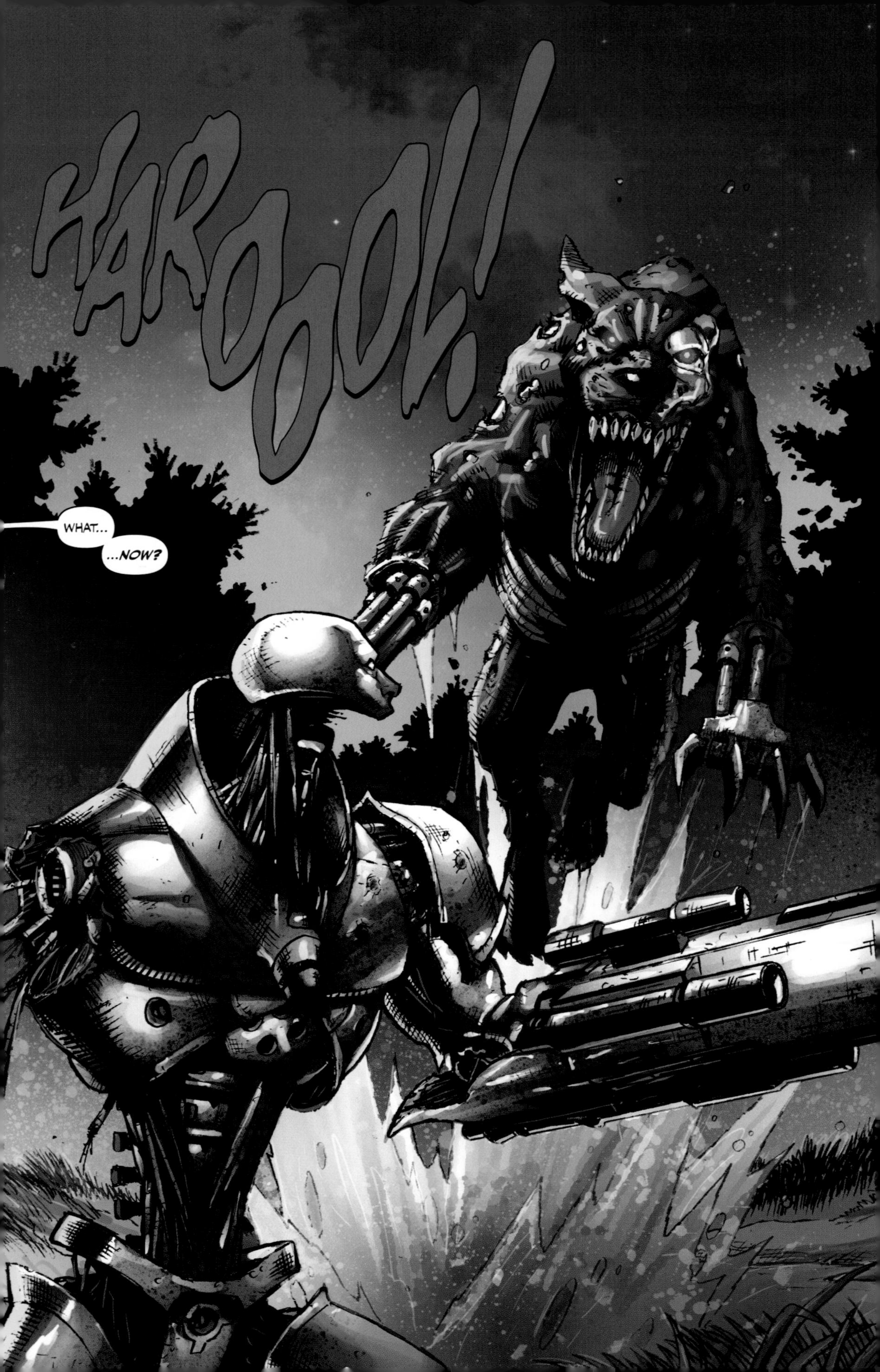
HAROOOL!!
WHAT...
...NOW?

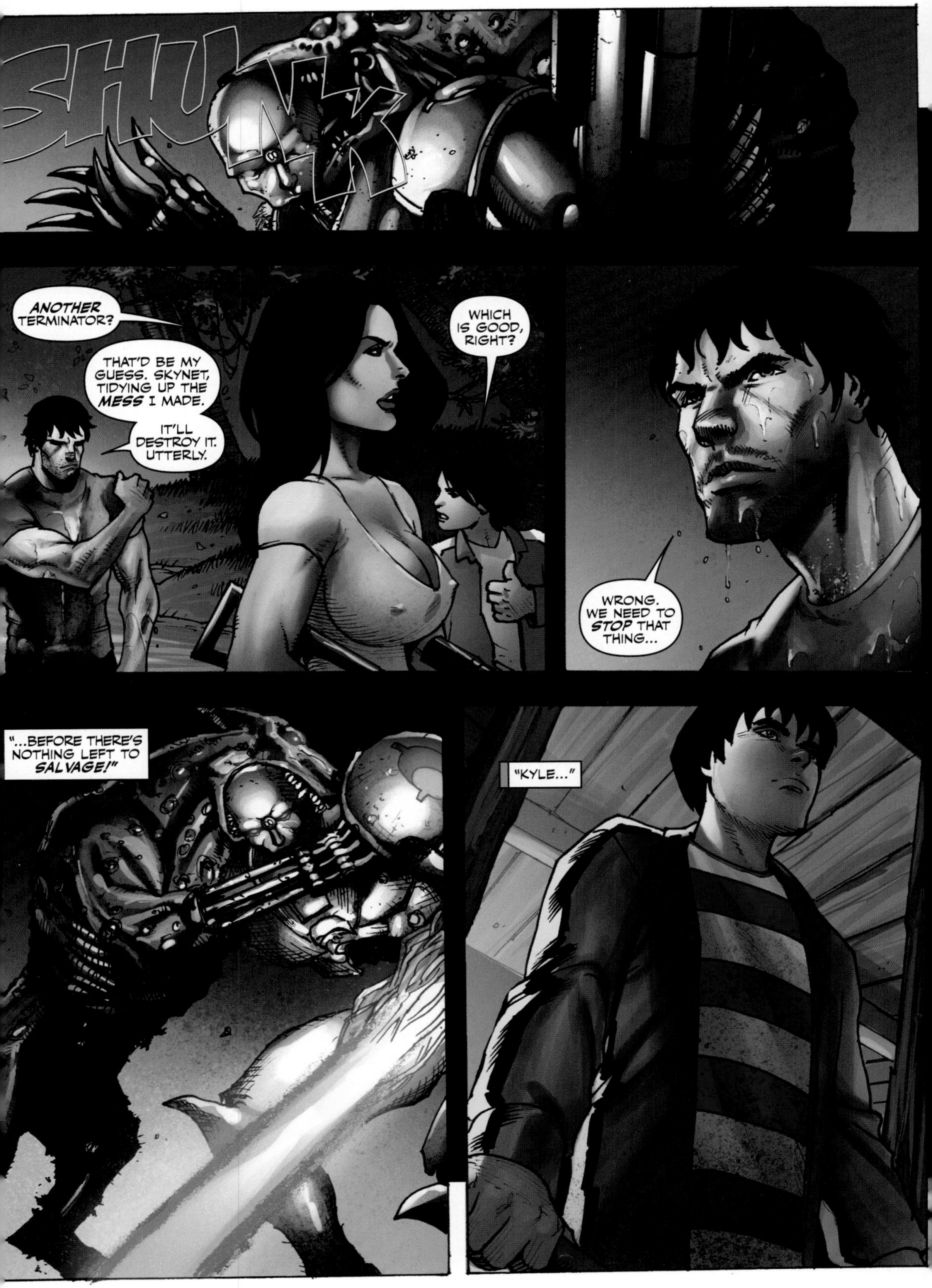
SHUNK
ANOTHER TERMINATOR?
THAT'D BE MY GUESS. SKYNET, TIDYING UP THE MESS I MADE.
IT'LL DESTROY IT. UTTERLY.
WHICH IS GOOD, RIGHT?
WRONG. WE NEED TO STOP THAT THING...
"...BEFORE THERE'S NOTHING LEFT TO SALVAGE!"
"KYLE..."

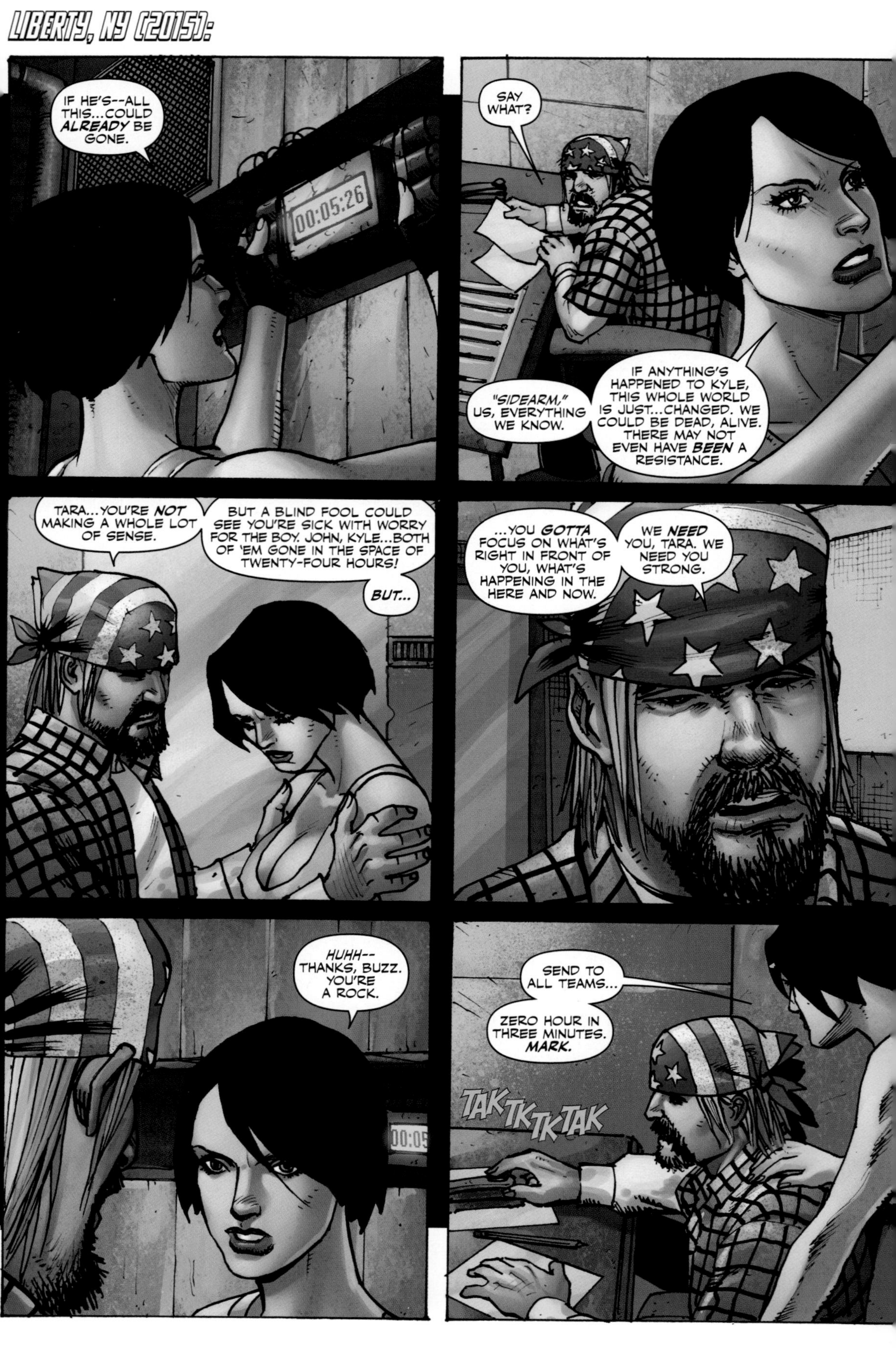
LIBERTY, NY (2015):
IF HE'S--ALL THIS...COULD ALREADY BE GONE.
00:05:26
SAY WHAT?
IF ANYTHING'S HAPPENED TO KYLE, THIS WHOLE WORLD IS JUST...CHANGED. WE COULD BE DEAD, ALIVE. THERE MAY NOT EVEN HAVE BEEN A RESISTANCE.
"SIDEARM," US, EVERYTHING WE KNOW.
TARA...YOU'RE NOT MAKING A WHOLE LOT OF SENSE.
BUT A BLIND FOOL COULD SEE YOU'RE SICK WITH WORRY FOR THE BOY. JOHN, KYLE...BOTH OF 'EM GONE IN THE SPACE OF TWENTY-FOUR HOURS!
BUT...
...YOU GOTTA FOCUS ON WHAT'S RIGHT IN FRONT OF YOU, WHAT'S HAPPENING IN THE HERE AND NOW.
WE NEED YOU, TARA. WE NEED YOU STRONG.
HUHH-- THANKS, BUZZ. YOU'RE A ROCK.
SEND TO ALL TEAMS...
ZERO HOUR IN THREE MINUTES. MARK.
TAKTKTKTAK

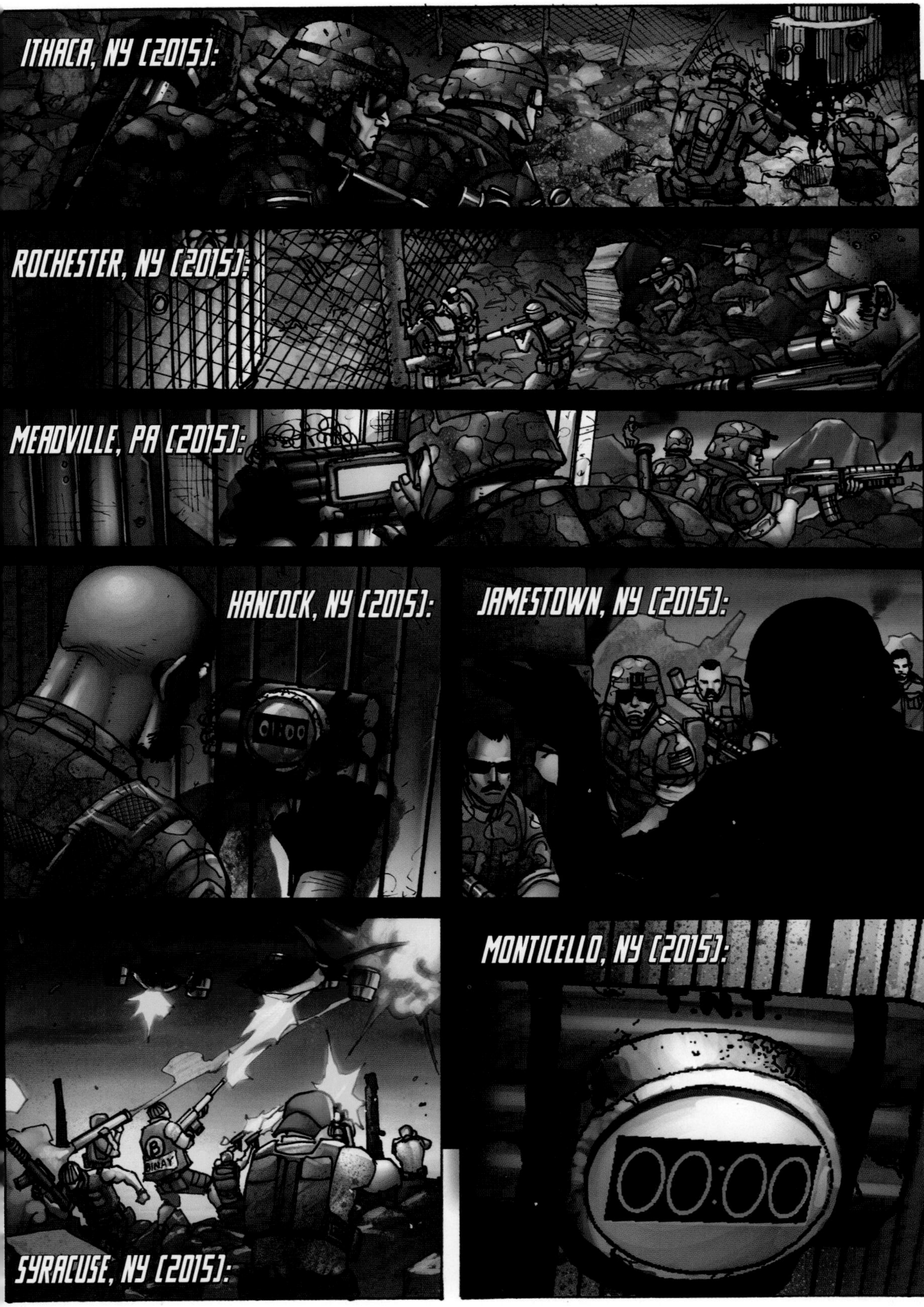
ITHACA, NY (2015):
ROCHESTER, NY (2015):
MEADVILLE, PA (2015):
HANCOCK, NY (2015):
01:00
JAMESTOWN, NY (2015):
SYRACUSE, NY (2015):
MONTICELLO, NY (2015):
00:00

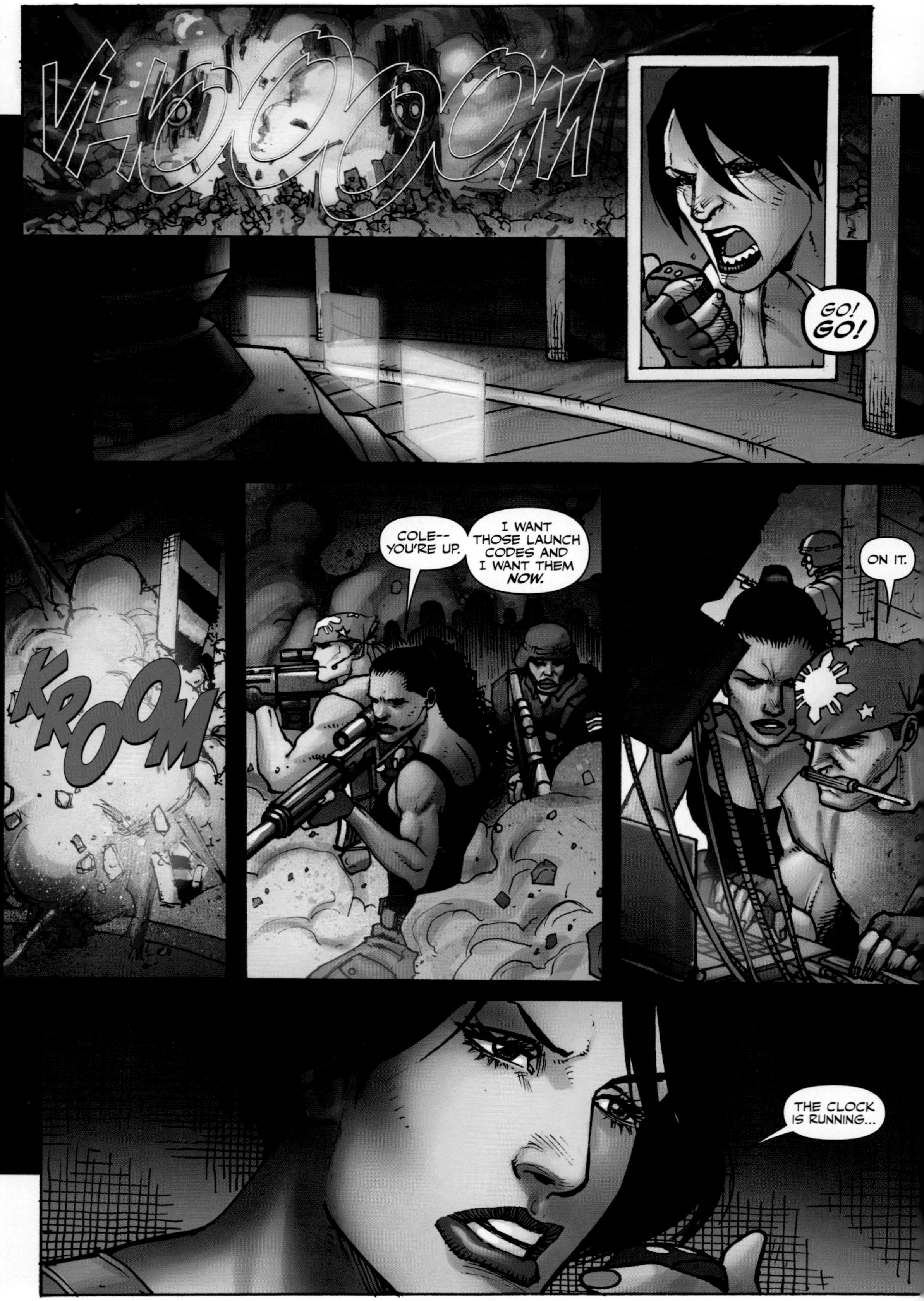
VHOOOOOM
GO! GO!
KROOM
COLE-- YOU'RE UP.
I WANT THOSE LAUNCH CODES AND I WANT THEM NOW.
ON IT.
THE CLOCK IS RUNNING...

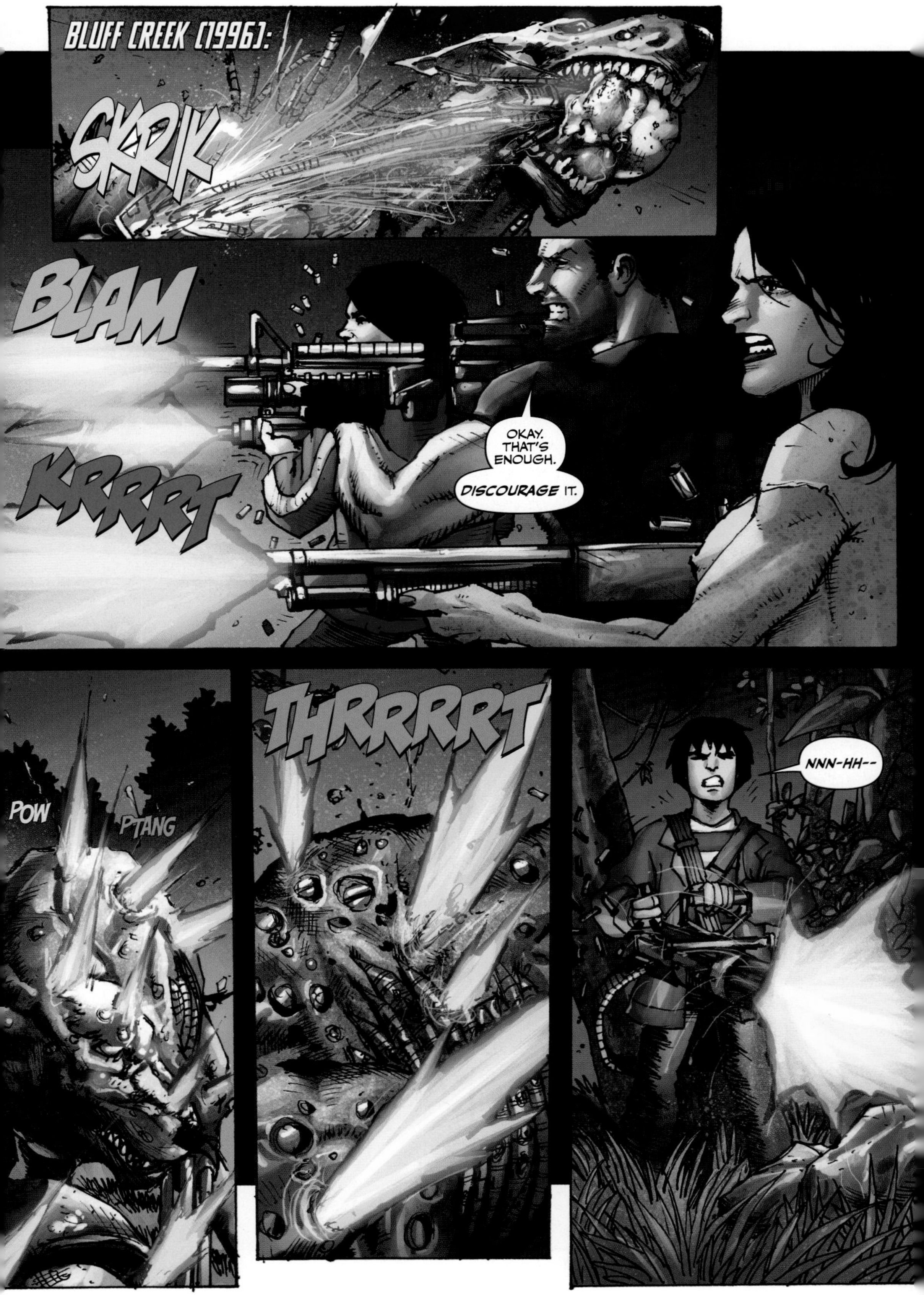
BLUFF CREEK (1996):
SKRIK
BLAM
KRRRT
OKAY. THAT'S ENOUGH.
DISCOURAGE IT.
POW
PTANG
THRRRRT
NNN-HH--

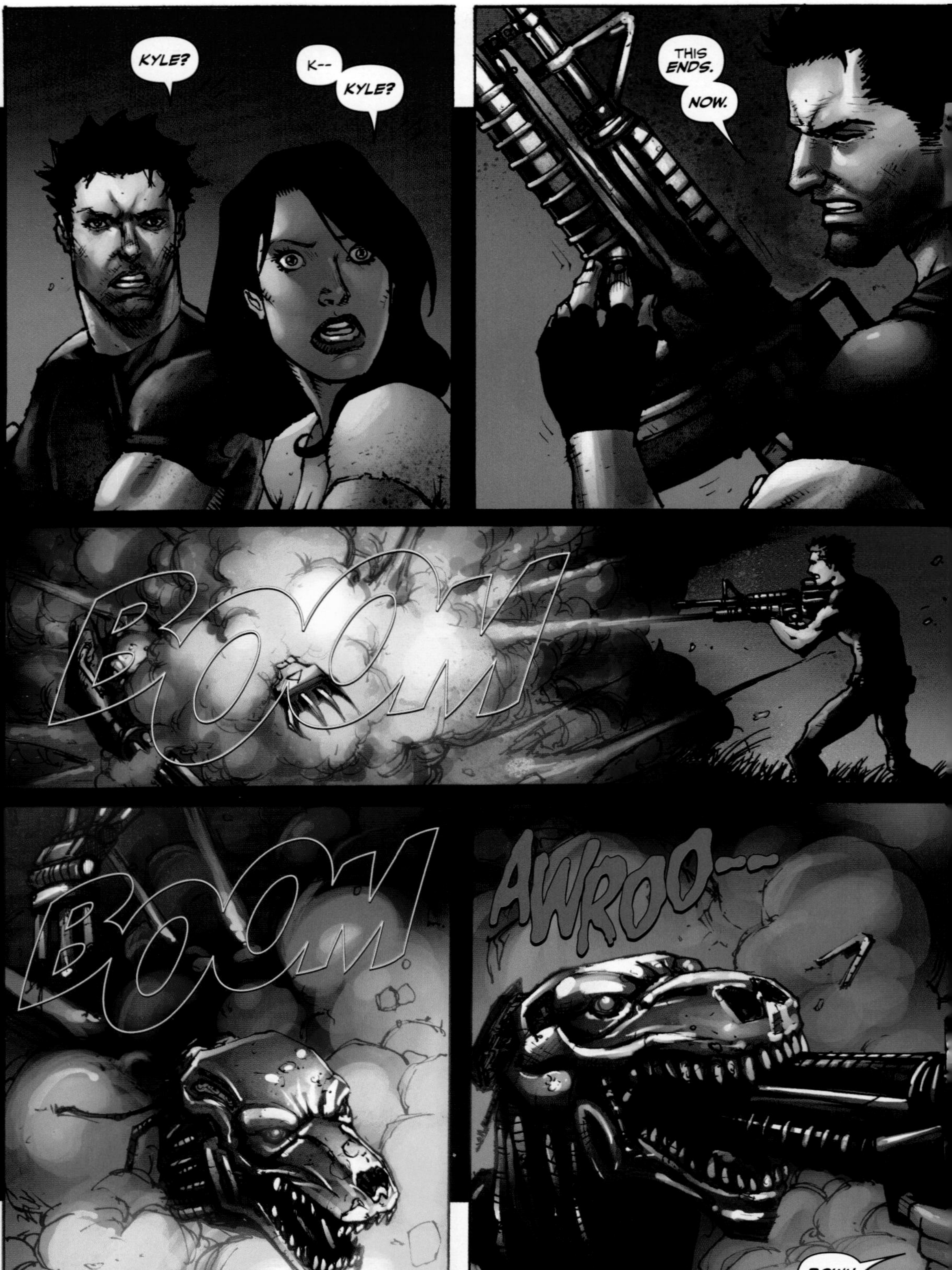
KYLE?
K--
KYLE?
THIS ENDS.
NOW.
BOOM
BOOM
AWROO--
DOWN BOY...

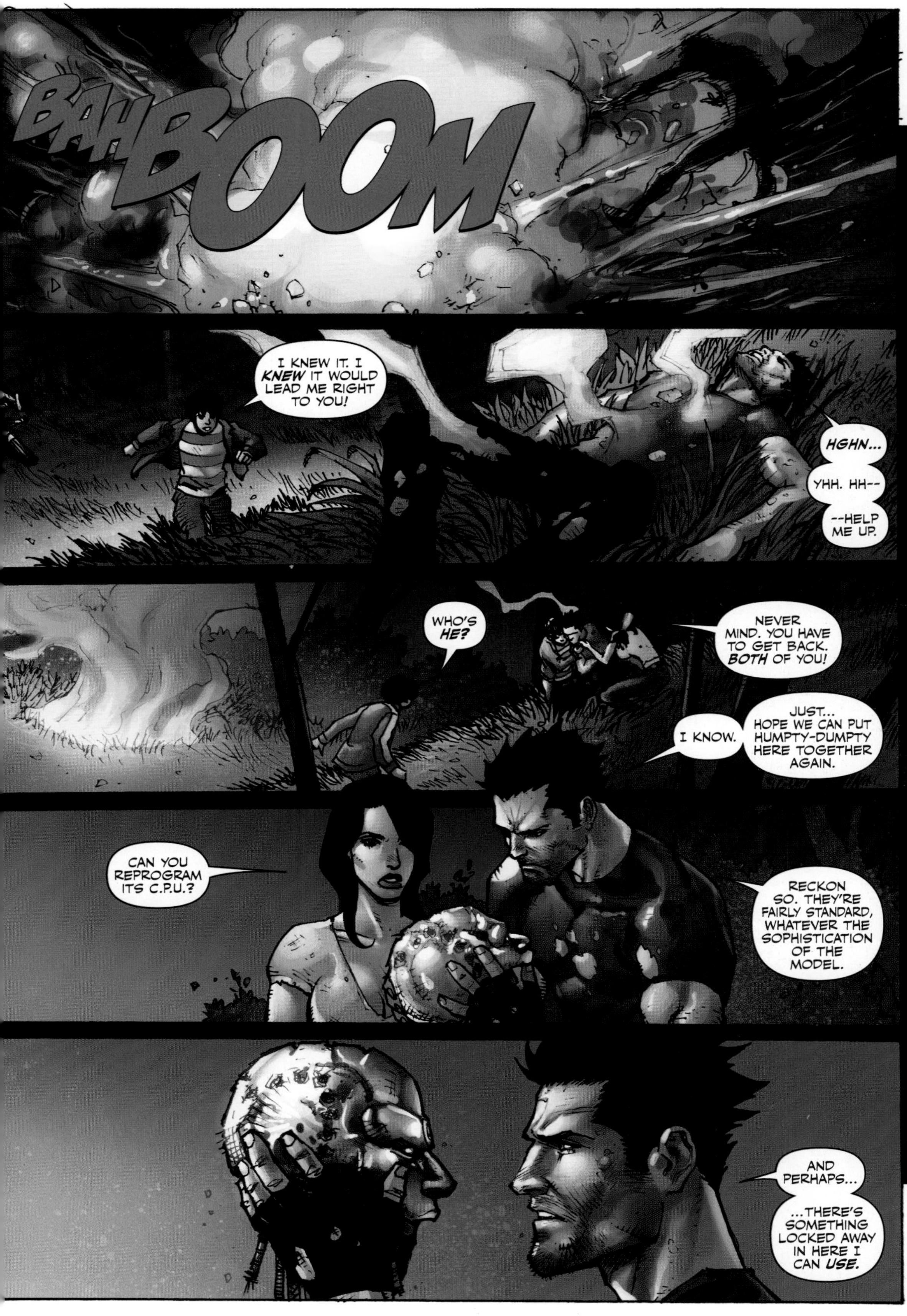
BAHBOOM
I KNEW IT. I KNEW IT WOULD LEAD ME RIGHT TO YOU!
HGHN...
YHH. HH--
--HELP ME UP.
WHO'S HE?
NEVER MIND. YOU HAVE TO GET BACK. BOTH OF YOU!
I KNOW.
JUST... HOPE WE CAN PUT HUMPTY-DUMPTY HERE TOGETHER AGAIN.
CAN YOU REPROGRAM ITS C.P.U.?
RECKON SO. THEY'RE FAIRLY STANDARD, WHATEVER THE SOPHISTICATION OF THE MODEL.
AND PERHAPS...
...THERE'S SOMETHING LOCKED AWAY IN HERE I CAN USE.

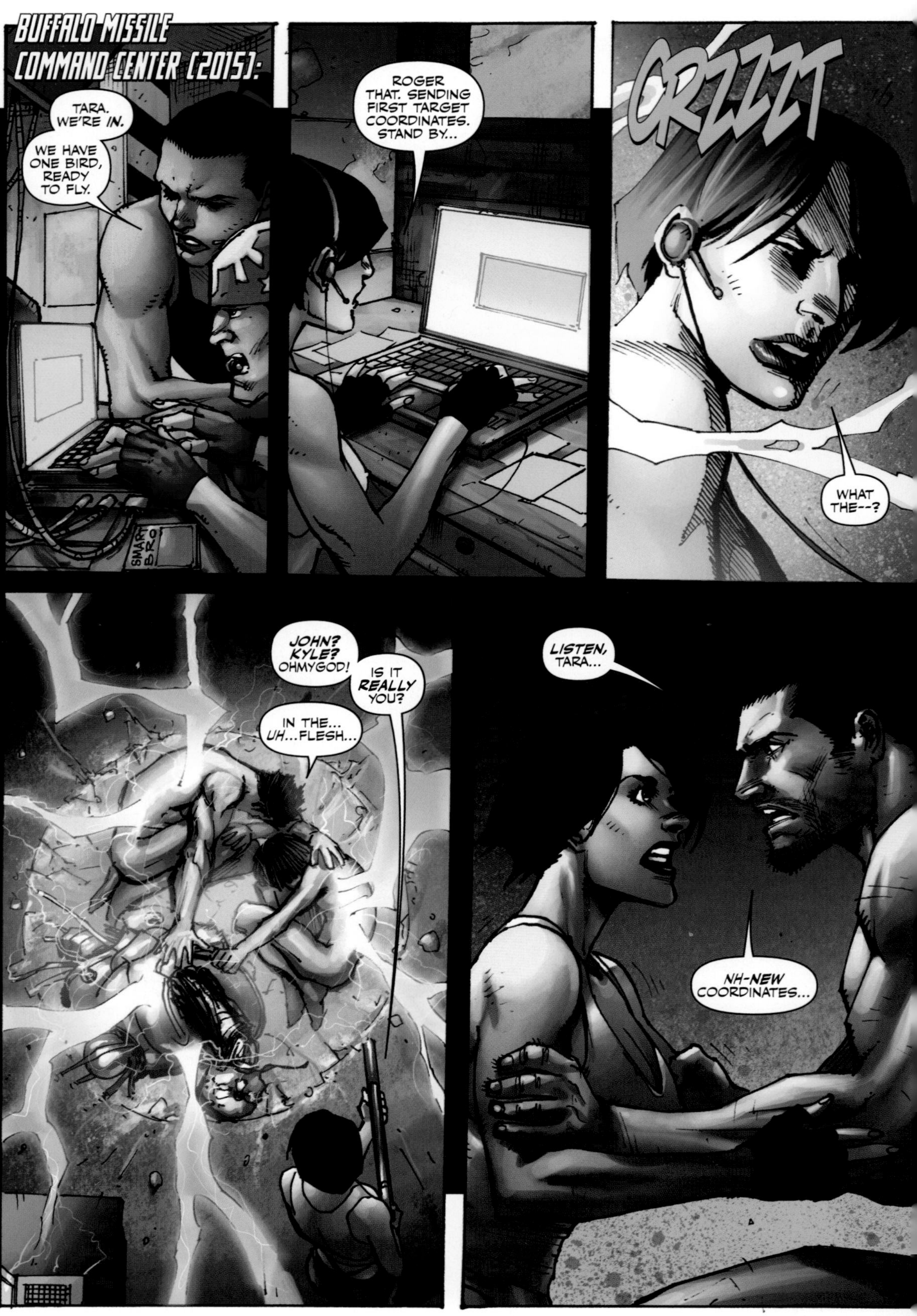
BUFFALO MISSILE COMMAND CENTER (2015):
TARA. WE'RE IN.
WE HAVE ONE BIRD, READY TO FLY.
SMART BRO
ROGER THAT. SENDING FIRST TARGET COORDINATES. STAND BY...
CRZZZT
WHAT THE--?
JOHN? KYLE? OHMYGOD!
IS IT REALLY YOU?
IN THE... UH...FLESH...
LISTEN, TARA...
NH-NEW COORDINATES...

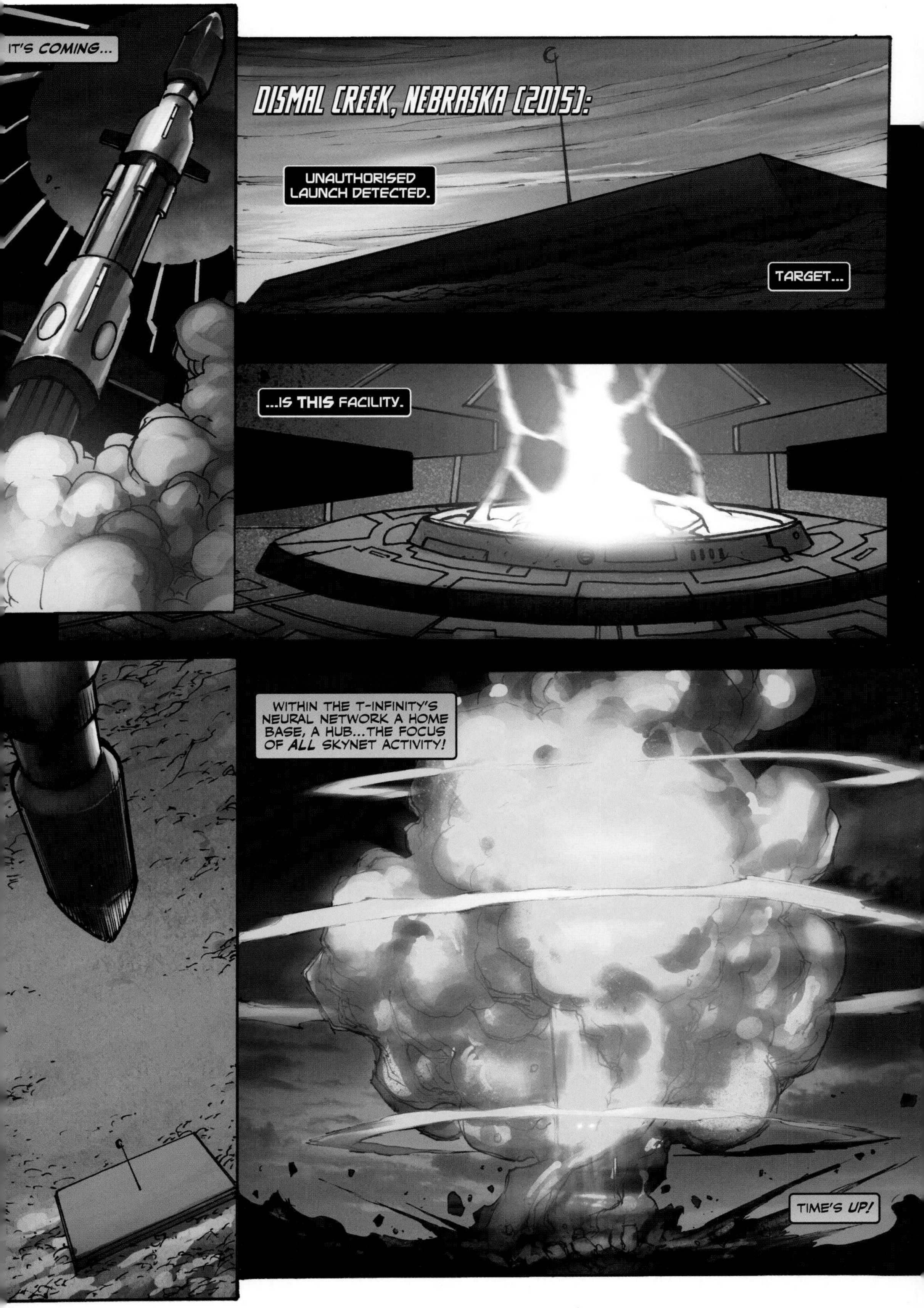
IT'S COMING...
DISMAL CREEK, NEBRASKA (2015):
UNAUTHORISED LAUNCH DETECTED.
TARGET...
...IS THIS FACILITY.
WITHIN THE T-INFINITY'S NEURAL NETWORK A HOME BASE, A HUB...THE FOCUS OF ALL SKYNET ACTIVITY!
TIME'S UP!

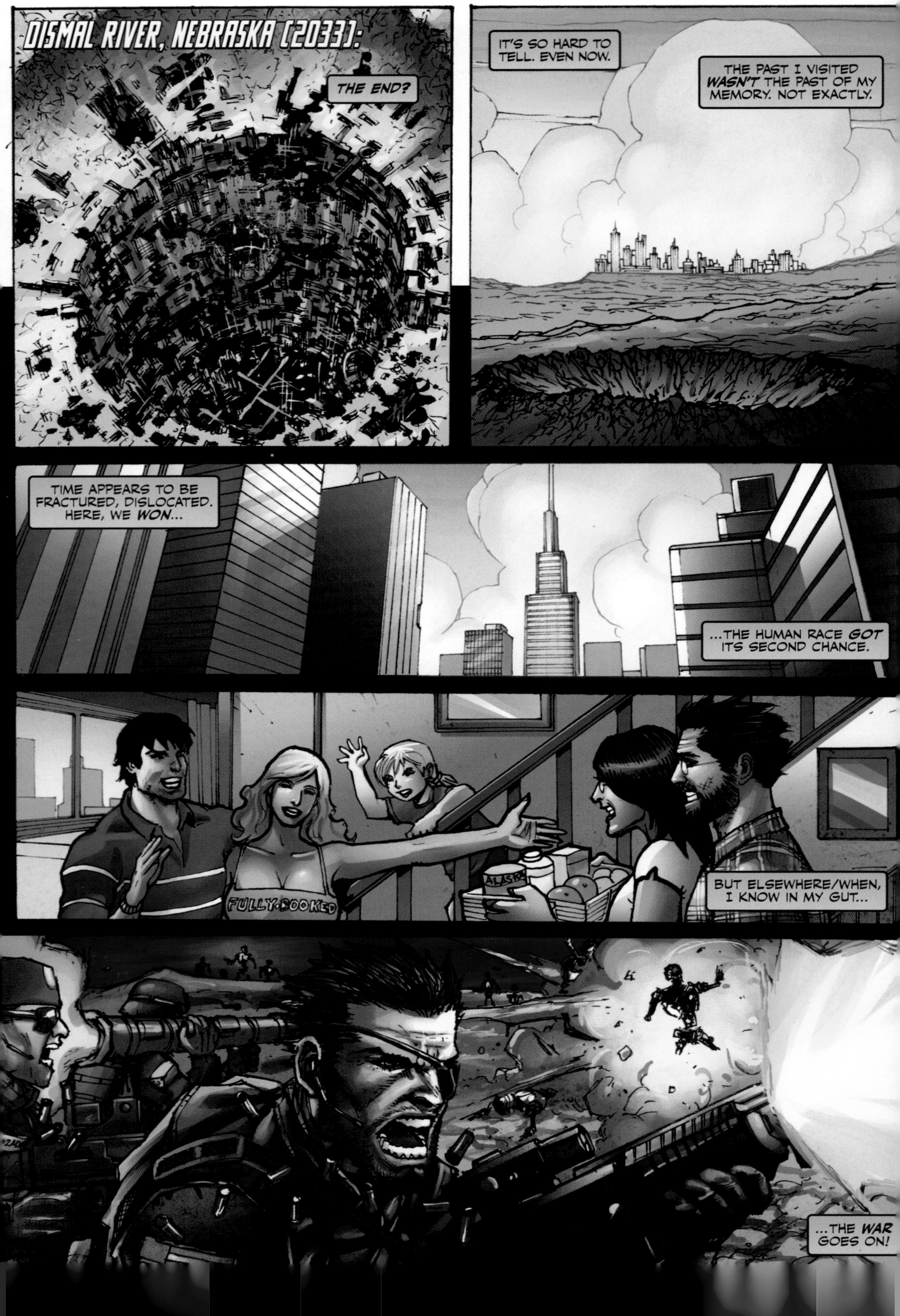
DISMAL RIVER, NEBRASKA (2033):
THE END?
IT'S SO HARD TO TELL. EVEN NOW.
THE PAST I VISITED WASN'T THE PAST OF MY MEMORY. NOT EXACTLY.
TIME APPEARS TO BE FRACTURED, DISLOCATED. HERE, WE WON...
...THE HUMAN RACE GOT ITS SECOND CHANCE.
FULLY BOOKED
BUT ELSEWHERE/WHEN, I KNOW IN MY GUT...
...THE WAR GOES ON!

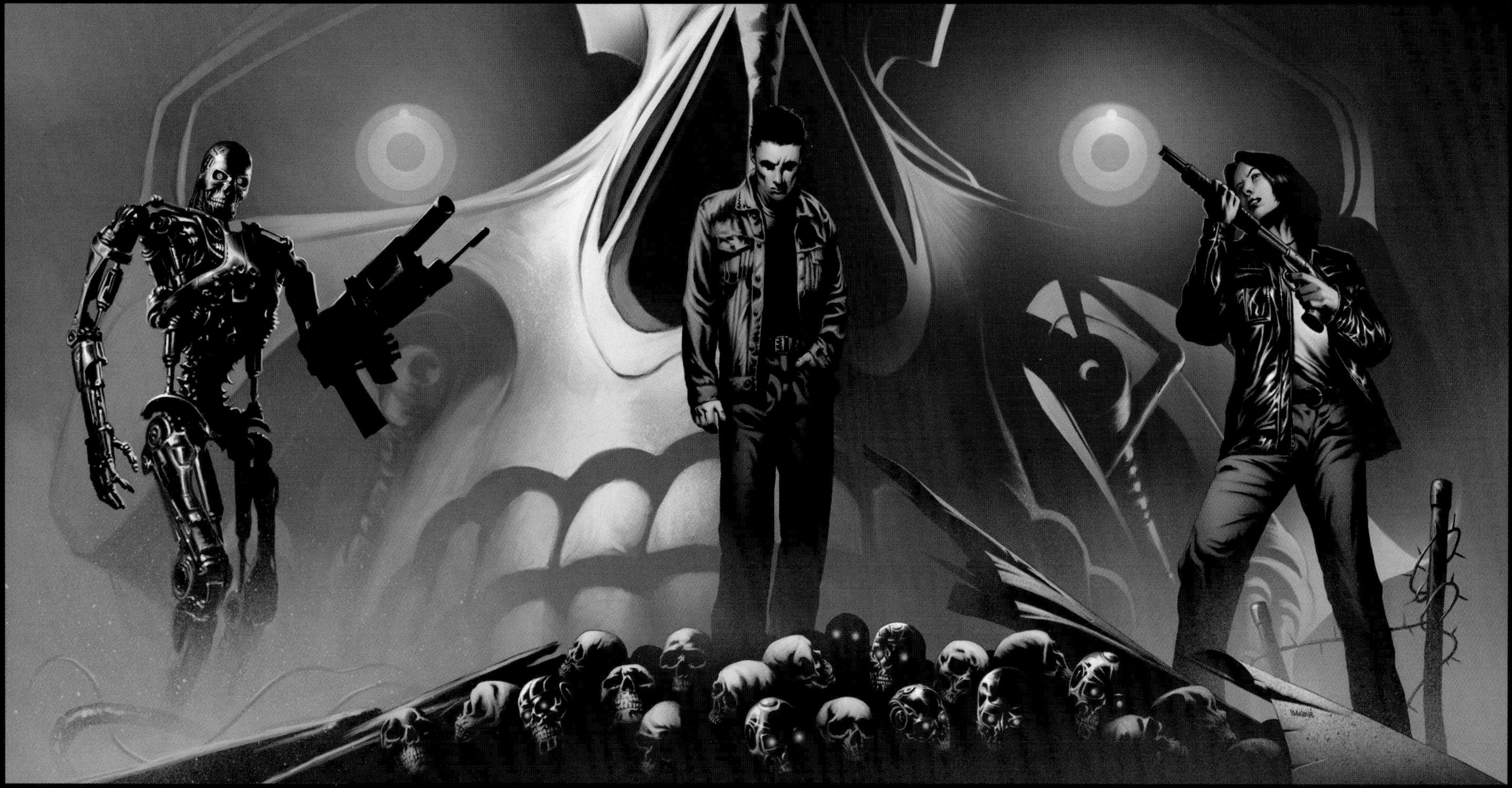

CONNECTING COVERS TO ISSUES ONE THROUGH THREE BY RICHARD ISANOVE

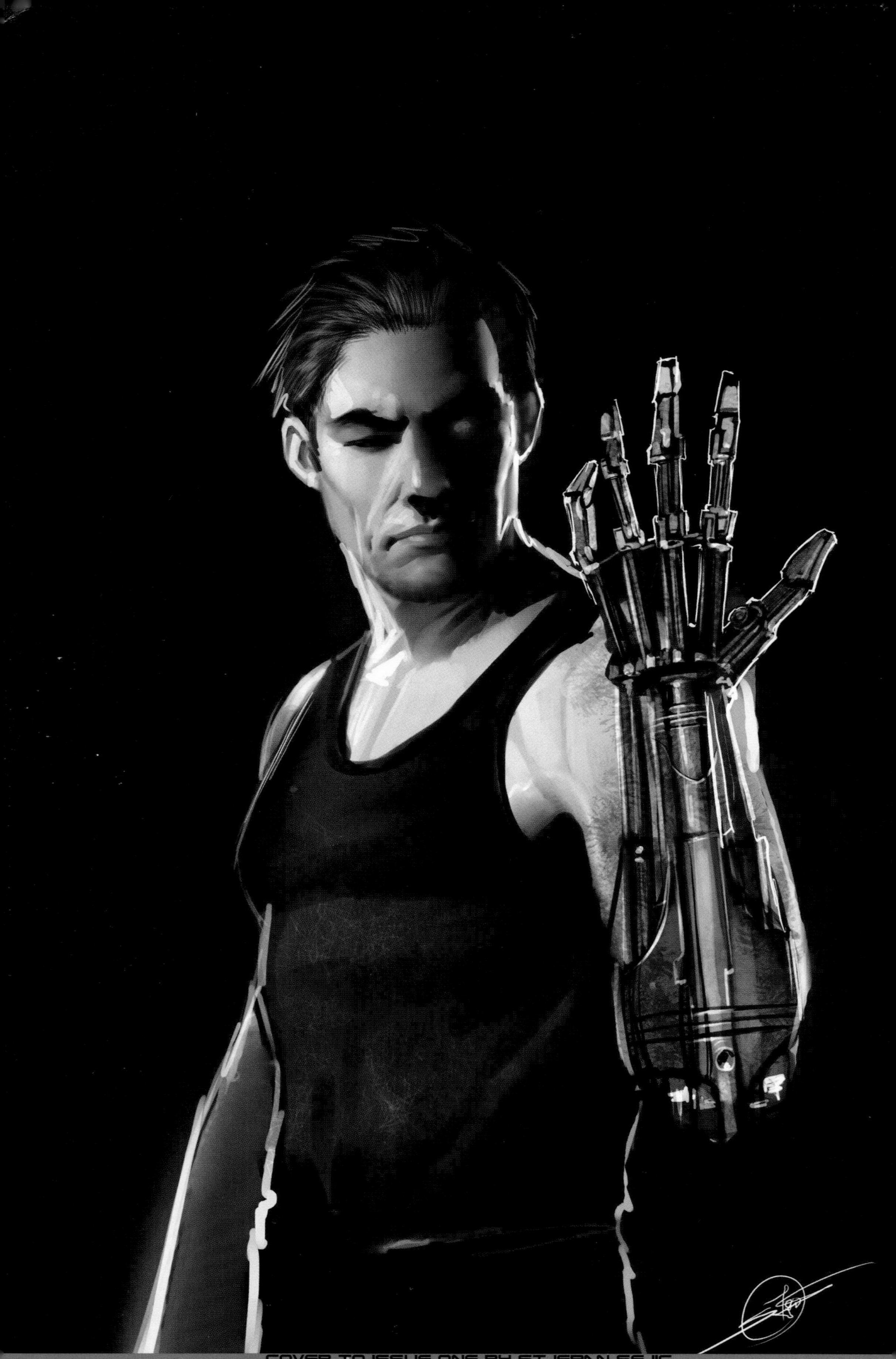

COVER TO ISSUE ONE BY STJEPAN SEJIC

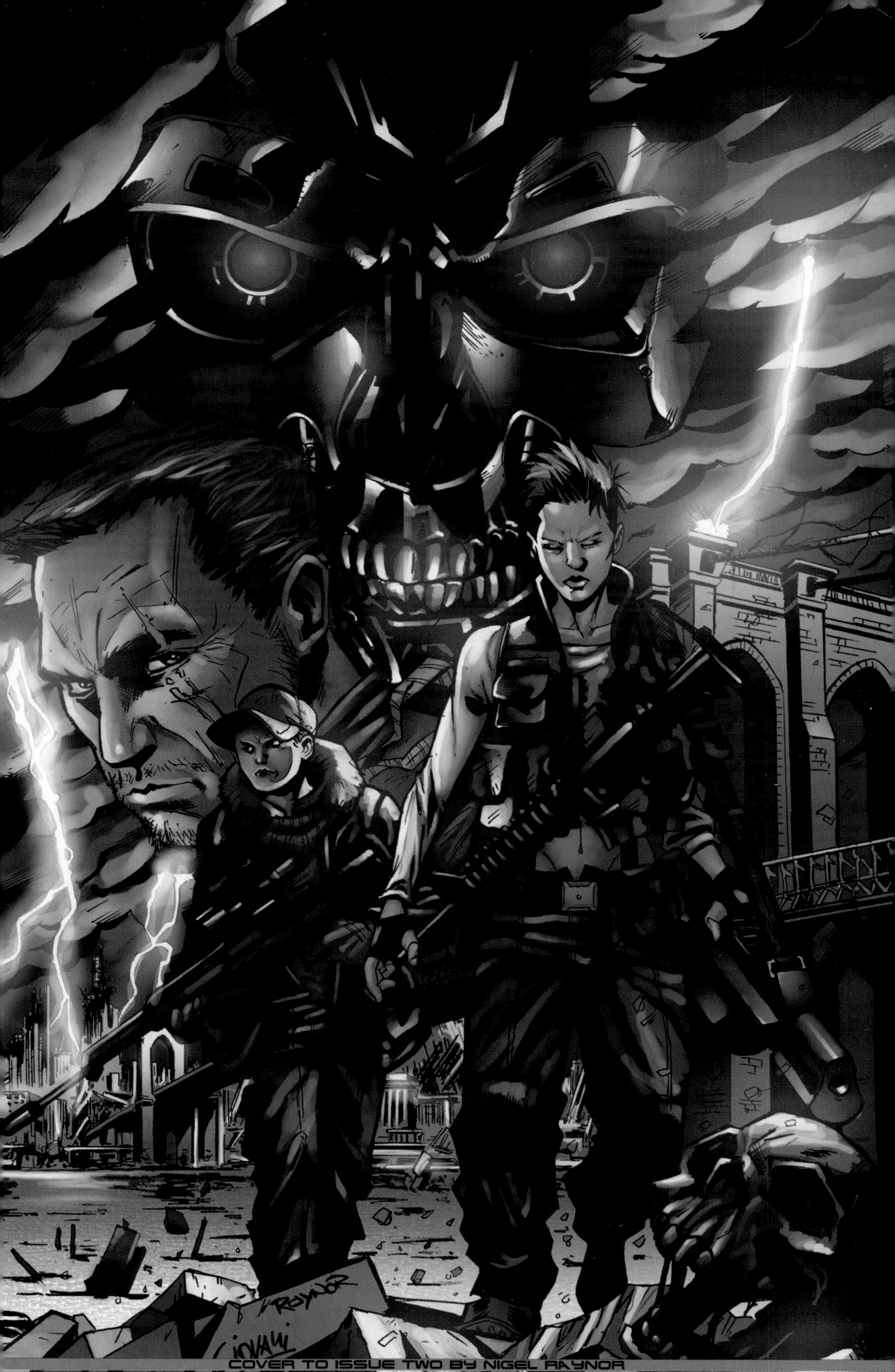
RAYNOR
GIOVANNI

COVER TO ISSUE TWO BY NIGEL RAYNOR

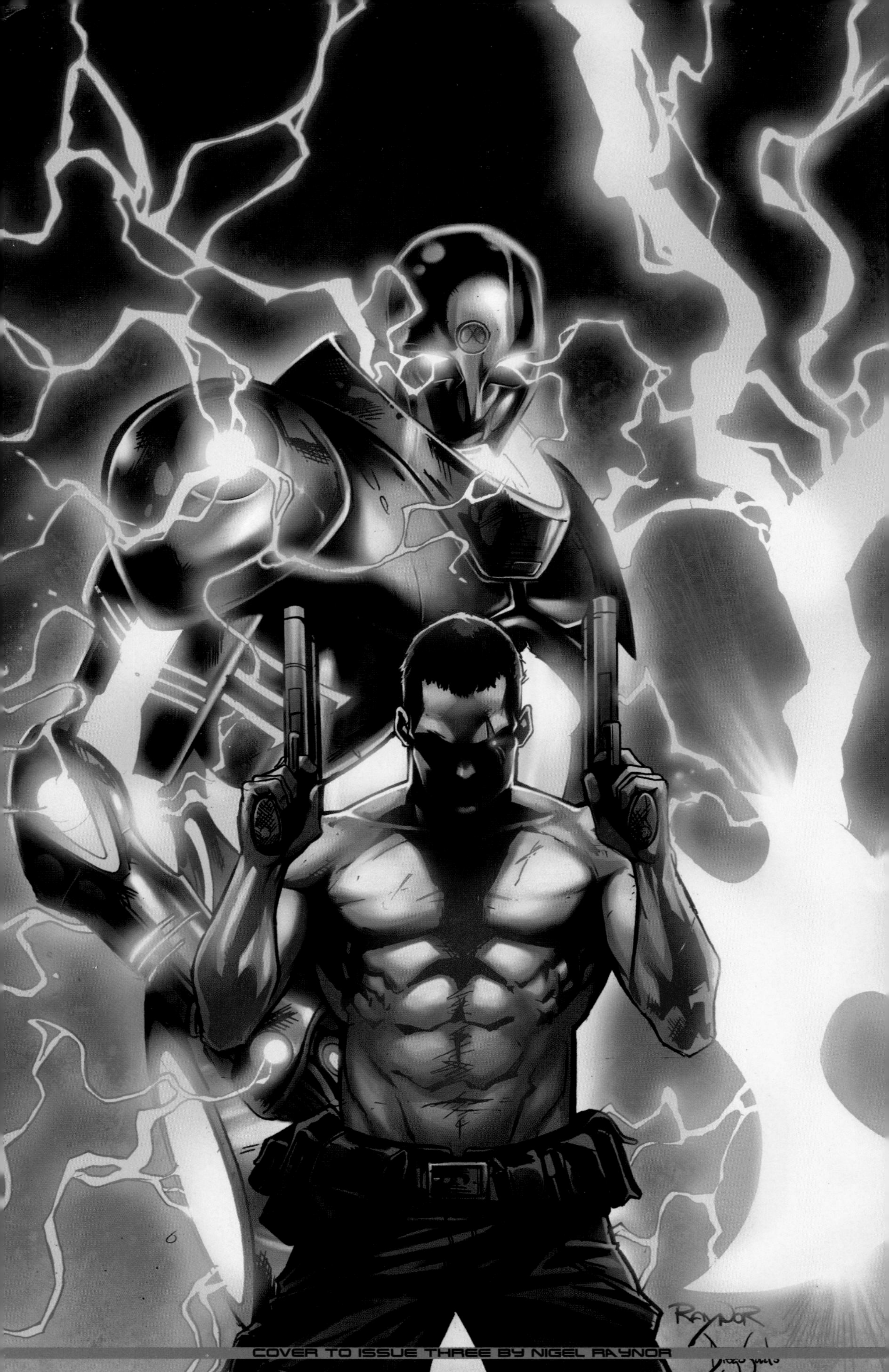
RAYNOR

COVER TO ISSUE THREE BY NIGEL RAYNOR

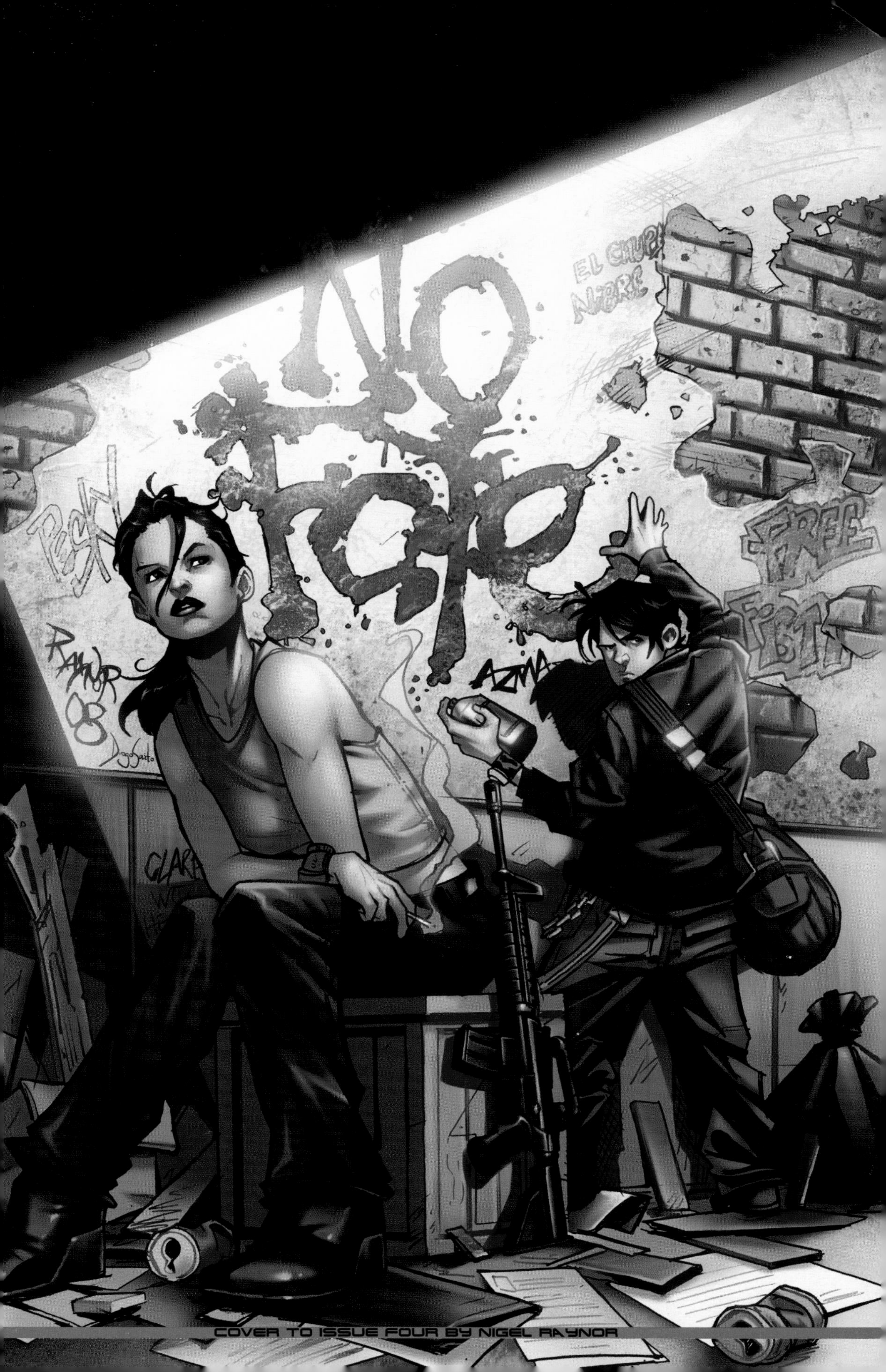
FREE
RAYNOR 08

COVER TO ISSUE FOUR BY NIGEL RAYNOR

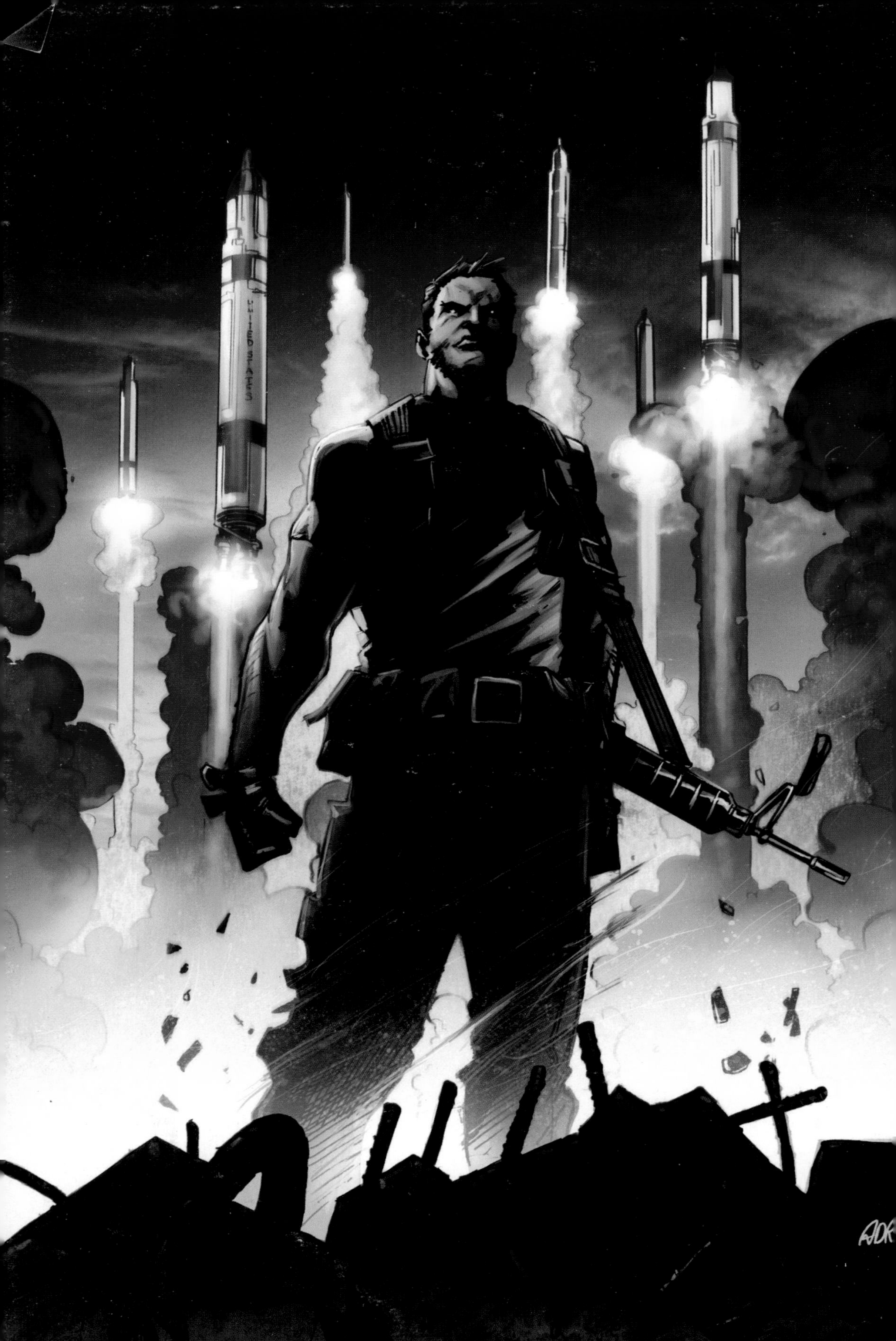
UNITED STATES

COVER TO ISSUE FIVE BY NIGEL RAYNOR